# RESISTANCE!

## OCCUPIED EUROPE AND ITS DEFIANCE OF HITLER

*D. A. Lande*

MBI Publishing Company

# Dedication

*This book is dedicated to all the men and women of the resistance in World War II, and especially to those who lost their lives in the quest for freedom.*

First published in 2000 by MBI Publishing Company, 729 Prospect Avenue, PO Box 1, Osceola, WI 54020-0001 USA

MBI Publishing Company books are also available at discounts in bulk quantity for industrial or sales-promotional use. For details write to Special Sales Manager at Motorbooks International Wholesalers & Distributors, 729 Prospect Avenue, PO Box 1, Osceola, WI 54020-0001 USA.

Library of Congress Cataloging-in-Publication Data
Lande, D.A.
    Resistance! : occupied Europe and its defiance of Hitler/D.A. Lande.
      p. cm.
    Includes index.
    ISBN 0-7603-0745-8 (pbk. : alk. paper)
      1. Anti-Nazi movement—Europe. 2. World War, 1939-1945—Europe.
      3. World War, 1939-1945—Underground movements—Europe.
      I. Title.
D8902.E9 L36 2000
940.53'4—dc21

Edited by Sara Perfetti
Designed by Katie Sonmor

Printed in the United States of America

# Contents

| | Acknowledgments | 4 |
| | Introduction | 7 |
| CHAPTER 1 | Czechoslovakia | 15 |
| CHAPTER 2 | Poland | 36 |
| CHAPTER 3 | Denmark | 52 |
| CHAPTER 4 | Norway | 70 |
| CHAPTER 5 | The Netherlands | 91 |
| CHAPTER 6 | Belgium and Luxembourg | 124 |
| CHAPTER 7 | France | 143 |
| CHAPTER 8 | Greece | 158 |
| CHAPTER 9 | Yugoslavia | 172 |
| CHAPTER 10 | The Baltic States | 186 |
| | Epilogue | 205 |
| APPENDIX | Resistance Organizations | 208 |
| | Notes | 213 |
| | Bibliography | 216 |
| | Index | 221 |

# Acknowledgments

I'm grateful to many helpful people and organizations for contributing to this project. In particular:

- Isabelle Engels and Jean-François Rase, who treated me like family on repeated visits and were instrumental in finding research contacts in Belgium and Luxembourg.
- Janet and Birger Henriksen, who *are* family in "the Old Country" of Norway and provided translation expertise, transport to historical sites, and other help.
- Reverend Clancy Kleinhans for translating letters.
- Graphic artist Julie Teclaw for her work on the maps herein.
- *Musée National de la Resistance*, National Museum of the Resistance, Luxembourg, and in particular Dr. Paul Dostert, a born teacher who has a passion for preserving his country's history and who so willingly imparts his knowledge.
- *Frihedsmuseet*, the Danish Resistance Museum, Copenhagen, and in particular, assistant curator Henrik Lundbak.
- *Hjemmefrontmuseum*, the Norwegian Resistance Museum, Oslo.
- *Nordsjofartmuseet*, the Norwegian Maritime Museum, at Tælevåg, and in particular, Mr. Simon Ovretviet, who shared his time and memories with me.
- Alexis Gibson of the Czech Embassy, Washington, D.C., along with Barbara Podoski, Lewis White, and Charles Kern, for their help in finding Czech contacts and information.
- *Verzetsmuseum*, the Dutch Resistance Museum, Amsterdam.
- The always helpful staff of the Dutch Department of Defense.
- *Centre De Recherches et d'Etudes Historiques*, Belgium's Documentation Center for World War II, Brussels.
- *Musée de la Resistance Nationale*, the French Resistance Museum, Champigny.

My thanks to the following sources of quotations (any omissions are unintentional and will be corrected upon future printings):

- Doubleday & Company, Inc. for Frantisek Moravec quotations from his book *Master of Spies* © 1975. Used with the permission of the publisher.
- Scientia-Factum, Inc. for Jerzy Kosinski quotations from his book *The Painted Bird* © 1967. Used with the permission of Kiki Kosinski.
- University of Illinois Press for Zygmunt Klukowski quotations from his book *Diary from the Years of Occupation, 1939–1944* © 1993. Used with the permission of the publisher.
- Holt, Rinehart and Winston for Julian Kulski quotations (and Winston Churchill speech in Chapter 2) from his book *Dying, We Live* © 1979. Used with the permission of the publisher.
- Funk and Wagnalls for Stefan Korbonski quotations from his book *Fighting Warsaw* © 1968. Used with the permission of HarperCollins Publishers.
- Hippocrene Books Inc. for Józef Garlinski quotations from his book *Poland in the Second World War* © 1985. Used with the permission of the publisher.
- McFarland & Company, Inc. for Leokadia Rowinski quotations from her book *That the Nightingale Return: A Memoir of the Polish Resistance, the Warsaw Uprising and German P.O.W. Camps* © 1999. Used with the permission of McFarland & Company, Inc., Box 611, Jefferson, North Carolina 28640, www.mcfarlandpub.com.
- Harcourt Brace Jovanovich for Joachim Rönneberg and Fredrik Kayser quotations, and the Gunnerside telegram, from Thomas Gallagher's book, *Assault in Norway: Sabotaging the Nazi Nuclear Bomb* © 1975. Used with the permission of Curtis Brown, Ltd.
- *Frihedsmuseet* for quotations from J.P. Jensen, Kaj Christensen, and Joergen Jespersen, which appear in Chapter 3. Used with the permission of the museum.
- Gerd Strey Gordon for quotations from Live Hiis Hauge, Gudrun Nielsen, Olaug Titlestad, Dr. Eilert Eilertsen, and Trygve Freyer, which appear in Chapter 4. They were drawn from Dr. Gordon's interviews for her Ph.D. dissertation. Used with the permission of Raymond Gordon.
- *Verzetsmuseum* for quotations from Remco Campert and for translation into English. Used with the permission of the museum.

- Fithian Press for Yvonne de Ridder Files quotations from her book *The Quest for Freedom: Belgian Resistance in World War II* © 1991. Used with the permission of the publisher.
- The University of Kentucky Press for George Watt quotations from his book *The Comet Connection* © 1990. Used with the permission of the publisher.
- Little, Brown and Company for Pierre Laval quotations from Blake Ehrlich's book *Resistance: France* © 1965. Used with the permission of the publisher.
- W.W. Norton & Company, Inc. for Elizabeth Barker quotations from Jean Lacouture's book *De Gaulle the Rebel 1890–1944* © 1990. Used with the permission of the publisher.
- McGraw-Hill Companies Inc. for Henri Frenay quotations from his book *The Night Will End: Memoirs of a Revolutionary* © 1976. Used with the permission of the publisher.
- From *The Secret Battalion* by Michael J. Bird, © 1964 by Michael J. Bird. Reprinted by permission Henry Holt & Co., LLC.
- Vanderbilt University Press for Ioanna (Jeanne) Tsatsos quotations from her book *The Sword's Fierce Edge* © 1969. Used with the permission of the publisher.
- Cambridge University Press for Marshal Tito's quotations from Stephen Cissold's book *A Short History of Yugoslavia* © 1966. Used with the permission of the publisher.
- Marshal Cavendish Ltd. for quotations by Olivia Manning, Phyllis Auty, and Rita Cavalouski from *History of the Second World War*, a magazine series published in 96 weekly parts. Used with the acknowledgment of the publisher.
- *Norges Hjemmefrontmuseum* (Norway's Resistance Museum, Oslo) for cartoon "Våpentransport." Used with the permission of the museum.

—D.A. Lande

# Introduction

*Asking yourself a question, that's how resistance begins.*
*And then ask that very question to someone else.*
—Remco Campert, poet

In the autumn of 1943, Nazi scientists began testing their devastating, new V-2 rocket bombs by launching them from a secret site and letting them fall indiscriminately on the Polish countryside without regard for the population living there. The V-2s' explosions became a regular occurrence within the striking area near Sarnaki and Rejowiec, sometimes killing and maiming the inhabitants. The peasant villagers had no idea what the aircraft were or why they were crashing there. All they knew was that each time one streaked out of the sky and exploded, German crews rushed to the scene to photograph and measure the resulting crater. Then, oddly, the soldiers meticulously gathered up every fragment no matter how small.

Despite the dangers, the peasants did not move from their humble shacks. Instead, after deliberating among themselves, they grimly resolved to beat the hated Germans at their own game—whatever that game was—by collecting the mysterious bits and pieces before the Germans could. They then sent the debris to resistance headquarters in Warsaw, which in turn forwarded it to London, where scientists were anxious to understand this new technological terror. And so ensued a lively competition. The villagers raced on horseback or on foot, while the Germans slogged through the swampy region in their vehicles. Being familiar with the land, the natives often reached the crash sites first, gathered up the pieces, and fled before the Germans arrived.

This is one isolated example in which oppressed people of occupied Europe defied the Nazi overlord. Alone, it did not bring Adolf Hitler to his knees. But when multiplied by untold thousands of acts of defiance, both large and small, resistance assumed epic proportions.

The story of occupation and resistance began with Hitler's bloodless seizure of the Czechoslovakian Sudetenland, after the major European powers feebly agreed to its annexation to Germany in 1938. Hitler went on to take the rest of Czechoslovakia in March 1939, then launched the blitzkrieg tactics of air, armor, and infantry against Poland in September. In the spring of 1940, he used the same tactics to slash through standing borders across Continental Europe, deftly occupying Denmark, Norway, Holland, Belgium, Luxembourg, and

France. By mid-1941, he had seized Greece, Yugoslavia, and the Baltic States (Lithuania, Estonia, and Latvia).

Conquered peoples left in the blitzkrieg's wake faced the grim reality of occupation. Their feelings followed a common pattern, something like what we today call the grieving process: It began with denial—a refusal to believe that anything as bad as Nazi terror could actually be happening. This disbelief was followed by the jarring realization that, yes, they *had* been brutally stripped of their rights and freedom, which led to unfocused rage. People then began "asking a question," as Remco Campert put it, and asking "that very question to someone else."[1] It wasn't long before like-thinking people banded together and defiance began smoldering.

Resistance wasn't instantaneously organized under some high-level authority and within some grand scheme of strategy against the enemy. It began with ordinary people joining together in reaction to a cruel occupation, and using whatever resources they had to combat it.

Resisters ranged from rail station clerks to royalty, from peasants to millionaires. They were men and women, young and old, from *every* political hue including communists after the German-Russian Nonaggression Pact was shattered. They included the villagers of Sarnaki and Rejowiec, who knew only what they faced locally in Poland, and in their isolation couldn't know the war's big picture or much about what others were doing in defiance. They and other resisters had no idea that their contribution would have ramifications on a strategic scale.

All resisters shared common motivations: Hatred of the Nazi occupier, and its oppression and tyranny. They could seethe over it privately amongst themselves; they could complain impotently about it in the obscurity of the shadows. But what, in their shadowy existence, could they *do* to confront a seemingly invincible foe? What form would their resistance take? They soon realized their obscurity was their greatest advantage. As T.E. Lawrence once phrased it, resistance was a "thing intangible, invulnerable, without front or back, drifting about like a gas. Armies were like plants, immobile, firm-rooted, nourished through long stems to the head. We might be a vapour, blowing where we wished, our kingdom lay in each mind." What the Nazi overlord needed more than anything else was the complete submission of its subjects. It could break their bodies and smash their cities, but that one key intangible—the will of the people to resist and win back freedom—was unbreakable.

As you'll see in the chapters that follow, resistance took many tangible forms, not all of them gun-wielding. Historians note the following as the mainline forms of resistance (with some variation in semantics[2]):

- Passive acts
- Underground newspapers
- Escape lines
- Intelligence
- Sabotage

- Assassination
- Guerrilla warfare—maquis and partisan
- Secret or "shadow" army

People of occupied countries usually started their resistance passively. Their first acts were spontaneous and small, such as slowing down work on assembly lines, absenteeism, giving bad directions to Germans at a metro station, and listening to the BBC (which was strictly banned).

The violent shock of Nazi brutality and imposition of Nazi ideology moved people from passive resistance to action. They abandoned the wait-and-see attitude about the Nazi occupation—or what was called *attentisme* in France—and took the leap to action. Once that was done, there was no turning back. They joined together in groups, and their first overt action typically was to establish an underground newspaper. Student associations, labor unions, and small nuclei of early resistance cells published them. Some were nothing more than a mimeographed or "roneoed" sheet of paper sent to a small readership once a week. Later, many were reproduced on high-capacity printing presses, like those used by regular newspapers. They grew in quality and popularity, with tens of thousands of readers. The largest issues of Poland's *Biuletyn Informacyjny* had a few print runs of 47,000 copies, the Netherlands' *De Waarheid* published 100,000 for a few of its issues, and France's *Combat* at times reached 300,000. Since copies were passed hand to hand, it's certain that readership far exceeded those numbers.

Escape lines were also typically created early in the progression of resistance actions. By answering an urgent need that arose early in the occupation, the lines worked to spirit away desperate citizens who were facing arrest for political reasons, avoiding forced labor, or Jewish deportations. In addition, fugitive Allied soldiers (many left stranded after Dunkirk), escaped POWs, and later, increasing numbers of downed airmen evading capture were taken in, fed and hidden, provided with false papers and civilian clothes, then ushered through the escape lines. The lines carried these "packages" or "passengers" from the Netherlands, Belgium, Luxembourg, and France to freedom (or internment) in Spain or Switzerland. They carried people from Denmark to Sweden, from Norway to the Shetland Islands or Sweden, and from the Baltic States to Finland.

Intelligence-gathering was another form of resistance vital to the Allies. In some countries, the professionals of a military intelligence service were able to move underground to continue working after surrender.

In others, intelligence information was transmitted via radio by amateur wireless operators who began on their own, or were equipped and trained by the intelligence services from Great Britain. This was dangerous work since the Germans had listening-in devices and direction-finding devices to locate the source of transmissions. Other intelligence information was sent by couriers over land for delivery (sometimes through diplomatic channels) to the Allies in Great Britain. Couriers carrying microfilm, maps, correspondence, and other messages typically followed routes similar to the escape lines.

Sabotage was a specialty of the resistance—and the first thing many people envision when they hear the term "resistance." It was more complex than Hollywood depicts it, however. Many steps preceded a shadowy saboteur gliding down through trees to set charges on railroad tracks or factory machinery. Intricate planning was necessary for each strike. Sabotage relied as much on people "above ground" as those underground. People who continued in legitimate jobs, like railroad clerks with knowledge of timetables, gave those working underground critical information to carry out the missions.

Assassination was a form of resistance warfare that targeted certain German leaders for their brutal regimes, or natives for their collaboration. In most of the occupied countries, assassination was used sparingly because horrific reprisal almost certainly would follow, or because the Germans would replace the individual with someone equally or more brutal.

Guerrilla warfare was the kind of resistance that had clear military value. It wasn't possible in most of the occupied countries, because many lacked remote forested and mountainous areas where guerrillas could set up hidden base camps from which they could launch hit-and-run attacks. Prime examples of guerrilla warfare took place in Yugoslavia's rugged mountains and France's great forested plateaus. Guerrilla warfare also took place in Carpathian Poland, areas of Greece, the Baltics, and to a lesser degree in several other countries. Heavily populated and urban countries of western Europe, like the Netherlands and Denmark, left few places for guerrillas to operate.

The ultimate stage of resistance in an occupied country was the formation of a secret army that would rise up in revolt at the right time, as the Allies were approaching and the Germans were retreating. The hope in most countries was for people throughout the urban and rural areas to rise up and liberate from within, so that when the victorious Allies came, the citizens already would be "masters of their own house." A magnificent rising was staged by Poland's Home Army, which rose in revolt against the Nazi occupiers of Warsaw as the Russians approached. In a massacre that has gone down in history as the Warsaw Rising, the Home Army seized much of Warsaw from the Wehrmacht. The Russians came within 10 miles of the besieged capital, close enough to see great fires and explosions, but halted their advance, allowing the Germans to send in reinforcements that crushed the Home Army in an unprecedented bloodbath.

All these forms of resistance were typical throughout Europe. However, the character of resistance in each of the occupied countries was unique. Resistance in each country had a distinctive personality, based mostly on the citizenry and the severity of occupation policies. Resistance sprang up homegrown—in reaction to circumstances at hand. The only constant was that resistance was *always* in response to the oppression of the occupier.

Much depended on geography—both topography and location on the conqueror's map. Some occupied countries were mountainous and forested; others were densely populated and urban. Just as forests and mountains encouraged guerrilla warfare, urban-based resistance encouraged sabotage, intelligence-gathering, and the infinite forms of passive (or "civil") resistance. Resistance in urban areas took place right under the nose of the enemy, because the Germans also were most heavily concentrated in those areas.

Much also depended on Hitler's whim or prejudice. Hitler clearly showed favoritism toward certain nationalities, at least initially, and his occupation policies reflected that. Race was a big determinate of the tolerance or brutality of the occupation. Particularly in eastern Europe, the inhabitants were regarded as inferior beings. Hitler showed no mercy toward the Poles, Czechs, Slavs, and Balts. Seizing their lands accomplished two objectives simultaneously: It opened new *lebensraum* (living space) for the expansive grand scheme of the 1,000-year Reich, and it predisposed the population to either enslavement or extermination. In western Europe, the racial "cousins" of the Aryans received relatively civil treatment. Among the unwilling kin were the Danes, Norwegians, Dutch, Flemish-speaking Belgians, and Luxembourgers. Hitler sincerely wanted these nationalities in his fold. So, initial occupation policies called for "correct" behavior by the German occupation troops. Jewish persecution in these countries started more slowly than in the East, where orders for the "final solution" were immediate. Hitler also somewhat favored the Greeks, admiring their age-old conquests for empire. He displayed a tolerant scorn for the French, unlike the typical German animosity of the time, but he lusted for vengeance just the same because of the still-deep wounds from World War I.

Within all these nationalities, whether embraced or despised, Hitler found collaborators. Some countries had few, others had many. The best-known collaborators, though of very different natures, were Norway's Vidkun Quisling, whose name has become immortalized universally as a dictionary definition for "traitor," and the Great War's French hero Marshal Pétain, who headed Vichy France and supported Nazi ideology, including the extermination of Jews. The rank and file of collaborators believed the Third Reich was permanent, and they settled into the "new order" with the motives of making the best of it, perhaps even enjoying financial or other gain. Some degenerates collaborated with the Germans to be given free license to perform sadistic acts against their countrymen. Others went so far as to join militias or police forces that were armed and trained by the Nazis, and served in direct opposition to the resistance.

While collaborationist forces usually received direct backing from the Nazis, the resistance received outside backing, too, albeit distant and not always reliable under the circumstances. By far the greatest assistance for the resistance came from the SOE, the Special Operations Executive of Great Britain. The SOE was founded by Prime Minister Winston Churchill in the summer of 1940, with the intent of enabling citizens to "set Europe ablaze." This was just after the evacuation of Commonwealth troops from Dunkirk, when Churchill realized that it would be years before he could hope to launch a military campaign on the Continent.

SOE's secret headquarters was in London on Baker Street, home to the legendary Sherlock Holmes. The front for SOE headquarters was an office of Marks and Spencer, a London department store. At various facilities in the United Kingdom, British experts in silent killing, sabotage, and intelligence-gathering trained men and women volunteers from the occupied countries. Outfitted with forged identity papers, inconspicuous clothing that would blend in with the locals, foreign currency, and an "L" pill (lethal cyanide capsule), the volunteers were then stealthily returned to their home country via air transport (parachute, glider, or short-takeoff aircraft) or by sea (submarine, PT boat, or Norway's "Shetland bus"). Other outside help for the resistance came later from SOE's American counterpart, the OSS, short for Office of Strategic Services.

Great Britain had another major role in helping the occupied countries: hosting exiled governments. By mid-1941, most governments-in-exile (and royalty, if any) from the occupied countries had fled to London. At one time or another, they included Czechoslovakia, Poland, Denmark, Norway, the Netherlands, Belgium, Luxembourg, France, Greece, and Yugoslavia. While in London, many exiled heads of state or military generals exercised what leadership was possible over their country's resistance activities. The British Broadcasting Company (BBC) generously offered a channel for these leaders to broadcast messages of guidance and hope to their peoples. Plus, for a long time, the BBC provided the only voice of truth that most occupied countries heard at a time when Nazi propaganda bombarded the airwaves, proclaiming inevitable German victory and making resistance seem futile. Where the BBC left off, the underground press in each country picked up, creating unity among the resisting population and informing them of local news.

It took tremendous courage to resist, because the Germans seemed invincible. The *Geheime Staatspolizei*—Secret State Police known everywhere as the Gestapo—seemed omniscient. Defiance under those circumstances was daunting, and the worst torture possible was used to extract information. Czech resister Radomir Luza later said, "The first rule in the Resistance was that you weren't to know any more than you needed to. If the Gestapo arrested you, they tortured you. It was difficult to keep silent."

Everyone became aware of the risks for even minor acts of resistance. Every day, men and women met torturous fates in the chambers of Gestapo headquarters and prisons throughout Europe. If captured, resisters were not prisoners of war like the uniformed military, and could expect no mercy. There were no "rules" accorded by the Geneva Convention. Thousands died. It made for unending fear in day-to-day life.

The culprits directly responsible for resistance acts weren't the only ones who paid in blood, if caught. Reprisals often meant death for anyone even vaguely associated. For instance, after the assassination of SS Obergruppenführer Reinhard Heydrich, the Gestapo searched the assassins and found a picture of one of the assassin's former girlfriends. Even though the woman had long since been married to someone else and had children from the marriage, they tracked her down and killed her. An even better known reprisal for Heydrich's death was the complete obliteration of the Czech village of Lidice and murder of its inhabitants, as covered in Chapter 1.

Each occupied country had its own mixture of horror stories and triumphs: Poland had the Warsaw Rising—the gallant stand of the 38,000 men and women of the Polish Home Army, which nearly liberated its capital, but ended in slaughter. Denmark is credited for its incredible feat of rescuing more than 90 percent of its Jewish citizens. Norway endured Quisling, as mentioned, but also saw the greatest sabotage raid of the war, which destroyed the Norsk Hydro heavy water plant at Vemork. The Netherlands was the home of thousands of *onderduikers* (fugitives hidden by the Dutch), but it suffered the devastation of *Englandspiel*, the counterespionage "game" that directly led to decimation of the Dutch resistance. Belgium had the largest escape line in the Comet Line, established by Andrèe de Jongh. Luxembourg rescued many Allied airmen and soldiers, as well. The French resistance, with great names such as Charles de Gaulle, Jean Moulin, and Henri Fornay, is the best known resistance movement and has a wealth of books about it—unlike some movements that have practically none, leaving them lost to history, or as in the East, where communists rewrote history. Greece's mountain warriors hurled back the Italian invaders though far outnumbered, and succumbed only to the powerful Wehrmacht. Yugoslavia had the largest and most effective guerrilla operations, doing great material damage and pinning down German divisions that otherwise would have seen bloody action against Allied soldiers. The Baltic States faced one horrific occupation after another—first Soviet, then Nazi, followed by Soviet again—while its resisters fought through it all.

The chapters that follow offer an overview of each country's distinctive resistance movement, presented in the order of German invasion and occupation. Here you will find the vanquished countries that lost their armies in humiliating defeat and were wholly occupied, yet dared to defy the control of the Nazi overlord.

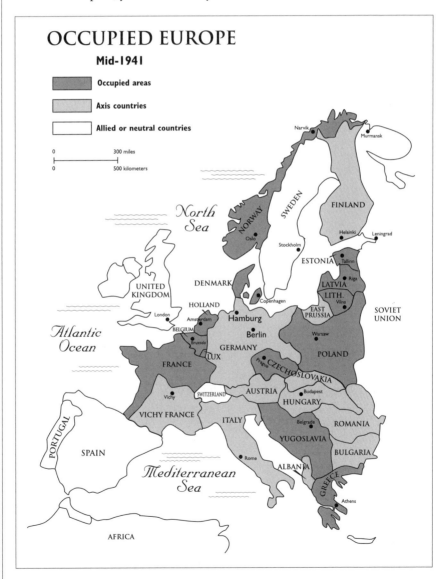

## OCCUPIED EUROPE
### Mid-1941

Occupied areas

Axis countries

Allied or neutral countries

## CHAPTER 1

# Czechoslovakia

In the late afternoon of March 14, 1939, eleven Czech intelligence officers traveling incognito boarded a chartered Dutch KLM airliner at Ruzyn Airport on the outskirts of Prague. They secretly carried aboard the most sensitive of their country's classified documents and a great deal of cash in bulging briefcases. The stewardess, like the rest of the crew, was unaware of who they were. After she helped them get situated in their seats, all sat in silence for an uncomfortable few minutes waiting for the engines to start. Finally, the Dutch pilot emerged from the cockpit to announce that weather might cause a delay. A terrible winter storm was bearing down on them from Germany and would likely envelope the area soon—words true in more ways than the pilot could know at that moment.

"How long do we wait?" spouted one of the passengers in the rear. The pilot hesitated before responding: "Could be indefinitely, until the storm passes." Sitting in obscurity until now, the leader of the small party arose authoritatively from his seat and spoke quietly with the pilot for several minutes. The man was Frantisek Moravec, head of Czech intelligence. As soon as Moravec retook his seat, the chocks were pulled, and the aircraft began rolling down the runway. The men breathed a collective sigh of relief. At 5:25 P.M. the aircraft lifted smoothly off the tarmac and banked toward a northwesterly course as light snow began to fall. Within hours, Germans were goose-stepping through the streets of Prague, but the Czechoslovaks had already taken their first steps down the road of resistance.

Leading up to the afternoon of March 14 had been months of international espionage and intrigue that would rival a good spy novel. In a series of clandestine meetings, a reliable informant had tipped off Moravec to Germany's plan to take Czechoslovakia. The informant was a high-ranking Abwehr[3] officer code-named A-54, who had stopped supporting the Nazi regime and was willing to provide information for personal financial gain.

A-54, whose real name was Paul Thümmel, first contacted Moravec in February 1936. Acting against the advice of his suspicious staff, Moravec accepted the German's offer and made the first payment of 4,000 Reichsmarks. Thus began a long-standing information-for-cash relationship that yielded some of the most valuable intelligence of

World War II, such as an accurate forecast of the seizure of the Sudetenland, and detailed information about the takeover of the rest of Czechoslovakia.[4]

A-54's information allowed Moravec and his 10 most valuable men to take flight from Prague to London—thereby saving their lives. In addition to stating the precise order of battle, complete with timetable, route, and the names of commanding generals, A-54 informed Moravec that all Czech intelligence officers would be immediately arrested and interrogated "with great severity" about information sources within the German army.

By arrangement of his superiors, Moravec met in urgent, secret meetings with Premier Rudolf Beran and ministers of the Czechoslovakian Cabinet to report the cataclysm to come. One of the ministers called the report "unfounded" and nearly all of them scoffed. Moravec continued to implore that the government should move to Paris, and recommended that the General Staff building that housed government records should be blown sky-high with no remnants left for the invader to find. He was ordered to "calm down" and take no action. The premier and his ministers followed their own direction— and were still in Prague when the Germans took the city.

Meanwhile, Moravec and his 10 men escaped from Prague, only to face near disaster over Germany—not from enemy action but Mother Nature. The flight path took them directly over Germany, the center of the blizzard that had concerned the Dutch pilot before takeoff. Blanketing the area with almost zero visibility, the snowstorm also caused violent downdrafts, which nearly caused the plane to crash more than once. The same blizzard played havoc with the advancing Nazi units on the ground. Bitter cold, snow, and high winds followed them across Germany and all the way into Prague. The Czechoslovaks would later call the snowstorm "God's judgment," in response to the Germans' aggression.

The KLM airliner landed in Rotterdam in the Netherlands for a brief refueling stop, then flew to Croydon, near London, and landed at 10 P.M. At the airport, the group was met by officials and quickly shuttled away by motorcade to the Grosvenor Hotel. Once there, Moravec reported the developments to former President Edvard Benes, who had resigned and left Czechoslovakia just after the Sudetenland annexation. Benes, aided by Moravec and others, would now set up Czechoslovakia's government-in-exile and provide leadership for resistance from abroad. Moravec's main interest was to set up an intelligence network that would supply his countrymen and the Allies with information. He had been in charge of military intelligence since March 1934, developing it into one of the finest organizations of its kind in Europe.

The laden briefcases brought by the 11 intelligence men contained key documents and cash (about 200,000 Reichsmarks and 100,000 Dutch gulden, the equivalent of about $128,000 at the time) to help start the operation. Most of the men, including Moravec, left families behind, and had not been able to even tell them where they were going.

The next day, newspaper headlines of London's *Daily Mail* read "Mystery Men Arrive by Air, Sign Secret Register." Later editions' headlines asked, "Who Are the Eleven Czechs?" Moravec himself had an answer to that question in his memoirs: "They were eleven Czechs who were tasting the bitter dregs, the most shattering happening a man can experience—the loss, the destruction, of his country."

It was clear from the start that Adolf Hitler reserved a special contempt for neighboring Czechoslovakia. To him, the people of Czechoslovakia were *Untermenschen* ("subhumans"), objects of deepseated hatred, and certainly no more than slaves destined to serve Aryan masters. His condemnation would set the tone for the occupation that followed. "The more blood the Germans shed, the more blood they desired to shed," observed Czech author Zdena Kapral in her war memoir, *Tomorrow Will Be Better*. "The more of us they killed, the more they hated us. However, while the Nazis had let themselves become monstrous, on another level they remained calm, cool, and organized. This combination of primordial brutality and modern efficiency was what terrified us most."

In September 1938, Hitler demanded possession of the Sudetenland, a western border region of Czechoslovakia where many Germans lived. He justified the demand by saying he needed to protect the "oppressed German families" living there from the "grasp of Czech treachery." Hoping to avoid war, British Prime Minister Neville Chamberlain and French Premier Edouard Daladier traveled to Munich to meet with Hitler and Benito Mussolini to discuss the Sudetenland. The result was a business-like memorandum written for Czechoslovakian signatures—the notorious Munich pact—granting the area to Germany. Helpless to resist in the face of an overwhelming military power, Czechoslovakian President Benes signed it.

Chamberlain and many in the civilized world sincerely believed that signing the papers would satisfy Hitler and that this small crisis was over. And why not? Hitler had *said* it would satisfy him. Then again, the world did not yet know Adolf Hitler.

Hitler would later say to the staff of the military high command: "From the very first moment it was clear to me that I could not be contented with the Sudeten German area. It was only a partial solution." With that, Czechoslovakia's fate was sealed.

Hitler put his propaganda machine to work turning the Slovaks against their Czech countrymen, and craftily setting the stage to divide and conquer, in the most literal sense. Using a justification parallel to the one he used for his intervention in the Sudetenland, Hitler fabricated headlines proclaiming "bloody Czech terror in Slovakia" and pleaded sympathy for Slovaks "under Czech bayonets." By churning up unrest, Hitler drew the Slovak portion of the country toward the Axis. At the same time, he tried to make the world believe Germany would be rescuing the "Slovak victims" when the Wehrmacht crossed the border.

With the Sudetenland already in the Germans' possession, Czechoslovakia's considerable western defensive fortifications had been taken away. So, early on March 15, 1939, German troops marched unimpeded across the border into Czechoslovakia and on to the capital of Prague. As deftly as the slash of a sword, the country was divided into its Czech and Slovak components, and Czechoslovakia no longer existed as a nation.

Hitler annexed the Czech portion of the country, Bohemia and Moravia, which together were labeled a "protectorate." Slovakia was severed from them so it could become the first German satellite—an independent puppet state. The division of Czechoslovakia into the protectorate (Bohemia and Moravia) and Slovakia made for two very different sets of conditions—and two very different natures of resistance arose as a result. So Czechoslovakia really had two separate stories of resistance, overlapping in some ways and even sharing direction from the same leadership of Benes and Moravec, but facing different types of control by the Nazi overlord.

## THE PARTITION OF CZECHOSLOVAKIA

MARCH 1939

Annexed To Germany

Axis Satellite State

0      50      100 miles

0              160 kilometers

Sudetenland

Lidice

Prague

Lezáky

POLAND

BOHEMIA

MORAVIA

Carpathian Mts.

Brno

GERMANY

SLOVAKIA

Banska Bystrica

Bratislava

Danube R.

HUNGARY

Czech resistance began even before Czechoslovakian President Edvard Benes left his country for England in October 1938. Because Benes had the foresight to know that Hitler would not settle for only the Sudetenland, he began talking with close friends about a future resistance network. Benes would be proven right within six months, when Hitler showed his true colors to the world by crushing what was left of the republic.

Although he'd officially resigned as president, Benes pleaded the case of his country to the United States, Great Britain, France, and Russia. He spoke for his country as a whole when he said in an address from Chicago: "The Czechs and Slovaks will never accept this unbearable imposition on their sacred rights." The fundamental part of his message, maintained from then on, was that Czechoslovakia "has legally never ceased to exist." In an unbending stand, Benes had declared the premise for his country's underground movement.

Resistance began slowly and cautiously after the shock of German occupation. Unlike some of the other countries, Czech resisters had almost no arms. The Czechoslovakian army had surrendered where it stood, by its government's own order, in a bloodless capitulation during the German march on Prague. Consequently, all its weapons had been handed over, almost down to the last rifle.

The general public was stunned into silence and disbelief, and remained that way for months. Hitler, after all, had said he would be satisfied by the Munich pact that awarded him the Sudetenland. The pact had implied assurances by the Western Powers, but the Western Powers, it turned out, had little power. Betrayal, in a sense, had come not only from Hitler but also from the leaders of France, England, and Russia, who had given lip service to the crisis at hand but, for individual reasons, nothing more in the end. By policy, the United States was isolationist. Hungary and Poland had had designs of their own on Czechoslovakian territory. Opportunistic in a neighbor's darkest hour, Poland snatched a portion of Silesia, and Hungary seized a portion of southern Slovakia. So, in the eyes of the Czechs, betrayal seemed quite complete.

Without missing a beat, the Nazis began installing a regime that completely shackled Bohemia and Moravia. All industry was converted to support the Reich, with the singular objective of milking every possible resource to feed the ravenous German war machine. There was direct German control politically and economically. Law and order was maintained by the iron fist of the Gestapo.

Leadership lay now in the hands of a collaborationist government under Benes' successor, President Emil Hàcha, and Beran's successor, Premier Alois Eliàs. Hàcha and Eliàs were under the thumb of the newly appointed *Reichsprotektor* Freiherr von Neurath.

Making matters worse was the attitude of the Sudeten Germans, who aligned quickly with the Nazi regime. The Sudeten Germans' familiarity with their Czech neighbors, their language, tendencies, and local nuances made them especially dangerous to any Czech giving thought to resisting. The Sudeten Germans gladly shared their insights with the Gestapo, which used that knowledge as a weapon of control, and oftentimes terror.

Anti-Nazis were forced underground immediately in March 1939, when the German army arrived in Prague. These individuals banded together in one of several underground movements, including one composed mainly of army officers.

The Munich pact had especially humiliated the Czechoslovak army's leadership. As early as September 1938, the army's officer corps had considered forming a military dictatorship that would refuse to surrender. But the following winter they tempered their aggressive thinking and instead laid out plans for opposition in the event of German occupation. When Germany invaded Bohemia and Moravia, the military underground spread through the Czech territory. With the clear objective of restoring Czechoslovakia to a free democracy, it attracted a large following. Many of the small grassroots groups throughout the land followed this military leadership in what came to be called the *Obrana Naroda* (ON), which translates to Defense of the Nation.

Radomir Luza was a teen-aged student when the Germans seized control in the protectorate. His father joined fellow army officers underground. "My father, Voatech Luza, was a five-star general, and the Gestapo came to arrest him," Radomir Luza said. "But before they could find him, he went underground. When they could not find him, they arrested my mother and myself, and kept us confined for six weeks before finally letting us go. After they released us, they tried to follow us to find out where my father had gone underground. We didn't know where he was—didn't know about specific, organized resistance groups. [Later,] I learned where he was when I went underground myself."

Also forming early in the occupation were two underground movements composed of politicians and intellectuals. One political group, called *Politicke Ústredi* (PÚ), or Political Center, drew together supporters of President Benes. Benes himself urged unification of all resistance activities in the anticipation of the German threat before the spring of 1939. The fact that this group was made up of high-profile political leaders and citizens, not clandestine resisters, resulted in many arrests that almost crushed the movement. Too free in their comments and too well known, these politicians did not make good secret conspirators against the ruthless professionals of the Gestapo. Only a few escaped arrest by fleeing the country. Younger activists and lesser-known politicians stepped in to fill the void, which later transformed the PÚ into a bona fide resistance movement capable of disrupting the Germans' regime.

Another political group was formed as early as May 1938, when a cadre of social democrats and leftist intellectuals sought to restore the territory of the fallen republic. They created a manifesto titled *Verni zustaneme* ("We Will Stay True") to communicate this fundamental aim. Although not contrary to the PÚ or ON, this group initially stayed independent of both. After the German takeover, the group increased its numbers by recruiting from the leftist individuals in the former army, trade unions and free masons, the YMCA, and universities and other schools. Support built steadily until it became the most popular and largest of the resistance groups. Known as the *Peticni vybor Verni zustaneme* (PVVZ) committee, members deliberately avoided affiliation with pre-Munich party politics. The group was forward thinking, already planning for an innovative new government without the old party system in postwar Czechoslovakia. The idea for structure would combine the best of economic democracy with a democratic socialist state. This was to happen within the restored borders previous to the Munich agreement. To punctuate its platform and to attract recruits, its final objective called for the ousting of all Sudeten Germans.

Members of the ON and PÚ applauded the ideals of this plan in 1941, and agreed to support them. This led to unity of the democratic resistance organizations into what was called the *Ústredni vybor odboje domaciho* (Central Leadership of the Home Resistance), abbreviated ÚVOD. Organizations taking part in ÚVOD included the ON, PÚ, and PVVZ, as well as a movement formed by the nationwide *Sokol* (Falcon) gymnastic organization called the "Falcon Organization in Resistance." As a security precaution, the groups within the ÚVOD remained segregated. Benes recognized the ÚVOD as his central contact for the home resistance.

Another pre-Munich group was the Communist Party of Czechoslovakia (KSC), which remained independent of the others until much later in the war. Communist resisters, as we'll read about in most other chapters to come, went through many adjustments and complete turnabouts, based on the on-again, off-again coalition of Germany and Russia. When Hitler first seized control in the spring of 1939 and before the German-Soviet Nonaggression Pact, the KSC ferociously opposed the German invaders. With the advent of the pact on August 23, 1939, an abrupt change of direction was ordered by Moscow. It wouldn't be until the June 1941 invasion of Russia that the KSC would resume resistance against the Nazi occupier. Many communists, too, wanted restoration of an independent Czechoslovakia but one closely aligned with the Soviet Union.

Apart from these organized groups, there was also nationwide passive resistance that stubbornly obstructed the Nazi occupier in any way possible. Untold thousands of Czechs participated in this. Collaboration among the masses was almost nonexistent.

There were many obstacles to active resistance, not the least of which was an almost complete lack of weapons and proper training. There was much to learn, and Czech resisters needed to understand the dangers quickly. "I was trying to organize an underground movement, but it had to be done very carefully and in a way that minimized the risks to the members of the network," Luza recalled. "The Gestapo was a very efficient organization. They sent informers into our groups and they learned about some of us and started to destroy the organizations. So we learned that you had to be careful that members of the network would not know each other. That relates to the first rule of the resistance: You aren't supposed to know more than you need to. That way, if [people were] seized by the Gestapo, they would be unable to give summary information about the network. We always built in 'dead ends' so that someone would not know more than necessary [to fulfill his role]."

The SOE sought to build up the fledgling organizations, and also to establish regular and reliable radio contact with London, much of it prompted by Moravec. During most of the first two years of occupation, there were two valuable radio sets operating. From August 1939 until June 1941, the PÚ used radio station "Sparta I" in Bohemia to beam more than 20,000 radiograms to London. Another 6,000 were sent through other countries. Astonishingly, this station transmitted the plans for Operation *Sea Lion*, the German invasion of Great Britain, and news of its subsequent cancellation. It even transmitted the date of the German attack on Russia, which Moscow foolishly ignored. The used "Sparta II" in a more specific way to continue contacts on behalf of the Czechoslovak Intelligence Service. Operated mainly under the charge of a Czech army staff officer named Captain Vaclav Moravek,[5] Sparta II communicated with A-54.

In May 1941, the Gestapo captured Sparta II. Moravek escaped and continued communication using Sparta I, but this set was also captured by the Gestapo about a month later. On October 4, 1941, a Czech agent named Frantisek Pavelka parachuted over Caslav with replacement radio components and codes for Moravek. Pavelka had been selected from the 1st Czech Brigade, the free Czech military unit composed of soldiers who escaped to Great Britain.[6] Pavelka made his way to Prague, but made the mistake of visiting relatives there. As a result the Gestapo found him later that month. He talked profusely. Gestapo records captured after the war reported that he was arrested in Prague on October 25, 1941, and betrayed six local resisters who had hidden him in their homes. The Gestapo apprehended all six.

The Gestapo tracked down transmitters relentlessly. Luza commented: "It was not difficult to trace the transmitters, so there were many narrow escapes. For a time, I was living with a peasant in an apartment building. One day, I heard someone suddenly blurt out, 'The police are here and they are searching!' There was a special hiding place behind a false wall in the room, so I quickly moved inside it when I heard the clump of the policeman's boots as he came down the hall. The Gestapo was searching the entire building. We didn't know who they were looking for. There was a moment when I was sure they had found me. The boots stopped right in front of the false wall I was hiding behind. I could hear the breath of the German policeman. If he had started to knock, he would have known immediately it was a false wall. I always carried poison with me in my pocket and was ready to take it. I knew I would be tortured and would have taken it, but I escaped safely."

During the first few years of occupation in the Czech regions of Bohemia and Moravia, there were no large-scale guerrilla activities, and little sabotage. Government-in-exile and underground leaders specifically called for restraint. They instead focused activities around the Sparta intelligence nets.

Moravec maintained contact from London with his large and well-developed networks of agents. Both Benes and Moravec had done a great service for the Czech resistance with their farsighted preparations for lengthy occupation and resistance, but neither could be accused of micromanaging resistance at home. They had their own preoccupations—Benes with diplomatic duties to win recognition for his government in hopes that it and the reunified country could be restored after the war, and Moravec with his vital and effective intelligence operations. This left the resistance leaders in Prague to decide what specific actions they would take—by no means a bad thing, since decisions made on firsthand observation were often better than those made remotely.

Underground newspapers flourished immediately without any outside encouragement. Among the most read were the ÚVOD's *Into Battle*, *V Boj* (*In Combat*), the *Red Law*, and the *Czech Mail*. The newspapers orchestrated some of the early demonstrations in Czechoslovakia. A series of strikes of Prague's public transportation began in September 1939, timed just after the British and French declaration of war on Germany.

The largest act of defiance during the first year of occupation was a massive demonstration by university students on October 28, 1939.

German security forces fired into the masses and injured many. Two students fell mortally wounded, and at a funeral that followed in mid-November, even larger demonstrations erupted. Nazi reaction was swift and severe: The Gestapo rounded up nine student leaders and executed them. About 1,200 students were also sent to concentration camps, but they were eventually released and allowed to return home. As a final exclamation point, Hitler himself ordered *all* Czech universities to be closed down immediately. Many of the campuses were then taken for use by German occupying forces; classrooms were turned into administrative offices and dormitories into soldiers' living quarters.

The early restraint of the resistance, deliberately limiting its activities mostly to intelligence gathering and other nonviolent activities, made the assassination of a major Nazi figure seem all the more abrupt and astonishing.

In September 1941, Hitler replaced Freiherr von Neurath with Reinhard Heydrich. Heydrich had been transferred from a similar post in Poland, where he excelled in all the Nazi "virtues." Blond, tall, and athletic, with piercing blue eyes, Heydrich was the picture of the Aryan ideal. He had already earned the moniker "Blond Beast" (which, had he heard it, might have made him smile in satisfaction).

The story given to the public was that *Reichsprotektor* von Neurath had requested a leave of absence for health reasons. But the actual reason was Hitler's dissatisfaction over the looseness with which von Neurath was running his protectorate. Czech patriotism was running high and resistance movements were gaining momentum. Boycotts of protectorate newspapers and continuing strikes were an ominous sign that Czechs still possessed the will to stand up to their masters. In the late summer of 1941, two four-man teams from the Czechoslovak army had parachuted into the country from the Soviet Union with the objective of establishing contact with the resistance. More came in the fall. Most of the activity was known or suspected by the Germans, partly because one of the parachutists promptly changed sides, leading to the arrest of 160 resisters. Commanders of the Gestapo, SD (*Sicherheitsdienst*), and SS met in Prague on September 17 to assess the declining situation and file the report that alerted Hitler.

Heydrich was the perfect replacement to remedy the situation. Some said the mere presence of Heydrich "caused chills down your spine." It had been Heydrich who eagerly accepted the assignment of devising the "final solution" to destroy all Jews.

Heydrich began by having puppet Premier Alois Eliàs arrested and sentenced to death. Other arrests and killings followed, including the execution of Josef Bily, the ON commander and Eliàs' friend. However, strikes and other resistance activity continued. On November 12, 1941, a month after Heydrich told Himmler he had matters well in hand, the Gestapo in Prague filed a report drawing attention to the communist activity. On November 14, Gestapo officers in Brno filed a similar report. Strikes orchestrated by the underground press paralyzed the Prague shipbuilding yards in Prague-Liben, the Úpice textile factories, the Ostrava mines, and many other places. With every act of defiance, Heydrich became more fanatical and murderous. Czechs were deported to concentration camps by the trainload.[7]

A dozen more teams of SOE-trained Czech agents parachuted in during the fall and winter. Most had the routine missions of establishing intelligence communications or training resisters. One team, under orders issued by Moravec, was code-named "Anthropoid" and had the very specific objective of assassinating Reinhard Heydrich.

Moravec explained in his memoirs: "The British and the Russians, hard-pressed on their own battlefields, kept pointing out to Benes the urgent need for . . . an increase in resistance activity . . . The President of course knew that I was sending parachutists into the country to maintain communications with the underground. In late 1941 he suggested that here was our opportunity for a spectacular action against the Nazis—an assassination carried out in complete secrecy by our trained paratroop commandos. The purpose of this action would be twofold. First, a powerful manifestation of resistance which would wipe out the stigma of passivity and help Czechoslovakia internationally. Second, a renaissance of the resistance movement which would provide a spark activating the mass of people. In discussions of the President's idea, two potential targets for assassination appeared suitable. One of them was the Czechoslovak quisling Emanuel Moravec, the former colonel in the Czechoslovak army who had been appointed to the Protectorate Cabinet by Heydrich. . . . The other was Heydrich himself."

The two principals of Anthropoid were Josef Gabcik and Jan Kubis, two young Czechs who had been sergeants in the Czechoslovak army. Neither had a wife nor living parents. They had been carefully selected and trained by the British for the singular purpose of assassinating Heydrich. They knew going in that their chances for survival were slim. Their mission was unprecedented: An assassination had not been attempted by the Czechs, let alone a targeting of a Nazi of such high rank and esteem within the Reich.

Gabcik and Kubis parachuted into the Prague area and made preparations for the attack. They knew Heydrich's office was at Hradcany castle. Both the castle and his home were crawling with SS guards, which rendered an attack at either out of the question. Little definite information had been known about Heydrich's daily routine, so Gabcik and Kubis studied the road leading from his residence at Panenske Brezany to the castle in Prague. After hiding in bushes and ditches on the road for many days, they decided upon a hairpin turn in a northern suburb of Prague as an ambush site.

On the morning of May 27, Heydrich bade his wife farewell and left for his office with only a chauffeur. He carried an overnight bag with him because he was to fly to Berlin that night. Initially, he had traveled with armed escort, but over time he became complacent about his own safety because no one had attacked him.

Lying in wait at the preselected hairpin turn, Gabcik saw Heydrich's open Mercedes approaching. Gabcik dashed into the middle of the road with a Sten gun cloaked by a raincoat. He flung the coat aside and leveled the gun at Heydrich. With the car just a few yards from him, Gabcik pressed the trigger and—nothing. The Sten had jammed without firing a round. The chauffeur panicked, had no idea what to do, and so slowed down. Heydrich drew out his pistol as the car rolled slowly onward.

From the side of the road, Kubis hurled a bomb into the car. The explosion, which shook an otherwise tranquil May morning, mortally wounded Heydrich. Kubis was also wounded by the bomb, but he was able to get away as planned on a bicycle. Gabcik melted into the crowd on a loaded trolley. Still clutching his pistol, Heydrich was taken to a hospital, where he suffered for a week, then died June 4 from blood poisoning caused by a bomb splinter.

Gabcik and Kubis were later betrayed for a cash reward of one million marks by another SOE-trained Czech agent, Sgt. Karel Curda.[8] Curda did not know where his two colleagues were hiding, but he was able to lead the Gestapo to members of the Czech resistance who were helping them hide. Curda identified a woman named Moravec (no relation to Frantisek known) and a man named Zelenka. These two, in turn, had sought help from Bishop Gorazd, and Fathers Petrek and Cikl of the Greek Orthodox Church. They had led Gabcik and Kubis, along with five other Czech resisters, through a secret opening at the front of the church altar and into the crypt. There, they stayed for three weeks, living on provisions brought by Mrs. Moravec and her son.

"The Gestapo burst in on Mrs. Moravec, who with great courage took poison and died rather than be forced to betray the brave men," recounted Zdena Kapral. "Mr. Zelenka also had time to take poison. This left the Nazis with young Ata Moravec, one of the boys who had transported food and water. He was taken to the Gestapo headquarters where he was brutally tortured, and when his resistance was at its lowest, he was stupefied with alcohol and presented with his mother's head floating in a fish tank. Broken by pain and shock, he finally gave his torturers a clue where to look for Heydrich's assassins."

In a shoot-out with SS troops at the church, Gabcik, Kubis, and their colleagues defended themselves as long as they could. Three were killed by gunfire. Then the Germans snaked in firehoses to flood the crypt, which the resisters prevented temporarily by cutting the hoses. Eventually, the survivors realized they could not escape the siege and committed suicide.

The plan to assassinate Heydrich had not been favored by resistance leaders in the know. They feared not only for their resistance networks, but also for the Czech population as a whole. Horrific reprisals that followed proved them right.

K.H. Frank, then Nazi state secretary, immediately declared martial law and followed Hitler's order for a bloodbath of "unforgettable revenge." The deaths of Gabcik and Kubis were far from being enough; every man and woman with the last names Gabcik or Kubis were rooted out and arrested.

The village of Lidice had been mentioned by chance in a note found on a captured agent. Despite the fact that the agent was not involved in the assassination, the SS chose the village for obliteration. On the night of June 9/10, the Gestapo, aided by Wehrmacht troops, encircled the village and called or dragged the inhabitants from their beds. They herded together 197 men, all males above age 15, onto the village green and executed them where they stood. They loaded all women and children aboard trucks for shipment to concentration camps—the women to Ravensbruck and children to Chelmno (86 of the children would die in Chelmno's gas chambers in July 1942). The 95 humble houses of the village were burned to the ground. Anything left standing was dynamited and plowed under, leaving nothing but a barren field. The smaller village of Lezaky was also obliterated and its 33 citizens murdered on the Gestapo's flimsy pretense that at some point they had harbored Allied parachutists.

Anyone arrested by the Gestapo or already held for even slight suspicion of association with the ON or any resistance activity was summarily executed. Even the communist resistance movement, which had no part in the assassination, was as much a target as the rest. Most of its leaders were found and captured, some having been captured and released before, but this time none of them left their cells alive. "I was aware that many people were arrested," Luza recalled. "Each week you saw big, new posters hanging on the walls of the cities that listed the names of persons that were hanged or sentenced to death. Sometimes two or three names, sometimes 20 or 30. Many names I knew, partly because my father was a general. Some had been guests at our house." Estimates range from 2,000 to 5,000 people were killed in direct retaliation for the death of Heydrich.

Heydrich's replacement, Ernst Kaltenbrunner, was born in Austria, near Adolf Hitler's birthplace at Brannau. One of the original Nazis, he was extremely loyal to Heinrich Himmler. Kaltenbrunner was a remorseless killer, even compared to others in the Gestapo ranks. He savored killing and delighted in innovative means of execution. By the time the reprisal killings were finally over and the Czechs fully grasped the brutality of Heydrich's successor, it was crystal clear that assassinations of high-ranking Nazis, especially in the occupied countries, did little good.

If an objective for the assassination had been to stimulate resistance activity, then it misfired badly. The immediate reprisals decimated the resistance groups and valuable time was lost in rebuilding. Nazi efforts to stamp out resistance increased. There were unprecedented house-to-house searches and mass killings. In the end, the result was greater fear and even more conservative resistance action than before. Plus, Dr. Joseph Goebbels' propagandists were given the opportunity to spin Heydrich as a gallant martyr—a heroic and tragic figure slaughtered mercilessly in cold blood. Something that Nazi propaganda lost was its myth that German leaders in Germany's protectorates were popular among the masses, which was obviously ridiculous now that all of them needed heavy escorts wherever they went. Allied propaganda made use of events in Czechoslovakia, too: Lidice was somberly held up as an example of Nazi savagery.

The years that followed Heydrich's assassination posed new challenges for the Czech resistance. As the fervor over the Heydrich slaying gradually subsided, *Reichsprotektor* Kaltenbrunner instituted a new strategy for handling the resistance.

Instead of terrorizing the population with continued mass executions and then widely publicizing them, the Gestapo used a more subtle, sophisticated, and systematic method of repression. They developed a large and effective network of informants. Constant threat of infiltrators into the resistance created widespread mistrust. Many resistance members had been skittish even before the massive purge in the wake of Heydrich's death. Now some became paranoid beyond reason. Kaltenbrunner's strategy worked. From 1942 though the summer of 1944, sabotage and other bolder acts of resistance were few, and mostly inconsequential to the German war effort.

During this time, the crippled remnants of the old organizations—the PÚ, ON, and PVVZ—became a nucleus for movements to come. News of Allied victories reached Bohemia and Moravia from the BBC, and Radio Moscow ignited a small flame of guarded hope. German defeat in the Battle of Stalingrad and North Africa during February and May 1943, Italy's surrender in September 1943, and, most of all, the Allied landings at Normandy in June 1944 gave resisters some reason to begin planning for a national uprising. Another reason for a hopeful future was the Czechs' renewed contact with Slovak resistance forces.

The Germans knew that news of Axis defeat was reaching the Czech population through the air waves, and that it was creating a powder-keg situation. "The Germans . . . immediately ordered the short-wave frequencies removed from all radio sets," later wrote Zdena Kapral. "However, an ingenious Czech invented a gadget that earned him undying gratitude of a nation starved for facts. It was known as a *churchillka*, a small attachment that could be snapped into any radio, giving it a short-wave capability."

Intelligence continued to flow to Moravec's group in London, including reports on Hitler's secret weapon, the new V-1, being tested at Peenemünde (more on this in Chapters 2 and 6). More SOE-trained parachutists floated down into Bohemia and Moravia to strengthen communications with leadership in London. Still, very little aid came in the form of airdropped weapons from England or Russia. It was a tiny fraction of what some of the western European countries received.

At the end of 1943, a Soviet-Czechoslovak alliance treaty was forged. This brought small groups of Russian solders, many of whom had been prisoners helped to freedom by Czech resisters, to serve in advisory positions for weapons and tactics. Some of these former prisoners helped form Czech partisan groups that lived secretly in the forested countryside. Escaped British prisoners of war also took part.

When the Slovaks launched an uprising late in the summer of 1944, the Nazis massed 10,000 specially trained antiguerrilla troops at the Slovak-Moravian border to prevent a link up of partisan forces from both regions. While Nazi forces were massed there, the Red Army approached the Bohemian border on September 30, 1944. Soon, joint Czech-Russian partisan forces were engaging Nazi troops on equal footing. The partisans won the upper hand in some areas, striking and withdrawing into the woodlands. For the first time, Czech resisters were hitting and winning.

By 1944 the remaining resistance leadership began a restructuring that resulted in the creation of several groups, each with a separate purpose. First and foremost was R 3, or the Council of the Three, which looked forward to postwar, and its social and economic reforms, much like the PVVZ platform had. R 3 also planned a nationwide uprising at the right time, as the Allied armies approached. The second was the Illegal Trade Union (ROH). And the third, working surprisingly closely with its democratic countrymen, was the communist resistance, which agreed with R 3 that a massive uprising was needed.

At the same time that resisters in the Czech half of the country were plotting a major uprising on their own initiative, the government-in-exile in London was in the process of organizing a major uprising for the Slovak half. The tragic reprisals following the Heydrich assassination made the Czechoslovak leaders in London gun-shy about ordering another major action in the Czech side. Action in Slovakia, as a satellite state, had been handled differently.

During the winter of 1944–1945, an infusion of Nazi troops trained for antiguerrilla operations reversed earlier Czech resistance successes in the countryside. The partisan groups were scattered and forced to go into hiding. By spring, more Russian partisans were on the scene, in both Bohemia and Moravia, and the Czechs again enjoyed the upper hand. In addition, the ranks of the Czech partisan groups swelled with volunteers as the tide began to turn. There was close cooperation between both democratic and communist partisan groups with the Russian partisans.

Eventually, all major partisan groups were directed on the tactical level by the partisan headquarters of the Red Army, located at the Ukrainian front. Central control of the Czech partisans remained in Czech hands, however. As the Allied forces began pressing in from all sides on the sputtering Nazi war machine, a central body emerged called the Czech National Council. The council united the R 3, the ROH, and communist resistance, as well as others that had arisen.

For two years, R 3 had been pleading with the Allies, through exiled leaders in London, for arms drops. Finally, in April 1945, the first substantial arms drops began. By this time, partisan warfare had become the main form of resistance throughout all of Czechoslovakia.

With a feeling of victory in the air, the resistance gained momentum. Uprisings were taking place across the land. Resistance leaders set about to plan an attack on the last remaining strongholds in Prague. By early May, with fever for freedom running high, Prague civilians spontaneously joined in the street fighting that erupted across the city. On May 5, resisters seized Prague's radio station and broadcast pleas for Allied help far and wide. No Allied help came, even though U.S. troops were less than 100 miles from Prague[9] and Russian troops were even closer in the east. Even without outside help, well-armed resisters battled with entrenched SS and Wehrmacht troops and, after several days, took much of the city at a cost of 2,000 Czech lives. On May 8, 1945, the German garrison finally surrendered, as did the Third Reich as a whole. The capital was in Czech hands again for the first time in six years.

While the Czech portion of the country went through all its trials, the Slovak resistance movement lived its own autonomous life. It began in spirit early, just after the Munich pact was signed in September 1938. But even the strongest anti-German Slovaks did not act, despite suspicions (partly as a result of warnings from Benes) that Hitler would not stop after annexation of the Sudetenland and would seize all of Czechoslovakia. Like their Czech countrymen in Bohemia and Moravia, the Slovaks were cautious. Blatant action seemed likely to provoke Hitler, or at least give him a convenient reason to use force on post-Munich Czechoslovakia.

When Hitler did take the next step to march into Bohemia and Moravia to make them a protectorate, he shrewdly drove a wedge to separate Slovakia. The wedge was not only physical, with barriers and guards at the new border, but also psychological—stirring up Slovak racial hatred and by tantalizing the Slovaks with promises of stature within the Third Reich. Appearances were important to Hitler at this stage, so he declared Slovakia to be "sovereign and independent." There was a lot of pomp and show around harmonious relations between Germans and Slovaks. Slovakia was to be a showplace in the "New Europe" proclaimed by the Nazis. A new government was installed in the city of Bratislava. Its new president was Jozef Tiso, who was a Catholic priest. He was assisted by a cast of Hitler puppets in all high government offices. The Nazis stayed out of most internal affairs, except that it kept a tight reign on the military. The military not only continued to exist, but demonstrated its loyal servitude by sending several infantry divisions to fight the Red Army.

Although some citizens accepted the situation and even initially welcomed it, they came to realize there had been a price—namely their freedom. Resistance began as a "whispering campaign" in opposition to the New Order of Nazi-dominated Europe.

Slovak resisters did not unite into large groups during the first several years, but instead joined together in small cells in nearly all towns and villages across Slovakia. Initially, communication between cells was almost nonexistent and there was no contact whatsoever with the Czech resistance. The reasons lay partly in a fortified border and partly in the fact that Slovak extremists had a hand in the severing of Czechoslovakia into two parts. Still, there was desire on both sides of the German-imposed border between Moravia and Slovakia to restore a democratic Czechoslovak Republic. As on the Czech side, there were both democratic and communist resisters. Unlike the Czech side, the Slovak resisters needed to challenge not only the Germans, but also their own government, because the Slovak government was pro-Nazi and willingly cooperated with the German masters.

The Germans wanted an illusion of prosperity in their model satellite state, which Slovak resisters set out to foil through "white-collar sabotage." Resisters doctored the books so that the new nation's economy did not appear so prosperous. The undertaking wasn't as difficult as it sounds, because resisters infiltrated numerous lower government posts and used their own accounting methods to adjust government statistics. They would compile two sets of statistics—a true one for their own benefit and an unfavorable one for published reports. The Tiso government was left scratching its head and stammering out explanations to the Nazi overlords, who were very concerned over production measures. But no matter what action the Slovak government took, it only seemed to get worse.

In 1940, more conventional sabotage began: Power lines were cut regularly, interrupting power to vital industries; factory machinery was disabled; fires were set. By 1942, sabotage had begun in earnest with more and bolder activities: The railway bridge at Kral'ova Lehota was dynamited; a German train carrying ammunition from the Skoda works at Brno was set on fire; a munitions warehouse near Novaky was demolished. The Tiso government reacted by instituting Nazi-like control measures, such as enacting the death penalty for sabotage and other "terrorist" activities.

Slovakia's youth eventually involved themselves deeply in the resistance. The Slovak Revolutionary Youth was responsible for a lot of sabotage. And the Association of Lutheran Youth was blatantly adverse to the government, following the example of their Lutheran pastors. Catholic priests did not oppose the government as openly, but urged the president—one of their own—not to support Nazism.

Through contacts established by Moravec's intelligence service, Benes kept contact with the Slovak resistance, as he did with the Czech resistance. In February 1943 he directed the resistance to step up its activities and to win support among the Slovak security forces, including the army, frontier guards, and police. Through his representatives and personal contacts, Benes implored many Slovak leaders and high-ranking army officers (although outwardly loyal to Tiso) to lead their troops in revolt.

Later in 1943 the first real effort was under way to establish a central leadership for the resistance. Democratic and communist leaders met and eventually reached agreement based on their anti-Fascist aims. It was called the Christmas Agreement of 1943, finalized and signed on November 20. It centralized control of the resistance in the *Slovenska narodna rada* or SNR, which translates into Slovak National Council. The SNR's first objective was to plan a national uprising.

At the same time, more and more partisans were massing in the mountains of central and northern Slovakia. Less and less the Tiso government was able to keep control. Some of the partisan groups were well armed and under the command of the Red Army, as were the Czech partisans.

One partisan raid intercepted a train at Turciansky Svaty Martin on August 27, 1944. Aboard was a German general named Paul von Otto, who was returning from Romania. He was accompanied by 27 German staff members. The partisans killed them all, to the outrage of the German High Command.

Those killings and other partisan raids, along with growing unrest among the general Slovak populace, pushed the Nazis too far. They finally tossed aside the facade of Slovakian "independence," revoked its "privileged" satellite status, and brutally occupied the territory.

At first the Slovak army was ordered not to resist, then later, certain units were ordered to attack the advancing German occupation troops. The first clashes between soldiers took place on August 29, 1944, at Bystrica, Cadca, Povazska, Trencin, and Zilina.

As this was happening, another major uprising was taking place in Warsaw, Poland, that paralleled events in central Slovakia. The Warsaw rising was happening more on a timetable of the Pole's choosing, however, rather than a series of precipitating events like that thrust upon the Slovaks. Critical to both Poles and Slovaks, however, was the fact that elements of the Red Army were approaching.

The SNR still was in the midst of planning a general uprising, but was far from complete in its preparations when it had to act. The SNR took to the airwaves of the "Free Slovak Radio Station" the next day and called on all Slovaks to rise.

By the beginning of September, more than 18,000 soldiers of the Slovak army joined in the rising, and by the middle of the month, more than 47,000 had joined the fight. This included about 2,000 Soviet-trained soldiers of the Czechoslovak 2nd Airborne Brigade flown into central Slovakia, along with the 1st Czechoslovak Air Fighter Regiment. Coming out of the mountains were what amounted to seven organized partisan brigades of all nationalities—15,000 men representing 24 European nations. Among them were Slovaks and Czechs, Poles, Hungarians, Germans, Russians, Ukrainians, Croats, Bulgarians, Belgians, Frenchmen, and Englishmen. This group succeeded in taking control of a large geographic area in central Slovakia.

Fighting centered around the town of Banská Bystrica, where the insurgents were headquartered. Tiso's government in Bratislava and several Slovak military commanders worked to undermine the revolt as much as they could. In some cases it was difficult to tell which military commanders were pro-Tiso or anti-Tiso, so the Nazis were able to create a general state of confusion within the ranks. In one case, this allowed units of a German armored division to easily crush some groups of insurgents.

In the east, where most of the Slovak army was concentrated, there was no armed military revolt. Errant orders from a commanding general delayed them and they never joined the rising. In the west, swift action by German commanders sent troops through Austria and Poland to take the Slovak army garrisons with little challenge. By mid-September, the German army had completely quieted all signs of revolt in both the east and west. In central Slovakia, many partisans and some army units continued the fight, but the Germans sent overwhelming forces of 40,000 soldiers to quell the remaining insurgents.

Success of the Slovak rising depended on Allied intervention. It would be an understatement to say the revolt was premature. Military leaders had concluded that the best timing for the national uprising would be when the Red Army captured Miskolc, in Hungary, and Cracow, in Poland. This would not happen for four and five months, respectively. When it was clear that help would not come and that Germans were attempting to encircle them from the south by traveling up through the river valleys, the rebel forces took to the mountains, giving up hard-won territory.

As rebel-held territory shrank, the SNR stepped in to propose a war council that could better coordinate the Slovak army and partisans. Slovak communists wanted to reorganize the army, aligning it more with the Red Army structure and political bent, but the democratic resisters opposed the communist plan, and most of the ranking army officers were non-Marxist and would not have supported it. The communists continued to diverge, attempting to organize at least the partisan units along Red Army lines. The conflict was never resolved.

In October, more German forces were dispatched through Hungary, and the rebel position became more desperate. Banská Bystrica, home to the rebel headquarters, fell on October 27.

General Rudolf Viest, who had been sent from London on October 7 to assume command of the army, announced by radio that "organized resistance of the army as a whole is no longer possible." The army was dispersed to undertake guerrilla-style warfare. Some individuals and units merged with partisan units operating out of the mountains. Others fought independently. But fighting continued incessantly until the Red Army and the Soviet-controlled 1st Czechoslovak Army Corps eventually broke through the Carpathian Mountains. Then all converged on the occupying Germans *en masse*.

From the beginning of the Slovak rising until war's end, an estimated 150,000 German troops were killed. Red Army losses were 60,000 wounded and 19,000 killed. Slovak army casualties numbered

7,500, about 2,500 of whom were killed. And 3,723 Slovakian civilians were killed by the Germans in mass reprisals; another 30,000 civilians were sent to Nazi concentration camps; 60 villages were completely destroyed.

The Slovak rising had a far-reaching effect on the future of central Europe. It demonstrated that, although Slovakia had been a satellite state with a government supporting Hitler, its people rejected Hitler's "New Order." It also demonstrated that the aims of both the Czech and Slovak resistance were the same: They wanted to be united in a single, independent, and sovereign state.

Many believe that it was the strong position of the resistance in the Czech lands and Slovakia that paved the way for three years of freedom and democracy that followed World War II, until the Soviet takeover of 1948.

## CHAPTER 2

# Poland

At the brink of dawn on Friday, September 1, 1939, Hitler's Wehrmacht stood poised at the border of Poland's western frontier. At the preset time of 4:45 A.M., nine German columns launched across the border in an act of undeclared war. This relatively small first step of conquest would explode into the unparalleled global war that we now call World War II. Poland had the dubious distinction of being chosen as the first victim in Hitler's blitzkrieg. The country would be characterized by another distinction as well: unremitting resistance against the Nazi occupier.

At the moment of invasion, Poland fielded an army of 1.7 million men. Against this formidable number, Germany sent invasion forces of only 800,000. The two-to-one numerical advantage in troop strength was Poland's *only* advantage. Germany had no less than a two-to-one advantage in firepower.

Poland's saber-wielding cavalry was hurled against Germany's armor. When the two sides clashed, it was almost as if Poland's soldiers on horseback and on foot had been sent through a time machine to confront a twentieth century nightmare of clanking gray steel. Using textbook-perfect, pre–World War I tactics, the gallant cavalry met the Panzer divisions. The results were predictably disastrous for Poland.

Following the "grand pincer" plan Hitler was so proud of, two German spearheads thrust deep into Poland. German mechanized units rolled across the sun-baked plains, which were perfect for tracked and even wheeled vehicles after an unusually dry summer. By September 8, they penetrated as far as the suburbs of the capital of Warsaw, severing communications and leaving Poland's forces leaderless and paralyzed.

In his home of Szczebrzeszyn, a small-town medical doctor named Zygmunt Klukowski wrote one of the first entries in his wartime diary: "the streets were full of marching soldiers. This time between the ranks of the unarmed Polish you can see German soldiers. This was a very terrible picture. I still remember that a few weeks before this mass of unarmed, dirty soldiers were members of the Polish armed forces, the pride of our nation."

On September 17, when it seemed that matters couldn't possibly become worse, and every surviving defense was oriented westward against the German onslaught, Poland was invaded by Russia from the east—accelerating Poland's inevitable defeat. The next day, military and government leaders fled south in panic to places unknown, but left behind orders for the last defenders of Warsaw to stand their ground. Nearly 100,000 troops aided by 800,000 civilian residents of Warsaw— really the first of Poland's resisters in World War II—kept the ferocious Wehrmacht at bay for a remarkable seven more days. During the siege, Poland made an eloquent statement of defiance through Radio Warsaw, which continuously played the first bars of the inspirational *Polonaise* in A-flat, Opus 53 (written by Poland's native son and most famous composer, Frédéric François Chopin), as if to proclaim, "We still live!"

The combined artillery of four German armies totaling 2,500 guns, and aerial bombardment by the Luftwaffe pounded the city for days, killing people by the score and leaving the rest without water, food, or electricity. Hitler became so infuriated at Polish defiance that he stepped up the saturation bombing. One wave of bombing followed another, around the clock. Finally, on September 27, Radio Warsaw played Chopin's *Death March* as the proud, besieged city surrendered.

In effect, Poland as a nation ceased to be—erased from the map of Europe. In rough accordance with the "prearranged fourth partition," Germany now possessed 72,500 square miles of the 150,000 square miles of Poland (as maps had defined the nation at the time). Within that territory were the bulk of Polish mines and factories, and 23 million Polish citizens—all of whom Hitler despised. Russia seized the remainder of the land, which included 12 million people and most of Poland's oil resources in a section adjoining Romania and oil fields near Lwow. Except for an agreement concerning the Baltics, these turned out to be the only real spoils shared under the German-Russian Nonaggression (Molotov-Ribbentrop) Pact. And even that "sharing" would be short-lived, because Germany would occupy the rest of Poland later when Germany invaded Russia during Operation *Barbarossa*.

It didn't take long for people from all political parties, all parts of the country, and all walks of life—truly, every aspect of society—to rise in unanimous resistance against the occupiers. Collaboration among the Polish population was almost nonexistent. With such widespread and wholehearted support, Poland's resistance movement became the largest, most autonomous of its kind in Europe. Before the end of 1939, the Polish resistance began forging false identity documents, printing underground newspapers, and building an arsenal of weapons.

With little Allied influence or support, the Poles successfully set up an underground network under the command of high-ranking army officers. Dispersed pockets of resisters steadily gathered together to form a secret army at first called the *Zwiazek Walki Zbrojnej* (ZWZ), which translates into the Association for Armed Struggle. Later, this force would become known as the Home Army, or *Armia Krajowa* (AK).

The Polish resistance's cohesiveness and spontaneity was not a surprise, since Poland had been battling for its freedom from larger, aggressive neighbors for centuries. The need for resistance operations seemed "perennial." With the end of World War I and the rebirth of Poland, there was a renewed and even greater patriotic passion to preserve its fragile freedom.

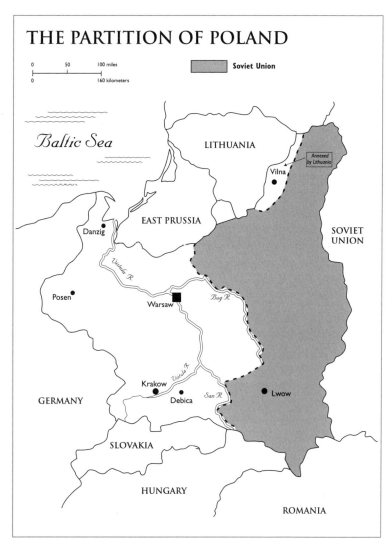

# THE PARTITION OF POLAND

Anti-Nazi resistance, in a sense, began in Poland even *before* the start of the shooting war. It had been the Poles who had pulled an espionage coup that would aid the Allied campaign immeasurably during the course of World War II. About a month before the invasion, on July 25, 1939, Poles absconded with two Enigma machines, used by Germany to convey their most secret cipher traffic.

It was an unequaled windfall for intelligence, not detected by the Germans even after the fall of Warsaw. The Polish deciphering team responsible got away, complete with the Enigma apparatus, to France. There, they turned over the treasure to the Allied intelligence organizations (France's Section D and Britain's MI6) and worked with Allied cryptologists to help break the code. While the antiquated Polish army had been humiliated by the Wehrmacht on the open battlefield, the Poles seemed to come into their own in the realm of clandestine warfare.

While the resistance was establishing itself, Poland's government-in-exile hopscotched its way to London. On September 18, 1939, the Polish political and military leadership found a temporary home in Romania. After relocation to France a few weeks later, it began to take shape with General Wladyslaw Sikorski as prime minister and Wladyslaw Raczkiewicz as president.

From Paris, contact with the nucleus of the resistance was restored, and General Sikorski assumed command. Sikorski, also serving as commander in chief of Polish free forces that would fight alongside the Allied armies, was delighted to learn that the resistance had become active on its own initiative, and that sabotage of German communication centers, industry, and railways had commenced almost immediately. But the Polish resistance had not yet structured itself for guerrilla warfare. Sikorski ordered restraint, directing the secret army to save its strength for an all-out uprising as the Allies brought about a general Nazi collapse. He appointed Colonel Stefan Rowecki to command the resistance forces at Warsaw, the most heavily populated and most important area of Poland.

While in France, communications between the government-in-exile and the resistance were not ideal. Through a radio network called *Regina*, Polish leaders were able to communicate with parts of Poland, but were unable to reach Warsaw, so couriers became the primary means of communications, their mission made easier by the fact it was possible to travel to Warsaw via Bucharest and Budapest by showing a diplomatic passport. From there they had to stealthily cross a stretch of German- or Russian-held territory to reach Warsaw.

In May 1940, when France was invaded, members of Poland's government-in-exile again had to uproot. Along with 17,000 escaped Polish soldiers and airmen,[10] they took refuge in London, new home to the governments of many occupied countries.

With the government-in-exile now in London, new, longer, and more dangerous routes had to be used by couriers. And a new radio network, called *Marta*, had to be established after almost all equipment was lost in the evacuation of France. By September 18, 1940, a direct link to Warsaw—sorely lacking since the surrender—was finally established. Despite the added distance to London, communications became regular and reliable. There were dozens of radios operating at any given time across Poland. Poles had done excellent work devising their own ciphers, but as the Poles came to know all too well, the Gestapo was everywhere, listening and finding ways to break codes. Stefan Korbonski wrote of the constant danger of "being discovered by the enemy's mobile radio interceptors or listening posts, which we called 'gonia.' [They] covered by means of a network the entire territory of Poland under German occupation."

Also early on, the BBC began beaming broadcasts in Polish, which prompted the Germans to confiscate all radios they could find. The Poles simply devised more radios.


Poland's new world of occupation was as harsh as any in Europe. Civilian bloodshed had not stopped with the bombardment of Warsaw during the blitzkrieg. That was only the beginning of a long, brutal occupation in which the general population was savaged on a daily basis. Hitler began a systematic destruction of even the Polish culture and national identity. In response, "the underground movement . . . had to embrace all spheres of national life," explained resister Józef Garlinski. It needed to not only concern itself with "sabotage, diversion, partisan war, and propaganda [as in western Europe] but also courts, education (on a secondary school and university level), the publication of books, protection of cultural relics, theater, and press," because all were banned or severely restricted.

From the day its army was crushed, the Polish population wholly adopted an attitude of defiance. Also from the very beginning, the Germans made clear there was zero tolerance for anything but complete submission in their new slave state.

"The Germans posted big red announcements saying, 'German Patience *Is At An End,*'" wrote Dr. Klukowski in his diary within only a few weeks of the invasion. Here, unlike western Europe where subtle gestures of ill-will toward Germans were commonplace in the beginning, nothing was tolerated. A western European caught in the east during the blitzkrieg observed, "After I was home again, I heard street vendors in Copenhagen speaking curtly to German soldiers. There, it might have brought an equally rude verbal retort by the German. *But that only.* In Poland, the response to the same vendor was apt to be a Luger drawn from its holster and fired at point-blank range."

Winston Churchill showed he understood the brutal treatment in Poland compared with other parts of Europe when he said in a BBC broadcast:

> *Every day Hitler's firing parties are busy in a dozen lands. Monday he shoots Dutchmen; Tuesday, Norwegians; Wednesday, the French and Belgians stand against the wall; Thursday is the day the Czechs must suffer; and now there are the Serbs and the Croats to fill his repulsive bill of executions. But, always, all the days, there are the Poles.*

The Gestapo was more bloodthirsty in Poland, fueled with racial hatred by their *Führer*. Its agents seemed to be everywhere, ruthless and omniscient. Every day, in the interrogation chambers of their dungeons, they tortured Poles—even those not specifically under suspicion—on the chance they might extract information. As Polish-born novelist Jerzy Kosinski wrote in his juvenile voice for his graphic war story, *The Painted Bird*: "Didn't they say . . . no one could resist the power of the German because he gobbled up the brains of the Poles, Russians, Gypsies, and Jews?"

Reprisals were the standard way of dealing with any Polish interference. Hitler "made examples" of people, especially in the regions of Silesia and Pomerania, by ordering mass executions. Citizens were killed without even the pretense of justification. That, in turn, evoked subsequent, greater action by the Poles. It became a vicious circle—the most vicious possible—in which *both* sides thought in terms of "reprisals" and "retaliation."

"The Gestapo has recently ordered mass round-ups of innocent citizens and the shooting of hostages," Stefan Korbonski wrote. "The Poles cannot be intimidated by such senseless and cruel activity. In reprisal for this kind of terror, additional retaliatory measures will be taken by the underground." With the very vulnerable and accessible civilian population, the exchange could not be even. A full 20 percent of the population would die.

It's no wonder that the Poles hated the Germans as mortal enemies. And it's also no wonder that the Poles felt they had nothing to lose in defying them in every way possible.

Resisters constantly sought intelligence for the immediate benefit of sabotage within the country, or to provide the Allies in London with information to be used on a more strategic scale. Poland's intelligence capabilities were second only to Czechoslovakia's, according to British historian John Keegan. Valuable intelligence about the Germans was already being collected by Poles forced to work in the Ruhr Valley and those conscripted into the Wehrmacht.

An important accomplishment of Polish intelligence gathering involved Germany's V-1 and V-2 flying bombs. The resistance not only provided information about the test and manufacturing sites for V-1s and V-2s throughout the war, but in one extraordinary instance actually offered a V-2 intact to Allied scientists.

Allied intelligence was aware of the existence of the V-1 testing ground in Peenemünde, on the Baltic Sea in northernmost Germany, because of reports from a Luxembourg laborer forced to help build the research facility. To gain more information, the Polish resistance dispatched an agent posing as a laborer seeking work in nearby Stettin. The agent was hired into a transportation unit tasked with regular delivery of food and supplies to the research facility in Peenemünde.

When the agent's report, complete with diagram sketches of the compound, reached Warsaw, the resistance recognized the urgent need to notify London. The Germans were already at the stage of mass production and the weapons had been seen loaded on trucks and trains. The report was photographed on microfilm and sent by courier without delay through Danzig, then to Sweden and ultimately London.

Churchill ordered a large-scale bombing mission to wipe out the facility. The RAF sent 600 heavy bombers on the night of August 17, 1943, to drop 2,000 tons of high-explosive and incendiary bombs on Peenemünde. Later reconnaissance revealed disappointingly light damage after this raid, which should have pounded the facility into dust. By comparing reconnaissance photos with the Polish agent's original diagrams, the British concluded that the most important parts, including the testing areas and wind tunnel, endured. However, the scientists' billets and 18 out of 30 forced labor barracks were leveled.

The air attack did not fully accomplish its mission, but nonetheless forced the Germans to relocate to a whole new facility for the testing of their next generation weapon—the deadlier V-2 rocket. A location in Poland's province of Krakow was chosen. At the time, in the fall of 1943, this was outside the range of standard RAF aircraft.

Because the Germans probably had no notion that it was actually Polish intelligence that had provided so much information about Peenemünde, they unknowingly put themselves squarely in the center of a resistance nightmare when they moved their main rocket experimentation facility from German to Polish soil.

The new facility was built at an SS troop training grounds called Heidelager, deep in the heavily forested region of southern Poland. The Germans took the precaution of sending away all Polish forced labor that had been at the SS training grounds and brought in Russian prisoners of war for labor. The small contingent of German guards was stepped up to 650 to safeguard this highest priority of the Nazis. The grounds bordered Blizna, a deserted village where the native population had long since been relocated or killed.

In an elaborate and failed ruse, the Germans went to great lengths to give the impression of normalcy in the village of Blizna. They hung wash on the lines of abandoned cottage gardens, placed plaster of Paris dogs in vacant kennels and wooden cows in pastures.

From the start, the Polish resistance kept close vigilance of the site. "Polish resistance," in this case, included old peasant women and men, younger adults, children—in short, everyone who encountered any German activity. All reported what they saw. The mosaic of information from these sources was transformed into a series of regular reports sent from Warsaw to London. They told of the construction of camouflaged buildings surrounded by antiaircraft guns and searchlights, the influx of German soldiers, the SS patrols with dogs, and a new branch line of the Krakow-Lemberg railway connecting the site to the outside world. At this point, the actual purpose of the site was still not understood. The Poles did not know they'd driven the Germans here after the Peenemünde bombing, and the world did not yet know about this newest technological terror, the V-2.

The first clue about the site's purpose came from a forest ranger at the area's forestry station, who told local resisters that he'd witnessed the incredible sight of a large, unfamiliar bullet-like shape roaring out of the dense forest, streaking up into the sky and exploding at high altitude on November 5, 1943. Resisters later stood by with cameras awaiting the next launch, and captured it on film. Other clues came from the railway station at Kochanowka, where the newly constructed line branched off to Blizna. Agents hiding there reported flatcars with what looked like aircraft fuselages. Although covered by tarps, a quick peak revealed an oddity: Exposed outlet valves were encrusted with ice even though the air temperature was well above freezing.

Another oddity was the Germans' urgency and meticulousness after a "crash" near the small town of Rejowiec, which piqued the residents' attention because after the "airplane" had come down, a German search party appeared almost immediately, cordoned off the area, took many photographs, and carefully measured the dimensions of the impact area. They then gathered up every discernible trace of the wrecked craft, which appeared to include no traces of a crew.

The suspicious activity tipped off the Allies that this was a matter of highest secrecy and priority. Perhaps the most telling clue was the fact that the commanding officer on the scene personally apologized to the Polish landowner and offered full reparation for the damages caused by the crash. In Germany, and perhaps even western Europe, that might have happened, but here, no! Reasonable and fair treatment of a Pole surely meant something sinister.

All information and photos reached Warsaw for analysis and then were forwarded to London, where scientists were beginning to piece together the theory of a rocket bomb. Over the course of weeks, the theory was confirmed when the tests reached advanced stages.

The Germans deliberately fired many V-2s across the Polish countryside, not caring where they fell. The first landed in the peasant villages around Sarnaki. Many more came without warning, as was characteristic of the V-2. Nothing was heard as it approached at 300 miles per hour and struck indiscriminately—killing, maiming, and destroying.

Instead of moving out of the impact zone, the resident peasants took it as a personal challenge. They saw how important the crash sites were to the Germans and resolved to collect up every bit of glass wool and wire, every rivet and bolt, right down to the tiniest piece of aluminum skin—just the way the Germans did. After fighting their way through thick forest undergrowth, the German crews often found a crater but no rocket parts. Finding crash sites became a lively competition for the Poles. The rocket pieces and information about precise locations reached Warsaw routinely.

The situation climaxed when a peasant named Jan Lopaciuk burst into the office of Dr. Marian Korczik, a fellow resister, in Sarnaki. Lopaciuk breathlessly uttered, "One has come down unexploded and buried itself in the banks of the Bug!" A V-2 test shot had failed. The rocket had plummeted to earth without exploding and buried itself in the muddy bank of the river Bug, near a village called Klimczyce about 80 miles east of Warsaw.

The German recovery crew, bent on keeping their new terror weapon a secret, sped to the scene to search for the intact rocket. At the same time, Lopaciuk and the doctor's brother ran back to the rocket and, with the help of other resisters, concealed the rocket fins visible above the water's surface by covering it with reeds.

A C-47 Dakota transport aircraft was dispatched from the Italian base at Brindisi to retrieve components of the V-2, and after a harrowing escape that nearly required blowing up the aircraft because it became stuck in the mud, the components were delivered into Allied hands. Secrets of the terror weapon were unveiled in London laboratories seven weeks before the first V-2 exploded there.

Compounding the brutality of the German occupation in Poland was the fact that the country had 3.3 million Jewish residents. Because Jews made up a large percentage of the population, Poland became Hitler's testing ground for the "final solution" in the chilling phraseology coined by Reinhard Heydrich. That, combined with the fact that Hitler despised the Polish as a nationality, added up to unequaled butchery.

Millions were sent by boxcar to concentration camps, many of which were built in Poland itself. An estimated 2,350,000 to 3,000,000 Polish Jews were murdered, most in the camps. Millions of non-Jewish Poles also died in the camps for their resistance activities, political views, education, social class, and for no particular reason at all.

In 1942, Dr. Klukowski witnessed horrific scenes of the "final solution" in his small hamlet:

> *June 24: A big ditch had already been prepared a few days ago. When the Jews were brought for execution, they were told to lie down in the ditch. They were shot with machine guns. Then the next few were forced to lie down on top of the dead. They killed them all in three rows. All were very old men who prayed and begged for mercy.*
>
> *October 22: It is a shame to say it but some Polish people . . . even helped the gendarmes look for hidden Jews. The Germans even killed small Jewish children. . . . It is so terrible that it is almost impossible to comprehend.*
>
> *October 26: Two gendarmes halted a Jewish girl. She was beaten, kicked, and finally when she was unable to walk she was pulled by her hair to the cemetery and shot. . . . On all sidewalks there are numerous blood stains.*

The resistance reacted with retaliatory executions. Dr. Klukowski recounted, "In Zwierzyniec Gestapo informer Kulik and his wife were shot. He had taken part in the Jewish liquidation." The Home Army's underground newspaper, *Biuletyn Informacyjny* (Information Bulletin), warned that "any anti-Semitic actions by Poles is considered traitorous and will be punished by death."

Another way the resistance figured into the holocaust was by aiding in escapes. Escapes from concentration camps were almost unheard of and considered impossible. Yet the Polish resistance, in this case the non-Jewish citizens living around extermination camps, took great risks to help in the escapes. At the camps west of Krakow, for example, nearly 700 are believed to have escaped. Many were recaptured and executed, but more than 300 cleanly escaped and survived the war.

Jews themselves established successful underground groups with the primary mission of aiding in the escapes. Contrary to the prevailing image of Jews as passive victims, many such groups rose in revolt— and desperation—against their tormentors. One celebrated group was the Bielski partisans who took to the forests of western Belorussia. The group, which grew to 1,200, was said to be the largest armed rescue operation of Jews by Jews in World War II.

One of the greatest acts of resistance on the part of the Jews themselves came in April 1943 at the infamous Warsaw ghetto. Hitler sent 3,000 SS troops and militia under the command of General Jürgen Stroop to destroy all Jews living there. Pitted against tanks, artillery, and armored cars, the heroic but weakly armed Jews rose up and lashed back. Stroop had been given three days for this mission, but it took four months. More than 56,000 Jews died in the fighting.

In a bizarre turn of events that characterized the complex situation faced by Poland, Russia and the Polish government-in-exile forged diplomatic relations in July 1941, a month after Germany invaded Russia. The immediate benefit was the release of some deported prisoners of war held in Russia. These troops then joined the Polish army fighting in the Near East. Russia's invasion of Poland's eastern half in September 1939 remained a delicate subject.

With the establishment of new relations, Sikorski ordered Home Army commander (now General) Rowecki, *not* to resist the Soviet troops, but instead to *aid* them as guides as the Soviets moved west.

Diplomatic relations between Poland and Russia were cut short early in January 1943, however, when Radio Berlin announced that Nazi troops had unearthed an enormous mass grave in an occupied area of Russia called the Katyn Forest. With German permission, the Polish Red Cross embarked on an investigation. The telling conclusion: The grave contained the bodies of 4,143 Polish army officers interned by the Russians since 1939. The mass grave *predated* the German invasion of Russia. For Poles, these were more than military officers. They were the elite—the intelligentsia and independent-minded future leaders.

Nazi propaganda pointed the finger at the NKVD, predecessor to the KGB. The Russians denied it (and later claimed that they found German bullets embedded in the skulls; moreover, they said, the method of execution—a single shot to the base of the skull—was a German method).

Poland immediately broke diplomatic relations with Russia.

To further complicate an already impossibly complicated circumstance as the Russian crisis reached its climax, General Sikorski was killed in a mysterious plane crash. Official reports simply state that Sikorski was flying from the Middle East to London. While circling over Gibraltar, his B-24 Liberator "somehow crashed on the airfield" on July 4, 1943. Sikorski died instantly. Announcing his death to the

House of Commons, Churchill called him "the symbol and embodiment of that spirit which has borne the Polish nation through centuries of sorrow and its unquenchable by agony." He was succeeded by General Kazimierz Sosnkowski.

In addition, another important Polish leader was lost: Within a week of Sikorski's death, General Rowecki was identified and arrested. Fourteen months later (during the Warsaw Rising) he was executed by Himmler's personal order. The loss of two key leaders was a setback to the Home Army, but as much support as ever came from the Polish populace in terms of volunteers and every conceivable aid.

The Warsaw Rising of August 1944 was the climax of Poland's resistance. As directed, the Home Army had deliberately avoided partisan-style combat (even though the mountainous Carpathian region provided adequate guerrilla terrain). By preserving its fighting strength until the final stages of the war, the entire Home Army, now commanded by General Count Tadeusz Bor-Komorowski (a former Austrian army officer), could rise up in force to oust the German occupier from Poland.

"The underground movement was passing through a phase of great excitement," Stephan Korbonski wrote. "We sensed the approaching hour of decision. . . . We discussed the existing situation and tried to envision the shape of things to come. The discussions showed clearly that a rising was inevitable."

It was to be *the* decisive lunge for independence. It needed to happen in the narrow window of time when Nazi Germany verged on collapse and before the Red Army arrived. As the logic went, the Poles then would be on equal footing as "masters of their own house" when the Red Army inevitably marched in.

The uprising was set in motion as the Red Army approached the banks of the Vistula near Warsaw. The Russians had gone on the offensive the month before, in July 1944, overwhelming the German Army Group North Ukraine in southeastern Poland and sending it reeling in headlong retreat toward Warsaw.

As the Russians advanced, all German occupation forces in their path became panic-stricken. Between July 21 and 25, German businesses and military commands packed their bags and fled Warsaw.

On July 26, the German High Command did a sudden about-face. It ordered the Wehrmacht to stand fast and defend the city. One hundred thousand Polish civilians were ordered to step forward to help build defensive fortifications for the Germans. That same day, a convoy of reinforcements rolled into Warsaw's southern outskirts. The SS "Viking" Panzer Division and "Hermann Göring" SS Panzer and

Paratroop Division had been moved up from Italy. On the following days, German infantry and additional police arrived.

As the Germans were returning in force to Warsaw, they were unaware that Russian troops were approaching the river Weichsel about 60 miles south of Warsaw, and that a Russian tank corps was rolling unopposed near Wolomin, only 10 miles from Warsaw. When General Bor-Komorowski learned of their close proximity, he was convinced that the time was nigh for the uprising. General Sosknowski and the government-in-exile in London agreed. In the same series of communications with London, Bor-Komorowski pleaded for deployment of a Polish paratroop brigade, but Warsaw was out of reach for Dakota troop transport aircraft. Plus, there was no suitable landing zone for such a jump. The Home Army would proceed regardless.

After five years of restraint, the exhilarating order was finally handed down and Poland would cast out the Nazi overlord. Events were developing quickly, so it needed to happen immediately—the next day, August 1. "W-hour," as the Poles called it, was set for 5 P.M.

The Home Army was composed of approximately 38,000 troops—34,000 men and 4,000 women. In preparation for the uprising, these men and women were organized into precincts, seven urban and one suburban. The eight precincts were further subdivided into sectors.

Two other small resistance organizations, not subordinated to the Home Army, also resided in the capital. The *Narodowe Sily Zbrojne* (NSZ), or National Armed Forces, was almost fascist in outlook and anti-Semitic. The *Armia Ludowa* (AL), or the People's Army, was made up of communists and was previously known as the People's Guards. NSZ and AL each had several hundred men in Warsaw that later joined in the uprising alongside the Home Army.

German troops numbered about 40,000. Units had pulled out and others later had taken their places in the panic at the end of July. The German foot soldiers were well equipped with weapons and ample ammunition.

By any comparison, the Poles were weakly armed. Some had old Polish infantry rifles, but many of the resisters had only crowbars, clubs, or their bare fists for weapons. Perhaps only one in five actually had heavy or light infantry weapons. About two-thirds of their weapons and ammunition had been cached after the 1939 capitulation; no more than a third (about 600 tons) had been airdropped over the course of the last three years. There was ammunition enough for only seven days' fighting. Polish rearmament over the course of battle depended on the capture of German equipment and supplies.

The Poles dressed for battle with whatever garb was available. They wore "a strange assortment of uniforms—helmets borrowed from the crosses over the graves of Polish soldiers who fell in the 1939 defense of the city, or combat camouflage jackets of the SS Panzer units taken from a nearby factory," explained Julian Kulski. ". . . red and white armbands [were] the only standard part of our otherwise crazy mixture of civilian and military outfits."

The two Panzer divisions were equipped with Germany's newest tanks, including the Panzer IV, Panther, and Tiger. For defense against them, the Poles prepared homemade Molotov cocktails. Concocted from household ingredients and chemicals available from any pharmacist, it was a bottle filled with a mixture of gasoline or diesel fuel, a few spoonfuls of sulfuric acid, and a small amount of potassium chloride attached to the outside of the bottle with a piece of paper. When the bottle shattered, the mixture inside combined with the potassium chloride and exploded in flame. It was a simple and deadly solution that rendered the tanks "useless in street fighting," according to Lieutenant General SS-*Gruppenführer* Heinz Reinefarth, in charge of German combat forces.

There was elation when the first gunfire erupted from rooftops, felling German soldiers on the streets below. "We finally were doing what [we] had dreamed of for four long years," wrote Kulski. "We were in the thick of battle against the Occupier."

When it became clear to the Germans that this was not a minor outbreak but a major insurgence, an infusion of reinforcements and weapons would surge in to augment the Warsaw garrison. Himmler issued orders brief and brutally to the point: "All inhabitants of Warsaw to be shot; no prisoners to be taken; the town is to be razed to the ground."

The Poles gradually made headway, street by street. Taking and holding, losing and retaking, neighborhood by neighborhood, district by district. After just three days, the Home Army reigned triumphant. "Much of Warsaw is ours again!" Kulski wrote that day. "In many areas, the red and white flag of Poland is flying over the scarred but proud city for the first time in five years, and the hated swastikas have been torn down." The only key objectives that remained were railway stations and bridges across the Vistula.

Then the tide turned—severely. The Poles could not sustain their victory against the reinforced and well-supplied enemy. The Germans knew it. The Russians knew it, too, and halted their advance at the most critical moment. With Red Army troops as close as Praga and other suburbs, Stalin shrugged that the Russian offensive had run out of steam.

Pleas from the other Allies to continue the advance were ignored. Furthermore, Stalin sneered, the Home Army leaders were "power-seeking criminals" and he dismissed the Warsaw Rising as "a reckless and fearful gamble." In addition, Stalin denied Allied requests to use Russian airfields to launch supply drops, just as he had denied other Allied requests to use Russian airfields throughout the war (except for a few strategic bombing missions against Germany). Some believe Stalin's true motive lay in the fact that the Home Army was as adamantly anticommunist as antifascist. There was obvious "convenience" in letting the two forces kill each other off, because then the Red Army could move in.

Meanwhile, the carnage continued in Warsaw. In the Wola districts retaken by the Germans, all civilians were flushed from their homes, and the houses were set ablaze, street by street. The civilians were gathered together at gunpoint, and Himmler's orders were carried out to the letter: Standing defenseless, fathers, mothers, sons, daughters, grandfathers, and grandmothers were riddled by machine gun fire until not one was left standing. The bodies were then stacked, doused in gasoline, and set ablaze.

Elsewhere, Polish women were made to walk in front of German troops and tanks as human shields, defying the resisters on the rooftops to shoot or toss their Molotov cocktails at them. Leokadia Rowinski, a member of the *Sluzba Kobiet* (Women's military service) of the Home Army, was at one point captured and forced to walk among the advancing Germans.

"Obviously, they did not know Polish women," wrote Rowinski. "The ones on and around the first tanks kept shouting to the insurgents, urging them to shoot and not give up." Not recognized as a resister, she was later released and rejoined her resistance unit.

Because of the obstacle of German-held streets, the only means of communications between some Polish-held sectors was by messengers, usually women. They could travel through the streets, risking bullets and explosions or creep through the city sewers, which provided a hidden network that connected points throughout the city. The Germans knew it too, so they made the sewer system a death trap. Rowinski commented: "One thing I could not force myself to do was to use this abominable underground route. I preferred death on the surface and in an open space to perishing like a rat in a dirty, stinky sewer. . . . We had news that the Germans were aware of the canals being used for communication and transportation and, at times, would block the manholes or throw hand grenades into them." German squads also jumped down to attack survivors in hand-to-hand combat in a subterranean nightmare of filth.

Gradually, the Home Army lost its momentum. At first, they pulled back building by building. Later, entire sectors had to be abandoned, and the Germans easily retook them. To the agonizing end, hope beyond all logic remained that "the British and Polish air units will drop paratroopers and that together we will liberate Warsaw," in Julian Kulski's words. Or that the Red Army would pick up its advance. Instead, the Russians sent help in the form of cursory artillery shelling from across the Vistula that accomplished little, and air drops of weapons and ammunition left over from World War I, "dropped without parachutes, so that three-quarters are smashed and useless. . . . That is good enough for Soviet purposes and for Soviet propaganda."

The resistance went into its death throes and with its last gasp of breath, Radio Warsaw broadcast: "May God, who is just, pass judgment on the terrible injustice suffered by the Polish nation."

"No one knew it yet, but I had heard about the signed capitulation agreement during my duty at the telephone switchboard," recounted Rowinski. "Although listening to transferred messages while making telephone connections was strictly against the rules, I could not force myself not to listen to this one. Frozen with helpless anger, despair filling my heart without almost physical pain, I could hardly believe what I was hearing. How could the leaders even consider a surrender? Did they not know that every man, every woman taking part in the uprising would sooner die than be part to such a shameful end?"

The survivors of the Home Army were permitted the dignity of marching out of their capital in formation, still armed, into the hands of the awaiting Germans. The entire civilian population was expelled from the city, and while the ragged citizens still thronged the outlying roads of once-proud Warsaw, the Germans commenced with a systematic destruction of any structure still left standing. Anything worth scavenging was taken back to Germany. Buildings were leveled with explosions and flame. Weeks later, Warsaw still burned.

When the Red Army's legions finally crossed the river Vistula, they entered a surreal, ashen expanse: Undulating gray mounds that had once been homes and shops were strewn with blackened bones that had once been living, breathing human beings. The outcome was as tragic as any resistance action in Europe. It was a magnificent and absurd sacrifice.

Over the course of the Warsaw Rising's 63 hellish days, the death toll was staggering: Losses of the Home Army troops were 10,000. Loss of civilian lives was estimated between 150,000 and 200,000 men, women, and children.

The Warsaw Rising virtually ended active Polish resistance in World War II. With its leadership captured and its Home Army's back broken, the people of Poland could do nothing but suffer through the last days of German occupation, all the while hoping for an intervention by Western Allied forces that never came.

## CHAPTER 3

# Denmark

An uneasy six-month lull followed the invasion of Poland. Then, with breathtaking suddenness, the next strike of Hitler's lightning war lit up the peaceful Scandinavian sky as both Denmark and Norway were invaded on the same day: April 9, 1940.

Copenhagen, the Danish capital, proved an easy objective for German seaborne invasion troops. By 5 A.M., three troop transports had plied the waters of Copenhagen's harbor unchallenged and landed an assault battalion at the Langelinie Quay. The battalion went directly to the center of Copenhagen and quickly overtook the King's Guard at Rosenborg Castle. Karin Stromgren, who lived in the Royal Observatory across the street from the castle and King's Guard garrison, later recalled, "The Germans marched right up and arrested all of the King's Guard. Of course, the 'Guard' didn't put up much of a fight. They were the soldiers with the tall black fur hats who stood in front of the bright red sentry boxes, played in the band, and marched for the tourists." Wave after wave of low-flying Luftwaffe aircraft thundered overhead, tossed into the mix more as a show of force than anything.

At the same time Copenhagen was being taken, German armored units entered Denmark at Krusaa, located on the 42-mile southern border Denmark shared with Germany. With no bridges blown, no roads mined, the panzers rolled unimpeded into the frontier of the Jutland (the Danish peninsula joined to continental Europe). Token attempts at defense with machine guns and small arms gave way quickly to surrender. To prevent unnecessary sacrifice of life in an obviously losing cause, King Christian X called for cease-fire.

The king and the Danish population never wanted anything but peace and, in the absence of that, at least neutrality (like the neutrality they maintained during World War I). They were so set on this hope that they had actually *reduced* the size of their armed forces in the months before the invasion, so as not to give any impression of a warring nation.[11]

With a grand total of 16 casualties by the end of the day, Denmark found itself an occupied country. Denmark was not officially at war—no formal declaration of war had ever been stated. The king and his ministers accepted German occupation as long as there was "no infringement on Danish independence." With that, Denmark became Hitler's "model Aryan protectorate."


On the surface, the German invasion did not change Danish life much: The king continued to reign and government officials remained in office. Students continued going to school, workers went to their offices or labored in factories, and farmers went on cultivating crops of carrots, potatoes, cabbages, and sugar beets. This normalcy put Denmark in a unique position among occupied countries—and with unique challenges for the resistance.

With collaboration as its policy, Denmark appeared to be Hitler's willing lackey. But beneath this impeccable veneer of calm acceptance were boiling feelings of defiance against the occupation. Danes gave *Den Kolde Skulder*—the cold shoulder—to the Germans. No place was this better manifested than in the daily horseback rides of the king through Copenhagen's streets. Christian X warmly responded to each citizen's "good morning," sometimes even dismounting to talk, but he shunned all German soldiers' salutes. And so the Danish resistance began—passively at first.

Next came a proliferation of underground mass communications. Among the many oddities in Denmark's new scenario as Germany's model protectorate, the news-reporting press was not censored. This permissiveness actually worked for a time, when news about Nazi victories in places like Russia and North Africa was true. But as the tides of war ebbed and flowed, the Germans didn't want news of setbacks to reach citizens, because it might encourage revolt. When the Germans began exerting control over what the Danes read, the Danes immediately responded with illegal flyers and chain letters. By the second half of 1941, underground newspapers were printed and distributed regularly. Some even became nationally distributed newspapers, as in the case of *Frit Danmark* (Free Denmark), established by an underground group of the same name.

First appearing monthly in 1942, *Frit Danmark* was a joint effort between strange bedfellows, the communists and the conservatives. The process of printing and distribution became highly efficient: Its editorial board in Copenhagen sent the articles in print-ready form to a network of resistance-run printing presses throughout the country. They, in turn, would print copies for local readers. The underground newspaper became so popular that by war's end over 6.3 million copies had been printed.

*De Frie Danske* was another popular tabloid that had a specialty of lampooning locals who consorted with the occupiers. It featured two regular columns: "*Vaernemagtens Damebekendtskaber,*" or "the

Wehrmacht's Female Acquaintances," which listed the names of women who fraternized with German soldiers, and "*Den Blaa Bog*," or "the Blue Book," which listed names and addresses of local businessmen and others who affiliated themselves with the Nazis. The embarrassing exposure invited harassment and ostracism by the reading public.

In time, the underground press encouraged more violent forms of resistance, particularly sabotage. The May 18, 1942, issue of *Boycott* read: "The least we can do—and we all can—is to boycott the Axis. But many of us have an opportunity also to sabotage the Axis—at shipyards, airfields, and factories." This paper and others praised the

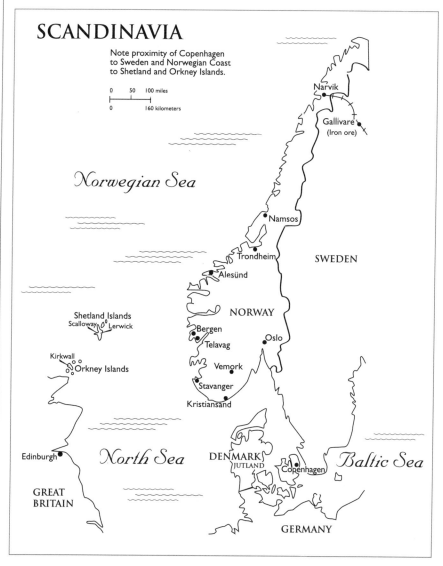

work of saboteurs (like the Churchill Club of Aalborg, covered later) and reported actual facts about targets and bomb damage, which were typically misconstrued in the "rump" (or legal) press.

Radios were not seized as in nearly all other occupied countries, allowing Danes to listen to local broadcasts. Of course, these broadcasts were rife with German propaganda, so Danes tuned in more distant broadcasts from Sweden and Great Britain, which the Germans immediately set about disrupting and jamming. Several Danes who were children during wartime remember gathering around the radio with their parents. One said, "I remember the frustration of my father straining to listen to the Swedish news—the real news—above the static interference." Resisters listened closely to BBC broadcasts in particular for code words in the form of nonsensical phrases to tip them off to arms drops and other covert activity.

Danes communicated to the outside world through a number of mediums. In July 1940, the Danish journalist Ebbe Munck went to Stockholm as a correspondent for the newspaper *Berlingske Tidende*. There he received communications from Denmark and passed them to the British legation which transmitted it to Great Britain. Like most occupied countries, Danish resisters used radio-transmitter equipment to provide valuable intelligence to Great Britain. But within the dangerous, technical world of intelligence communications, with its secret radio transmissions always in danger of being traced by local German direction-finding detectors, agents in Denmark discovered a simpler, safer means of communication: The telephone. Telephone calls placed to Stockholm and relayed to Great Britain offered a ridiculously easy and sure-fire medium for many vital messages, right under the noses of the Germans. There were simply too many lines and too many calls, making it impossible to cover them all.

The first intelligence gatherers in the Danish resistance were professionals—a group of junior officers from the army and navy intelligence services, who came to be known as "the Princes." Since Denmark was not at war, the young officers remained on active duty, with the Germans' awareness and blessing. They continued collecting intelligence, although not the kind the occupiers would have approved—namely about movements and numbers of German troops, planes, and ships! These were communicated regularly to Great Britain via Munck in Stockholm for three years.

One particularly notable accomplishment of the Princes happened in August 1943, when the group obtained photographs of an unexploded V-1 flying bomb that had crashed on the Danish island of Bornholm, northeast of the launch site at Peenemünde. Knowing the value of the photos to Allied intelligence, the Princes reproduced eight sets of them and sent eight couriers on different routes and schedules to ensure delivery in London. The Germans caught one courier. His capture led to the arrests of several other Danes, because the Germans recognized the crash site on Bornholm in the photographs, and from that deduced who witnessed it. None talked. Other couriers completed their missions and detailed photos were delivered safely to Allied hands.

Despite these clandestine acts even within the military, the policy of the Danish government remained officially "accommodation" to the occupier. Soon after the invasion, the Danes appointed Erik Scavenius foreign minister to replace Dr. P. Munch, who was mistrusted because he adhered to the policy of reconciliation with Germany. Scavenius had been the foreign minister during World War I when neutrality was remarkably preserved. People assumed he knew how to deal with the Germans, but Scavenius began with the pessimistic premise that Germany would win World War II and that Denmark should act accordingly and "agreeably." The population soon vocalized its rejection of this and called for "Norwegian conditions"—casting off the façade of accommodation.

The Danish population reached its own hopeful conclusions, which were completely opposite from those of Scavenius. Their belief that Germany would lose the war was fueled by the events of 1941, when Germany invaded Russia and reached a standstill at Stalingrad, and the United States entered the war. By reading underground newspapers and listening to the Swedish radio and the BBC, the Danes knew the truth about all of it as early as the free world knew it.

Rallied by the thought that "Denmark has been occupied but not conquered," early resisters on the extreme ends of the political spectrum committed minor acts directed not against the Germans, but against their own government. When the Danish police caught them, they were tried as criminals in Danish courts.

On the left end, the forbidden Communist Party formed the first sabotage groups. Many had experience as volunteers in the Spanish Civil War in the mid-1930s. The Danish Communist Party had been legal and even had three members in parliament. However, after the German invasion of Russia, the party was banned and the Germans demanded that the Danish police arrest all the communists they could find. During the summer of 1941, 295 people were arrested and of those, 117 were quickly released for lack of evidence. It was enacted into law that communists could be arrested on suspicion alone. Later that year, in November, Denmark joined the Anti-Comintern Pact, directed against the Russians. This forced all remaining communists underground and into more active roles of resistance.

Others joining in active resistance were patriots (who had volunteered in the Finnish Winter War 1939–1940 against the Russians), conservatives, and activists from a small right-wing party called *Dansk Samling*. This party saw its wartime mission as motivating Danes throughout the country to rise up and take back their country by force when the time was right, in the same vein as Poland and others to follow.

By the spring of 1942, groups of saboteurs were striking key places throughout the country. One of the first groups heralded in underground newspapers was the Churchill Club, a group of teenage boys and girls from Aalborg's Cathedral School.

Saboteur groups like the Churchill Club sprang up and struck in other places. The communists also banded together in small groups for sabotage, using homemade firebombs and later, stolen explosives. The Danish police were in the awkward situation of maintaining order. There were obvious advantages to law enforcement remaining in Danish hands rather than the Gestapo's. But the Gestapo allowed this only if the Danish police maintained order. Danish authorities apprehended the Churchill Club in May 1942 and were able to keep acts of defiance in check.

By the end of 1942, damage done by sabotage was only minor. Still, German patience was growing thin. Sabotage would remain "one of the most troublesome" issues in the Dano-German relationship.

Perhaps *the* most troublesome issue was the "Jewish question"—that some 8,000 Jews lived freely in the presence of the anti-Semitic occupier in Denmark. The phrasing of the "Jewish question" is said to have come from the German ambassador, Cecil von Renthe-Fink, in a conversation with King Christian X. The latter is said to have replied, "There is no Jewish question in this country. There is only my people." During the first years of occupation, von Renthe-Fink and other German authorities sent numerous reports to Berlin punctuating that, unlike some other occupied countries, Denmark would not accept persecution of Jews. And, in fact, revocation of Jews' civil rights would likely set off violent revolt that would greatly disrupt relatively stable relations.[12]

"Danes never had considered Jews anything but just other Danes," Karin Stromgren Campbell echoed her king's sentiment. "We were astonished and indignant when we learned of the Germans' hatred."

In late 1942, when the Nazis experimented with anti-Semitic acts, such as painting swastikas on the walls of a Copenhagen synagogue and then setting the building ablaze, the Danish police rushed to the scene and stopped them. Then the police went the step further to create an all-Jewish auxiliary police squad armed with guns to protect the synagogue—a bold move unprecedented in Nazi-occupied Europe.

When word of the Jewish support, increasing sabotage, and strong suspicion of intelligence activities reached Hitler, he was enraged and decided it was time to gain a much tighter grip on his model protectorate. He replaced von Renthe-Fink with Dr. Karl Werner Best, one of the architects of the Gestapo and its former administrative chief. With the title of German Reich Plenipotentiary, Best was empowered to decide and act largely on his own. When Best arrived in Denmark on November 5, 1942, no one expected a Gestapo officer of this high rank to have anything other than a no-nonsense solution to the Jewish question. But Best surprised many Danes and Germans by maintaining the moderate position of his predecessor. Best, too, thought these pure Aryans should administer the affairs of their own state. Furthermore, he concurred that acting against the Jews would bring about unnecessary turmoil. Above it all was the ironclad logic that there could be adverse effects on Danish production, upon which Germany had come to depend: Denmark produced much-needed agricultural products in large quantities (even more than demanded by heavy quotas) and her factories supplied industrial products, such as components for aircraft, tanks, and ships.

Since the Nazis seemed destined to live with this aggravating permissiveness in Denmark, they assigned a tough-minded Wehrmacht officer, Lieutenant General Hermann von Hanneken, to head the occupation forces, with specific orders to bolster coastal defenses against Allied invasion. At the same time, the Germans demanded that Foreign Minister Erik Scavenius should become prime minister to replace Prime Minister Vilhelm Buhl. Increasingly unpopular among his own people, Scavenius reluctantly accepted the post. Appointment by German command put Scavenius in a difficult position, because it was the first time a prime minister had not been elected by parliament. However, Scavenius soon realized he had the majority of parliament behind him, because its members feared the consequences of defying Germany.

An unprecedented event arose out of Denmark's highly unique situation during World War II: a general election in an occupied country. In accordance with the Danish constitution, 1943 was an election year, and consistent with his theory that "good races" should administer themselves, Best decided that parliamentary and other elections should go on in March. It was an experiment that would not be repeated. Voter turnout was an unprecedented 89.5 percent—the highest in Danish history. More than 97 percent of the vote was anti-Nazi, leaving candidates of the Danish Nazi Party with less than 3 percent.

More boldly now the Danish citizenry began asserting itself in opposition to the Germans. Subtle taunts, such as wearing the U.S. and U.K. colors of red, white, and blue, gave way to much more aggressive forms of resistance. Many who initially had opposed violent acts changed their minds. Sabotage against the armament industry sharply increased through late winter and spring of 1943:

February reports tallied 34 acts of sabotage; 70 for March; and 78 for April. The success of these acts was compared in the underground press to the RAF bombing raid on Burmeister & Wein shipyard in Copenhagen. High Danish casualties and unintended damage there helped convince the general population that sabotage executed by its own underground was "safer" and less costly in the long run.

Aware of increased action and changing attitudes, the Allies sought to fan the flames of resistance. The BBC renewed its campaign urging resistance. With this nucleus of resistance forming and the tempers of the general population simmering, the SOE stirred up the pot by dropping arms and agents. The SOE got off to a tough start. The first agent, dropped in December 1941, was captured and killed after landing. Two more out of the first eight agents dropped were also killed. Three others were arrested, leaving only two to operate. In all, 53 SOE-trained Danes would return to their homeland as agents, and enough arms were dropped to equip 25,000 resisters. Along with that came plenty of explosives, transmitters, receivers, and other supplies. A continuing struggle throughout the war was that the SOE needed to coordinate its efforts with, or at least act with diplomacy toward, the Danish Military Intelligence Service.

The first successful arms drop took place on March 11, 1943, when cylindrical containers with small arms were parachuted into Jutland. This was one of many that had as its larger objective equipping a whole secret army that would be ready to rise up when the Allies invaded. "Reception organizations" were set up by the resistance expressly for the purpose of retrieving materials from drop zones. These men and women listened intently to the BBC's Danish news broadcasts for codes indicating drops. Despite their careful preparation and secrecy, things still went wrong.

A leader in a reception organization, J.P. Jensen, recounted, "When the plane came it circled three times. That was too much. And when it finally dropped six containers they fell some distance away from where they should have landed. So we had to dash across the fields to get them, and they aren't half heavy. We got them on the lorry and then away we went. But unfortunately we had been spotted. A German patrol vehicle saw us and hailed us. . . . We were 12 men plus the containers in the lorry. We were shot down right on the edge of the Rold forest. One of my men, Niels Erik Vangsted, was killed on the spot. Another, Poul Kjoer Sorensen, was taken prisoner and executed some days later in Arhus. The rest of us got away."

General von Hanneken linked the increased sabotage with the SOE or, at least, Great Britain. In his mind, this could mean only one thing: impending invasion. He sought authority from the German High Command to disarm the Danish military and increase his own forces to combat the resistance and stiffen coastal defenses. While von Hanneken wrestled with his own bureaucracy that would not support this, the internal situation deteriorated further.

Mass labor strikes were another headache for the Germans. A succession of strikes followed German reversals on several battle fronts. July and August 1943 were active months for the Danish population and the Allied war effort as a whole. On July 10, the Allies gained a first foothold in Southern Europe by taking Sicily. Italian dictator Benito Mussolini toppled from power soon after. During the last week of July, the large port at Hamburg, Germany, was reduced to ashes when the RAF bombed it with 7,500 tons of explosives. The German offensive against Russia stalled at Kursk on July 9, and Hitler was forced to pull forces from the Russian front to cover "the soft underbelly" of Europe from the next Allied jump from Sicily.

Strikes began on July 28 at the shipyard at Odense. A German minesweeper there was sabotaged two days before launch. German troops picked up their guns and marched in, then shipyard workers dropped their tools and walked out. In an act of solidarity, workers throughout Odense in every factory also walked out. Clashes with German authorities followed. An officer drew his Luger and fired into a crowd wounding several people including a young boy, whereupon he was promptly overpowered and beaten by the mob that engulfed him.

Next was Esbjerg, where a strike began at a fish warehouse; soon, everyone in the town, including police and civil servants and other laborers, walked away from their jobs. The Germans imposed a curfew, which was entirely disregarded. People thronged the streets, leading to confrontations with police and soldiers. The Germans lifted the curfew, hoping to appease, but the fever of defiance had already spread. More strikes followed in Odense, then to nearly all towns throughout the Jutland, all the way from Aalborg over to Zealand.

This nationwide uproar occurred despite the lack of a central resistance leader. Unions headed by communists had some rabble-rousing effect, but it was mostly begun by like-thinking workers who had harbored discontent long enough and felt surging hope that the war would end soon.

The Scavenius government in Copenhagen became desperate. The Germans were furious. No one could quell the strikes, not even union leaders on the local level.

Meanwhile, sabotage continued—220 acts by the end of August. Danish government officials implored its citizens to remain orderly, while Best, the Reich plenipotentiary, watched order unravel before his eyes. It seemed as if the state of the nation couldn't get any worse.

Then it happened. One more act of major sabotage committed in the full light of day was the proverbial straw that broke the camel's back. On August 24, the resistance group *Holger Danske* sent five saboteurs to the Forum, the largest public hall in Copenhagen, and blew it to smithereens.

Two days later in Berlin, Best stood meekly before Foreign Minister Joachim von Ribbentrop, who unleashed a tirade about this confounded "policy of understanding." The next day, back in Copenhagen, Best handed Scavenius a black-and-white ultimatum: "The Danish government must proclaim a state of emergency throughout the whole country" or it would be ousted. Along with it came a ban on strikes, in addition to imposing the death penalty on convicted saboteurs.

The government rejected the ultimatum, voting unanimously to resign rather than support it. On August 29, 1943, German forces declared martial law and, in effect, Denmark was now finally in a state of war with Germany.

The Wehrmacht's first act was to carry out the order General von Hanneken had wanted all along: to disarm the Danish military. The Germans actually launched a surprise attack and demanded surrender of the Danish army, killing 23 of its soldiers in the process. Denmark's navy took action immediately to prevent its small fleet from falling into German hands. Aboard his flagship, the ranking admiral at Copenhagen Navy Yard signaled to all ships in the harbor: "Scuttle or escape to Sweden." Immediately, 29 ships were scuttled and 13 small craft crossed the Oresund to Sweden. The Germans captured only six ships intact.

King Christian X declared himself a prisoner of war. Parliament dissolved and the Scavenius government ceased to exist.

As the central authority for government exited the picture, a central authority for the resistance entered. On September 16, 1943, Denmark's Freedom Council was established. The council united the leaders of the four largest resistance organizations: *Dansk Samling, Frit Danmark, Ringen*, and the communists. This unification of supreme leadership was a major step toward coordinated resistance throughout the nation. It organized the country into six regions, each of which had direct radio contact with London. But the council itself remained the direct link between the Danish resistance and the SOE.

Ultimate command for virtually all functions of resistance now rested with the Freedom Council. Subcommittees reporting to the council had particular responsibilities: The "K-Committee" coordinated major sabotage activities, as well as quartermaster duties of parceling out supplies from the Allies. The information committee gathered news from many sources and provided the information to the underground newspapers. The reception committee continued to receive and hide guns, explosives, and equipment air-dropped by the Allies, and also material sent across the water highway from Sweden. The escape (or transport) committee helped evaders and escapees get out of Denmark. The intelligence committee reported to both the council and to London all troop and ship movements, continuing the excellent intelligence work of the Princes, after the Danish military had been interned.

Financing for the resistance came largely from civil servants on local levels who took over certain roles in the fallen national government. Civil servants did their part in the resistance by doctoring books and diverting millions of Danish kroner directly into the coffers of the resistance.

At the same time, the Germans pounded into place a totalitarian regime much like that in other occupied countries. In September 1943, the Gestapo brought in many seasoned men skilled in torture to extract information and launch a reign of terror. With them came a new chief, SS General Günther Pancke, who did not report to Dr. Best. What followed was the same brutal pattern of reprisals and using a country's own people as informers and collaborators. In a small country with areas of dense population like Denmark, informers were a valuable source of information to the Gestapo. The resistance had to liquidate them as quickly as they were identified.

Laws like the newly enacted death penalty for sabotage were enforced to the letter: Between August 1943 and the end of the occupation, 102 Danes were formally tried by German military courts and executed. Thousands more were killed in the act or sentenced to concentration camps and later died.

Reprisals, in the form of murder and wholesale property destruction, had been what many Danes feared most with the occupation. What was supposed to be a deterrent turned into bloodlust. It happened almost daily from September 1943 on. Liquidation of an informer was answered automatically with the shooting of a Dane— usually an innocent bystander on a street or a well-known citizen. In this way, Denmark's renowned poet and priest, Kaj Munk, met his death—beaten almost beyond recognition and shot point-blank five times.[13] Each incident of sabotage had a reciprocal retaliation, such as closing down shops, popular entertainment spots, and businesses not involved in the armament industry.

The Gestapo was supplemented with the *Schalburgkorps*, a military unit made up of Danish Nazis (mostly local thugs and criminals freed from prison) that was called back from the Russian front expressly to hunt down resisters and to begin the nightmare of Jew-baiting. But this nightmare led instead to Denmark's finest hour, as the remarkable story of Jewish deliverance unfolded. Rarely in history have the people of a nation acted in such unanimity.

Even by late 1943, the Holocaust had left Danish Jews almost untouched. But after the catastrophes that summer, Best was demoted from his position of plenipotentiary. Angry and humiliated, he remembered his trump card: The final solution.

Whereas Best himself had adamantly discouraged the idea before—in fact told Hitler that "irreparable damage" would be done to German-Danish relations—he now proposed deportation of all Danish Jews. After receiving Best's telegram, Hitler was so delighted that he immediately reinstated Best as plenipotentiary. Von Ribbentrop was instructed to provide all the resources Best would need to carry out the deportations, and *Reichsführer* Heinrich Himmler prepared the order to send additional SS and Gestapo.

The Germans had done their homework: The membership lists of synagogues, seized sometime before, became the lists of the "wanted." Names and addresses of all Jewish families were known.

Best set about briefing his own staff on the details of the coming roundup. Among the staff was Georg Ferdinand Duckwitz, head of the German embassy's shipping operations. In 1928, Duckwitz had moved from his German homeland to work in Denmark, and over many years he had made many close friends there. Among those friends was Hans Hedtoft, a leader in the Danish Social Democrat party.

A firm date and time were set for the arrests: Using diabolical logic, the plan was for Nazi troops to burst into Jewish homes at 10 P.M. on Friday, October 1, the start of Rosh Hashanah when, by Jewish doctrine, all should be home for the night.

At the first opportunity, Duckwitz tipped off Hedtoft about the plan. From there, the news spread fast. The day before Rosh Hashanah, the Jewish New Year, Rabbi Marcus Melchior stood before his congregation of the Copenhagen Synagogue to announce, in no uncertain terms, that all Jews must immediately go into hiding. Whether the news was announced by a rabbi or delivered in whispers from a Christian friend, almost all Jews learned of the imminent Nazi roundup.

One Dane who immediately took action was Dr. Richard Ege, a professor in the biochemistry department of the Rockefeller Institute in Copenhagen. Ege was at the institute when another professor, Dr. Poul Astrup, told him of the Nazi plans. Ege knew Astrup was a communist resister and thereby had reliable inside information; Astrup knew of Ege's caring nature and friendship with several local Jews.

Ege wasted no time in leaving the institute to find Jewish friends in their offices and homes. A few of them required convincing; they'd been lulled into complacency over the years of occupation when no action had been taken. Others immediately accepted it as fact. For those who had nowhere to go, Ege was quick to offer his own home, living quarters above the laboratory at the Rockefeller Institute.

In his haste to spread the word, Ege had neglected to inform his wife of the news or that these guests would be arriving soon. After his breathless explanation, Mrs. Ege immediately also set out to warn her Jewish friends. Fearing the telephone was not secure, she informed most in person. But there was one long-time friend that could be contacted by telephone: Annemarie Glanner, a childhood friend of Mrs. Ege who had known her while living in Siam. The warning, spoken over the telephone in Siamese, was, in a pinch, as good as any secret code.

Other people who put out the word were long-time members of the resistance. Jens Lillelund had many Jewish acquaintances in his role as a cash-register salesman, as did Mogens Staffeldt, a bookshop owner. Both used the guise of their occupations to secretively broadcast the word far and wide.

When nightfall came on October 1, the Nazi terror squads divided up in precincts to canvass the width and breadth of neighborhoods wherever Jews lived. The squads found nothing but dark windows and burst through doors to find nothing but silent rooms and no one home. Nearly every Danish Jew had vanished into the home of a Gentile neighbor, to an out-of-the-way friend's country cottage, or directly to the fishing boats in rural harbors for escape to Sweden.

Only 284 Jews were arrested that night, out of a total of 8,000. It helped that 95 percent of Denmark's Jews were concentrated in Copenhagen. But that very fact gave Himmler confidence that they could be tracked down. After all, he reasoned, those Jews could run but they couldn't hide "for more than a few days."

"My dad had a good friend, a professor who was Jewish," said Karin Stromgren Campbell. "His two little girls, ages 8 and 6, were smuggled to our house and had to live in our attic. We never told even our best friends in school. My father sat us down and said, 'We're hiding Jews. If we're found we'll be shot on the spot.' I was 9 at the time but simply took it as part of life. Every day I'd come home from school and go to the attic to play with them. Talk about scared kids. Can you imagine? A strange house, no parents, hiding in an attic."

One day, Stromgren came home from school and the Jewish girls were gone. They had been smuggled out of Denmark. More than 7,000

Jews had been safely harbored by the defiant Danes until, boat-by-boat, they could be spirited to neutral Sweden.

Even Adolf Eichmann's personal presence, starting on October 3, and all the ruthless methods of the Gestapo were to no avail. During the remainder of October, the Germans' frustrated search yielded not even 200 more.

Two huge transport ships floated forlornly in Copenhagen harbor. The cavernous *Wartheland* could have crammed thousands of prisoners in its hold. Instead it steamed out of the harbor with only 202. The other ship left empty, presumably to travel to a foreign port where the Jewish population had not been so fortunate.

A grand total of 481 Danish Jews were arrested in the roundup. They were sent to the concentration camp of Theresienstadt in Czechoslovakia, where 52 of them died from natural causes or from harsh conditions. But thanks to the continued efforts of the Danes on their behalf, no Danish Jew is known to have died in the gas chambers.

Instead of the journey to concentration camps, 90 percent of Denmark's Jews were transported by fishing boats along the illegal routes to Sweden. As part of the organized escape group of the resistance, certain individuals were responsible for arranging for transports and others for smuggling the travelers in manageable numbers to the boats. These developed into "permanent" underground units used to secretly convey other refugees to and from neutral Sweden.

One of the most famous Jewish passengers in the boats was Nobel Prize-winning physicist Niels Bohr, who made the trip on the first day of the roundup, October 1. Before leaving Denmark, Bohr had heard of the German plot directly from Hans Hedtoft himself.

Special provisions for escape had been made for Bohr by the Allies, who needed his genius for work on the atom bomb in the United States. The plan was for Bohr to fly from Sweden directly to London without delay, and then on to the United States. But Bohr would not agree to go until he met with Swedish authorities, and thereby played a critical role in the rescue of the Danish Jews.

The plan had always been to get the Danish Jews to Sweden, but it was not a given that neutral Sweden would condone such a plan, officially or unofficially. Bohr demanded an audience with the Swedish foreign minister about the matter, but the foreign minister gave no assurance. Using a bit of coercion that had a touch of genius in its own right, Bohr stood fast until he had that assurance. Knowing the desperate need for his nuclear physics expertise by the Allies, Niels Bohr brought to bear all the pressure in the world on Sweden. When the foreign minister dodged the question, Bohr went to King Gustav himself, who eventually gave that assurance. Bohr went on to assist in the Manhattan Project, which created the weapon to end World War II.

As the daughter of another world-renowned Danish scientist, Karin Stromgren Campbell recounted her own wartime connection to Niels Bohr. Her father, astro-physicist Bengt Stromgren, and Niels Bohr were professional colleagues and good friends. She recounted:

> *We awoke to a loud pounding on the door downstairs. My father opened it to find German soldiers standing there with guns. Some Hungarian prisoners had escaped from the German headquarters nearby our home and they were out searching for them. We were all herded downstairs in our nightclothes—no shoes or robes—to stand shivering on the hardwood floor. A sixteen-year-old soldier kept a rifle pointed into my father's stomach for the two hours the search lasted.*
>
> *My father, who was active in the underground, was white as a sheet. He had a trunk full of papers to be distributed to other resisters. These papers contained information on where the RAF would drop weapons. But the Germans left without finding anything.*
>
> *There was something else we had that the Germans would have been most interested in, but we didn't know it at the time. We found out after the war that, before he left for Sweden, Niels Bohr had buried his important papers in our yard. If my father had known that, he would have been whiter still!*

The greatest turning point for the Danish resistance came with the Jewish evacuation. After that, there was no turning back; the resistance pulled out the stops and the Danish population as a whole became an instrument of defiance.

More strikes followed during the summer of 1944. Protesting German oppression, especially a curfew from 8 P.M. to 5 A.M., imposed on June 25, workers in Copenhagen and towns throughout the country didn't report for work. The Germans took swift action to break the strike, unleashing the *Schalburgmen* and cutting off food supplies to cities, along with water and electricity. The Freedom Council urged all workers to continue with the strike and demanded a lifting of the curfew and withdrawal of the *Schalburgkorps*.

Workers supported this. On July 3, the last night of the strike, an estimated 5,000 fires illuminated the streets during blackout hours. It was a shining punctuation point to their demands, during days when the last thing the Germans needed was a direction marker on the ground for the high-flying RAF night bombers on the way to the Fatherland. The Danes knew they had the upper hand in one respect: The German military needed their industrial and food production for their war effort. The Germans backed down, revoking the curfew and withdrawing the *Schalburgkorps*.

Through the events of the summer and before, it was increasingly evident that law enforcement in Danish hands was not working. On September 19, 1944, the Germans arrested Danish policemen and eliminated all local police departments. Approximately 1,900 policemen and 141 border guards were deported to Buchenwald and other concentration camps (80 policemen and 41 border guards would perish in the camps). Another 7,000 policemen went into hiding and many joined the resistance.

Danish prisons were now bulging at the seams with inmates, and thousands of Danes were in concentration camps. The Nazis' terror was reaching epidemic proportions. The same horrific torture methods perfected in eastern Europe were now employed on Danish men and women. People in the street were picked at random to be gunned down in reprisal.

All this served to further bolster the resolve of the resistance. Within Denmark's borders a secret army, formidably equipped by the Allies, was growing to number 40,000 strong. More than 225 underground newspapers were in circulation now. About 20,000 Danes sought refuge in Sweden, traveling by way of the same fishing-boat routes used during the Jewish evacuation. Of those, about 5,000 had been recruited into Danforce, an Allied military unit that trained for retaking their Danish homeland when the time was right. The "model Aryan protectorate" by mid-1944 had become the "model defiant," spiraling wildly out of German control.

Germany was losing on almost all fronts. The Fatherland itself was being bombed around the clock by U.S. and British strategic bombing units. German morale had reached a low ebb. Most devastating of all, the Allies had landed at Normandy and were making steady progress eastward. To aid their progress, the Freedom Council sent teams of saboteurs to the Jutland as the Germans desperately attempted to dispatch reinforcements to the battle of the Ardennes. Sabotage to railways and other harassment delayed a German division for three days. All told, sabotage to railroads caused more than 1,500 interruptions, lasting from hours to days.

One seasoned saboteur, Kaj Christensen, remembered a railway sabotage incident, "I saw the train the following day. It was a perfect blow-up, with railcar after railcar lying in layers like layers in a layer cake. Talk about destruction. And on the very top of this pile of destroyed carriages stood a brand-new . . . big German truck. They could only get it down one way, namely by pushing it, and then it was smashed anyway."

Other forms of sabotage continued relentlessly. German communications and war industry remained high priority targets.

Joergen Jespersen described an armed attack against the Globus factory in Copenhagen: "We knew we couldn't get in by stealth as we had done it on previous occasions. We couldn't take these sentries by surprise. They were well-trained soldiers, and there wasn't much we could do about them, especially if they retreated into their pillboxes. We had tried to get people employed in the factory, so as to possibly smuggle something in. But it was impossible. The security checks were very thorough, so we decided to carry out our first partisan attack."

Talk of a secret army or "partisan attack" was unheard of early in the war. But by the closing days of the war in Europe, Denmark too had reached this mature form of resistance. With the seed planted by the SOE, an underground army composed of the resisters had grown steadily since early 1944. Leadership came mostly from the former officers in the Danish army and navy. This army was not expected to fight in the open until Allied forces reached Denmark. By the time Allied armies finally approached Denmark's borders in mid-1945, the secret army numbered about 45,000.

At this time, the Allies were making final plans for the liberation of the Scandinavian countries. The fear was that, during the thrust into the Nazi heart of Berlin, the formidable garrisons of German soldiers remaining in Scandinavia might make a last-ditch stand, at great cost to the citizenry. But on April 30, Hitler committed suicide in his bunker in Berlin; the next day Admiral Dönitz became Hitler's successor. With northwest Germany under British control, Dönitz sent Admiral Hans von Friedeburg to Field Marshal Bernard Montgomery's headquarters at Luneburg. And on May 4 at 6:30 P.M., von Friedeburg signed the instrument of surrender for German forces in northwest Germany, the German islands, Schleswig-Holstein, Holland, and Denmark. The announcement of surrender came on the BBC's news, spoken in Danish, at 8:35 P.M. After the long struggle in occupation, Denmark was spared a land battle between the surging Allied armies and the retreating Germans. After Germany collapsed, a quarter-million German refugees fled to Denmark.

The island of Bornholm was the last part of Denmark to be liberated. The Germans on Bornholm held out until May 9, after the island cities of Ronne and Nesko were bombed by the Russians on successive days. Russian infantry then invaded and occupied the island. Some tension arose over Russian intentions, especially after Denmark had joined in the Comintern, but the Russians finally pulled out of the island in the spring of 1946.

Celebrations in the streets after the liberation were combined with retaliation against collaborators. Eventually, 40,000 people were arrested. Of those, 13,500 were convicted of crimes during the occupation. Sentences ranged from years in prison to death; 78 death sentences were handed down, but only 46 were executed.

The postwar government included representatives from the resistance. A general election, the first since March 1943, was held on Oct. 30, 1945. Elections restored a government much like that previous to the war. Newly freed newspapers wrote: "Although the physical landscape of our nation is cratered and strewn with the wreckage of war, the political landscape of Denmark has not changed."

# Norway

On the gray morning of April 9, 1940, a northbound train lurched away from Oslo's East Railway Station. Its departure time of 7:23 A.M. was not scheduled on any railroad timetable. Aboard were wide-eyed, harried passengers not accustomed to being harried. They were Norway's royal family: 68-year-old King Haakon VII (widowed in 1938), along with his son Crown Prince Olav, the princess, and their three children. Also aboard were the parliament, the cabinet, and numerous key government employees.

At that same moment, a vanguard of German shock troops already stood on Norwegian soil. The first of what would number 1,600 airborne troops had landed at Fornebu Airport, 3 miles west of Oslo, and 2,000 seaborne troops had come ashore 12 miles south, at Sonsbukten.

That afternoon, when German soldiers goose-stepped into downtown Oslo for their victory parade (complete with a marching band), their intended "honorary grand marshal"—the Norwegian king—was missing, as were 50 tons of pure gold from the Norwegian treasury. In the form of bullion and coins, the gold had been packed into wooden crates and barrels at the Bank of Norway early that morning, then rushed out of Oslo by truckers who had been flagged down on the street by desperate bank employees. The gold was en route to a secret prearranged vault for temporary safekeeping in Lillehammer.

The plan for the king to take flight, rather than stand fast as had his brother in Denmark,[14] was decided at an emergency meeting of the Norwegian Cabinet early that morning. All agreed that the king and the government should withdraw to a safe place and orchestrate opposition from there. When the Germans realized this, they dispatched a contingent to find him. Roughly deducing his whereabouts, the German pursuers sped north in an attempt to find and return the king to Oslo that day.

About 70 miles out of Oslo, Colonel Otto Ruge, inspector general of the Norwegian infantry, quickly drew together civilian volunteers from a local rifle club to supplement his small army detachment, and prepared to intercept the pursuers. At Ruge's roadblock, a shoot-out left the German commander mortally wounded, while the other German soldiers fled. For the beloved king, this was only the beginning of a lengthy evasion in which he would be aided by hundreds of his subjects who hampered the Nazi's search.

The king's flight and the smuggling of the treasury's gold amounted to Norway's first acts of civil resistance.

With a watchmaker's precision, Germany struck both Norway and Denmark on April 9. At the same time that the Nazis were seizing key parts of Denmark, they were also invading the Norwegian ports of Trondheim and Egersund, which fell easily. German landings at Norway's coastal cities of Kristiansand and Bergen were challenged, but both fell later in the day. Narvik far to the north was also taken.

German forces moved inland with the utmost efficiency, knowing in advance exactly which airfields, government buildings, and communication centers to secure. But letting the Norwegian king slip through their fingers was not in their plan. Neither was the explosive reception at Oslo's harbor that began their day. During the predawn hours, the brand-new cruiser *Blücher* and pocket battleship *Lützow* escorted German troopships up the deep recession of Oslo Fjord. As the enemy flotilla plied the inky waters of the fjord, they drew closer and closer to the old Oscarborg Naval Fortress guarding Oslo's harbor. The fortress was plainly on their charts. Even the weaponry was known. But the danger was discounted. Ironically and almost humorously in the German sailors' minds, the old fortress' guns had been forged and installed in 1895 by the German manufacturer Krupp.

At 4:21 A.M., the old fortress' searchlight suddenly snapped to life and the captain of the *Blücher* found himself staring down the barrels of three antiquated 11-inch guns of the shore battery. The Norwegians immediately fired a 700-pound shell, scoring a direct hit at 1,800 yards—point-blank for an 11-inch gun.

In the next heartbeat, the *Blücher* was blown to kingdom come with the loss of 1,000 German lives. As the shore battery continued its salvos, the *Lützow* sustained damage and quickly turned tail. The invasion fleet followed, regressing to a safe distance south to land its two battalions at Sonsbukten. The troops would now approach Oslo by land.

This sudden change in landing plans delayed the German march toward the vitals of Oslo. And as a result, the king and a king's ransom—50 tons of gold—were long gone.

King Haakon and Prince Olav's flight transformed royalty into fugitives. The princess and three children left the group after they reached Hamar, where they crossed over the border into neutral Sweden. The king refused the sanctity of Sweden, saying, "As long as any part of Norway remains free, I must stay." The Germans dogged the royal duo, using every means available, including air surveillance by aircraft equipped with cameras. Aided by the long days in the land of the midnight sun, the Germans had many good hours of daylight to scour the roads and trails.

On the second day, Haakon took refuge in the small ski resort village of Nybergsund. From there, in an appeal repeated by radio throughout the land, he implored his three million subjects to resist the invaders. At nearby Elverum, Norwegian representatives met with German officers, who again demanded Norway's surrender. The Norwegian foreign minister refused capitulation once more, retorting sarcastically that "Hitler himself said that a people who submitted did not deserve to be free."

By the time the meeting adjourned, the Germans were furious. This time the Luftwaffe was dispatched in pursuit of the king, not only with cameras and sharp-eyed observers, but with explosive and incendiary bombs to blast and burn Nybergsund and Elverum to ashes. The two villages were destroyed, but Haakon and his son hid in the surrounding forest and escaped.

After more days on the run, they took refuge in the backwoods cabin of an acquaintance's farm. Knowing the threats he faced and that he had to be prepared to leave on a moment's notice, the king made a practice of sleeping in his clothes. "[Hitler] has chased me off roads into woods," the king reportedly muttered. "But I'll be damned if he'll ever get a picture of me in my pajamas."

Meanwhile, for lack of alternatives, representatives in Oslo attempted to negotiate some sort of compromise for the occupied regions. In the uncaptured northern regions, open warfare continued as the last remnants of the Norwegian army continued to fight.

At Narvik, the British navy sank 10 German destroyers and their support ships between April 10 and 13. A week after the German invasion, the Allies returned with land forces to help. British landings came north and south of Trondheim, followed by landings at Namsos and Aandalsnes. But these forces were withdrawn during the first days of May in favor of concentrating on Narvik. There in the north, they sought to wrest at least part of Norway from Nazi control and, in particular, to sever the vital flow of iron, copper, and nickel from Swedish mines needed to feed the German war machine. Royal Marines, along with French and Polish soldiers, were dispatched to Narvik, and initially made headway inland. But then came the German offensive in western Europe, biting deep into France. That left no chance for reinforcement.

As the Allied expeditionary efforts failed, so did the faltering Norwegian army. Narvik fell again on May 28. By early June, uniformed military opposition was all but crushed. The Germans firmly clutched Norway, as it already had Czechoslovakia, Poland, Denmark, and now, with the new offensive in the west, Belgium, Luxembourg, and the Netherlands.

Now that none of Norway remained free, mass evacuations took place the first week of June. The Allies withdrew, taking with them the king, the crown prince, and government officials, along with the gold, on June 8. As the king left, he appointed Otto Ruge to general and commander of Norwegian forces.

Norway's government-in-exile set up administration in London, and resistance continued, as King Haakon VII had called for and demonstrated himself.


A young Norwegian named Simon Ovretviet was among the soldiers demobilized in northwestern Norway. "When we saw they had no chance in the south, my regiment was demobilized," he later commented. "We had to turn in our rifles. We were given civilian clothes and told to return home to our families." Almost as soon as they were in civilian clothes, many members of the bloodied and beaten Norwegian armed forces went underground to begin resistance. Their defiance mirrored the willful attitude of their king.

All over Norway, resistance groups sprang into existence, albeit small and isolated. The very first groups were composed of young men freshly mustered out of service, or who had known each other before the invasion and now united with only vague direction. In Bergen, a former Norwegian army captain drew together ex-soldiers into an underground army unit. West of Oslo, in the Vestmarka forest, a former lieutenant struggled to keep a group together. He put his 30 men through ski drills and basic infantry tactics. In Oslo, the Student Athletic Association formed "teams" that practiced, not sports, but military drills.

With few knowledgeable instructors, training was extremely limited. Even the former military officers, proficient as they were in military discipline, bearing, and protocol, were not versed in the ways of irregular warfare, and there were few weapons.

Still, there *were* a number of factors working in favor of the Norwegian resistance. Of all the occupied countries in Europe, only a few regions had terrain conducive to guerrilla warfare. In east central Europe there were Carpathian Poland, Yugoslavia, and Greece. But in the northwest, only Norway north of Oslo provided the mountainous and wooded terrain needed. Other geographical advantages were a long jagged coastline, and equally as good, a border shared with neutral Sweden. But in the region, civilians were few and the German occupation troops were many—densely concentrated in anticipation of more Allied landings. Eventually *1 person of every 10* in the region would be a uniformed German.

Resistance among the wider population started slowly, for the same reasons it started slowly in Denmark. With a "gentlemanly" occupier, people did not feel compelled to act. It took *something* to push people from the threshold of passive resistance into active, and that something wasn't there initially to break the static inertia.

The German commander in Bergen told the citizens to remain calm, and that his soldiers had "come as friends." He pledged: "We shall not take away your personal freedom, and we wish you to continue in your regular work."

Except for isolated incidents with the SS and Gestapo, German occupation troops *did* act like perfect gentlemen, as was initial policy in western Europe. As a Bergen citizen named Live Hiis Hauge commented, "I felt safe walking at night even on the streets of Bergen, because German soldiers were so well disciplined."

Average Norwegians began with their own form of civil resistance, showing contempt in only certain, proper ways. For instance, when Germans entered restaurants, Norwegian patrons would demonstratively pull out their timepieces and position them on the tables in plain view. The rule of the occupation dictated that no one could leave a restaurant until 15 minutes after a German entered. And, 15 minutes later to the second, there was a mass exodus out the door.

"Our civil resistance . . . made the Germans uncertain and hesitant, surrounded as they were by a nation of enemies," noted Asbjoern Stensaker, wartime mayor of Bergen.

The nature of Norway's occupation policies diverged from those of Denmark, because of Norway's formal declaration of war and the flight of the Norwegian king. Otherwise, Norway might have been considered a "model protectorate," too. Hitler had hoped for that. He also hoped that all Scandinavians would accept his sincere invitation to join the Germans as racial cousins in Nazi ideology. But neither Scandinavian country welcomed the "kinship."

Unlike Denmark, Norway's government administration would not remain intact. Also unlike Denmark, Norway had a man named Quisling.

Major Vidkun Quisling had been Norway's minister of defense from 1931 to 1933 and afterward became the founder of his own Fascist party, the NS or *Nasjonal Samling* (National Unification), which was in effect the Norwegian Nazi Party. It was Quisling who first hatched the plot for a Nazi coup in Norway. Armed with the idea, he approached Hitler in December 1939. He left with a declaration of "Heil Hitler!" accentuated by the clack of his heels and thrusting of his right arm—"a poor attempt without the proper snap in giving the Nazi salute," one observer said, adding that it was something Norwegian collaborators could never seem to master. It was a salute nonetheless, and a strong statement of affinity by at least one faction in Norway.

Still, Hitler preferred a neutral Scandinavia. As long as Germany received iron ore on schedule from mines in Sweden and the British stayed away, there was no reason to invade. But the British forced his hand.[15]

When Germany finally moved against Norway, Hitler had expected submissive and even willing prey, based on Quisling's exuberant description. But Quisling had only told the Germans what they wanted to hear: That the *majority* of Norway's three million citizens were ready to adopt and, in fact, cherish the "Pan-Germanic ideal."

The fact was that Quisling rallied no appreciable help for the Nazi invasion. Once Oslo fell, however, Quisling and his stooges muscled into a local radio station and commandeered the microphone to announce proudly to his countrymen that the Germans had intervened to protect Norway from the British invaders—*and* that he was Norway's new prime minister.

The announcement naturally outraged the Norwegians. And it stunned the Germans.

During the week that followed, the Norwegian public and government officials snubbed Quisling at every turn. To the embarrassment of the Germans, he became the laughingstock of the country, and later the world. The efficiency of the invasion had shown how well prepared the Germans were militarily. But allowing Vidkun Quisling to take office showed that the Germans had not done their homework to understand the Norwegian people.[16] A quick look at the political record told the story: The NS had never attracted more than two percent of the vote and was never able to place a member into parliament. Six days after taking office, the Germans turned him out (but he would be back).

Removing Quisling was an attempt to respond to the popular feeling of the Norwegian people. But feeble attempts to "understand" and appeal to them were soon abandoned. The Germans stopped recognizing any Norwegian leaders of government unless they belonged to *Nasjonal Samling*. At the same time, the Nazis brought in Josef Terboven, a World War I pilot and later Brown Shirt street thug, who was elevated from *Gauleiter* of Essen to *Reichskommissar* of Norway. He was hand-picked to preside over a typical Nazi regime.

The new regime was enough to push some passive resisters over to active. What began as simply military occupation, turned more and more into an imposition of the Nazi ideology. With it came a flood of propaganda and an attempt to isolate Norwegians from the influences of the outside world.

Radios were confiscated, but underground newspapers soon found their way into the hands of grateful readers. The writers of the newspapers drew much of the news from the BBC. Just outside Bergen, one woman would climb into the loft of the chicken coop where her radio was hidden. By flashlight, she listened to the radio and scribbled wildly in shorthand, while an accomplice kept watch for the boarder upstairs, who was a Norwegian Nazi. The notes were then transcribed and put in the newspaper format.

"Initially, we listened to the BBC to get information," Gudrun Nielsen explained. "Later, when we lost the radios, we gained the clandestine newspapers. People risked their lives to get us the news, which we so badly wanted."

At peak, there were about 300 underground newspapers in Norway. Equipment and staff for as many as 120 were traced and destroyed. About 20,000 people, mostly in their 20s and 30s, took part. Of those, between 3,000 and 4,000 were arrested. When an underground newspaper abruptly stopped distribution, the rump press occasionally ran a story telling the fate of the defunct paper's writers—often a prison sentence (usually meaning Grini Concentration Camp) or even summary execution.

As time went on and resistance increased, leniency diminished and any sort of suspicious activity was likely to be met with an abrupt response, like a knock on the door in the middle of the night and arrest by the Gestapo.

"When someone had been arrested by the Gestapo, we used to watch his family, and we invariably found what we were hoping for: new recruits for the resistance," explained resister Olaug Titlestad. "The Gestapo prompted more people to become active resisters than we could have hoped to ourselves."

A physician and resister in Bergen, Dr. Eilert Eilertsen, stated, "I am convinced that the Gestapo's violence and terror actually created the Norwegian resistance movement."

Gradually, numbers grew and organization of the fragmented Norwegian resistance groups improved, under the leadership of General Ruge. Leadership on a higher level meant communication between the groups. During 1941, resisters were united into a network known as *Milorg*. Initially, the government-in-exile was suspicious of Milorg's motives and chose not to recognize it.

Milorg's primary mission was to rise up (in the same vein as the Polish Home Army and the other countries covered so far) and take control of the country when the Allies invaded. Its founders and leaders were mostly former army officers. SOE sponsored Milorg from its early development and provided instructors and weapons.

Other resistance organizations were specialized:

*Civorg* (civil organization) resisted against imposition of Nazi ideology. It dealt with national Norwegian issues such as politics, labor, and religion. And it provided leadership for the underground press.

X-U was Norway's intelligence network, which was responsible for providing information via clandestine radio transmitters to Great Britain. Its accomplishments included alerting the Royal Navy to the location of the German battleship *Bismarck*, leading to its sinking. Its reports helped protect the North Atlantic convoys. From their secret observation posts, X-U reported on troop movements and air operations as well.

*Norge Fritt*, or Free Norway, the communist group, was very active and carried out an especially violent agenda. As in all the other occupied countries, the communists kept a low profile and did not act until Operation *Barbarossa*.


On July 19, 1940, little more than a month after the Allied evacuation from Narvik, the Special Operations Executive was formed. While the Norwegian resistance developed cautiously, SOE matured quickly.

SOE sought select volunteers from each of the occupied countries and promised immediate action against the occupier. This appealed to some Norwegians. During the first months of occupation, in the summer of 1940, some volunteered for training with the SOE. Based on ability and dedication to the mission, only a select few could be chosen. Among the handful of agents trained that summer was Martin Linge, a famous actor in Norway. Linge (pronounced like "ring" but with a soft *e* at the end) emerged as leader of what was formally called the Norwegian Independent Company No. 1. It was more popularly known as his namesake, "Company Linge." The company would support the more aggressive approach to resistance that the British wanted.

On December 11, 1940, SOE drew up a statement of purpose for its role in Norway, thoughtfully covering long-term and short-term aims. In essence, for the long-term, Norway would be liberated by an Allied invasion eventually. To prepare for that invasion, there would be secret arms drops gradually over many months to equip an underground army that would fight when the Allies landed. This precisely matched the aims of Milorg and the government-in-exile. However, the short-term aims didn't match. The SOE called for a regimen of sabotage and raids inside Norway. SOE's purpose statement finished with "Norway must become and remain a thorn in the German side."

The first major raid happened in March 1941 in the Lofotens, a chain of rugged islands off of Narvik's shore. The islands held no military significance, so the Germans had only a small garrison of occupation troops stationed there. But these were dismal days in Great Britain, with defeat after defeat—at Dunkirk and in North Africa. If for nothing else, Churchill needed a victory for morale at home, and also to fire the imagination of resistance leaders in Norway. The Lofotens were selected.

The natives of the Lofotens were mainly fishermen and their families. Many living there were fiercely patriotic and pro-British. There had been no members of Quisling's *Nasjonal Samling* in the community council before the occupation, but now a few had found their way into local government office.

On March 4, 1941, 52 men of Company Linge, along with 450 British commandos, landed on the two largest islands of the Lofotens. The Germans were taken completely off guard and quickly surrendered: 213 Germans and 12 Norwegian NS members were taken prisoner. The Allied invaders proceeded to blow up a total of six Norwegian and German ships, amounting to 19,000 tons sent to the bottom of the ocean. They exploded 18 facilities that produced glycerin for the German explosives industry and four large factories, which produced half of Norway's fish oil.

The civilian population was very supportive. In fact, when the Allied forces pulled out, 314 natives volunteered to return with them to join forces against Germany; among them were eight women who volunteered for the Norwegian Red Cross. Many of the men would later become part of Company Linge.

Once the force returned to Great Britain, *The Times* of London and other newspapers trumpeted the Lofoten Islands raid as "an unqualified success." It was held up as an example of Allied cooperation.

At that point, no one was thinking ahead to the consequences. When the Germans returned to the Lofotens, there was a price to pay. After a cursory investigation, German authorities launched reprisals. Dozens of houses were burned to the ground and at least 70 citizens were rounded up and sent to the concentration camp at Grini.

Fearing reprisals from the beginning, the Norwegian government-in-exile protested the raid, saying the British didn't have the right to execute such operations without consulting them. Milorg joined in to protest that the reprisals were not worth what was gained.

In June 1941, Milorg's leadership wrote a letter to King Haakon himself outlining a cautious resistance policy that would avoid activity likely to provoke reprisals. They also echoed the protest of the government-in-exile over the raid on the Lofotens, calling it "hazardous" for the citizens, and wanted all future British activity to be coordinated with and approved by Milorg.

The letter didn't reach the king. Passed by courier into the hands of a British liaison officer in the Shetland Islands, it was intercepted by SOE. Reading it in the context that SOE's charge was to "set Europe ablaze," British officers scoffed that Milorg was nothing more than a "military Sunday school." Instead of receiving a reply from the king, Milorg received a response from the agency it had criticized. Attempting to be diplomatic, SOE's response began with affirmation of Milorg's intentions, but then moved quickly to point out immediate needs for action—sabotage and training for its secret army. Furthermore, the message read, it was Milorg that would take orders from SOE, not vice versa. The exchange did nothing to improve Anglo-Norwegian relations.

A chasm between SOE and Milorg continued until October 1941, when two Milorg leaders were invited to travel to London to meet with SOE officers and Norwegian government officials. It turned out to be a double benefit for the Norwegian resistance: Milorg had not actually received the backing of the government-in-exile before then. Norwegian officials had suspected Milorg of a counter-government agenda, perhaps even a takeover after liberation. Those suspicions dissolved with the London meetings. From that point on, Milorg was formally condoned as part of the Norwegian military by the government-in-exile. And it narrowed the gap with SOE. By the end of the meetings, a pledge was struck and drafted in the form of a memorandum with the subject line: "Anglo-Norwegian Collaboration Regarding the Military Organization in Norway."

The memo acknowledged that neither SOE nor Milorg could hope for success without the support of the other, and that both would cooperate in actions in Norway. But the unsteady legs of the coalition would stumble two months later when the Lofoten Islands were raided a second time by British Commandos supported by the Norwegians of Company Linge. This time, the islands of Vagsoy and Maloy were also targets.

Landing on December 27, 1941, the Norwegian commandos of Company Linge in particular had every reason to believe they were part of an effort to gain a permanent foothold in Norway. They were geared for it, having been issued advance pay for three months and sent with a vanguard of several hundred troops and a substantial naval support. While the raid overall was successful, the Norwegians suffered one particularly harsh blow. After their commander, actor-turned-soldier Martin Linge, delivered a masterful pep talk to his company, he was immediately killed in action. Following a mere 10-minute siege, the entire German garrison thrust up their hands and marched out to be captured. All objectives were quickly achieved on the Lofotens and in the two villages of Vagsoy and Maloy. The group again capped their raid by sinking many ships in port, this time totaling 15,000 tons. Again, many local Norwegian residents volunteered for training in England to fight the enemy.

For the 77 Norwegian commandos, the mission was tragic. The death of Major Linge left them feeling directionless and demoralized.

Worse still, the hope to fight for their homeland for permanent victory was dashed. The British goal had been to establish a permanent sea base in the north, but supply problems killed the idea. The British then changed their objective to holding the Lofotens for several weeks. However, when the Royal Navy commander in charge of the mission learned through intercepts that German counterforces were massing at Narvik, the plan was scaled back to another hit-and-run raid.

Convinced that theirs would be a sustained operation, the commandos emphatically assured the villagers that they were there for the long run. This won the confidence and support of the Lofoten Islanders again. But again, the troops left.

Predictably, reprisals followed, worse than before. All family members of Company Linge volunteers, whether they had taken any part in support of the Allies or not, were sent to concentration camps. Many died there.

Milorg and the Norwegian government-in-exile did not find out about the raids until after the fact. They were outraged, especially in light of the collaboration pledge two months previous. From then on, Milorg took an immovably firm stand against sabotage and other military actions that would evoke reprisals; instead it would wait for the "right time." The British recognized and admitted the blunder, and did their best to patch up relations by forming a Norwegian section within SOE. Heading the section was a British officer, Lieutenant Colonel J.S. Wilson. The Norwegian government-in-exile selected a staff to work with Wilson, beginning in mid-February 1942. The group had the hopeful title of Anglo-Norwegian Collaboration Committee. The committee did reach some acceptable compromises.

For all the miscues and struggles between the Norwegians and British during the first years of the war, one bright spot existed: the "Shetland Bus." This was not a yellow vehicle with wheels that ran a regular route on a regular schedule, but it did have clockwork reliability and safety that earned it its name. The Shetland Bus was a covert sea ferry service linking Norwegian ports and the Shetland Islands, 100 miles northeast of the northern tip of Scotland.

Within the same month of the German invasion, experienced Norwegian seafarers began using their own weather-beaten fishing smacks to make the three-week crossings through frigid and stormy seas. Hundreds of Norwegians escaped to the Shetland Islands that way. SOE took due notice and during the same summer of 1941 that the first Norwegian SOE agents were in training, agents began asking the crews if they'd volunteer on a regular basis to return to Norway on secret assignments. When many agreed, the British army then ordered Major L.H. Mitchell to set up a system to handle regular traffic to and from Norway. Unlike the Lofotens raids, this truly became a model of Anglo-Norwegian cooperation.

Mitchell began with about 40 intrepid Norwegians and four fishing smacks that crossed the North Sea and reached landfall at discreet docks at Lunna and the village of Scalloway. Norwegian seaman earned regular pay of 4 pounds a week, and a bonus of 10 pounds upon completion of each trip. They deliberately chose the worst possible weather, assuming that German naval patrols would stay safely in port. During the spring, the increasing daylight made crossings too dangerous. During its first season, the Shetland Bus completed no less than 40 round trips, delivering 49 SOE agents to Norway, along with 150 tons of arms and communication gear, and on return trips retrieved 46 Norwegians, including known resisters sought by the Germans.

The sea link was beneficial in many ways, delivering arms and equipment to Norway, and ferrying passengers both ways. For the entire war, it was a regular and direct lifeline with Great Britain not enjoyed by any other occupied country.

All told over three seasons, the Norwegians ran up a total of 207 round trips, delivering 219 SOE agents and 314 tons of supplies. It lost eight fishing boats and 50 men. By 1943, the Germans had become aware of the regular traffic, and air surveillance had become so effective that the rugged old fishing boats could no longer cross safely. At that point, the U.S. Navy offered three of its fast sub chasers so the Shetland Bus could continue. Until war's end, the sub chasers darted in and out of Norwegian waters without trouble, making 105 round trips without a loss.

In February 1942, in a political move that couldn't have been more upsetting to the general population, the Nazis brought back Vidkun Quisling as puppet prime minister. The Germans found, over the long run, that his NS had been the only faction of the Norwegian population they could rely on, and Quisling remained its leader even after he had been pulled from political office in 1940. The NS had grown to about 45,000 during the first two years of occupation.

Quisling envisioned himself as a significant individual, leading a country prominent in the Axis. However, Terboven remained *Reichskommissar* and retained the power.

With Quisling's new appointment, the NS benefited. The NS spun off a number of other organizations, including women's and youth organizations, and the elite *Foregarden* that served as Quisling's bodyguard. Best known and most hated was the Hird (a name derived from Viking history) comprised of thugs and criminals turned loose to terrorize the general population. The Hird was structured as seven regiments. This included even naval and air sections, called *Hirdmarinen* and *Hirden Flykorpset*, which served as sources of volunteers for the Kriegsmarine and Luftwaffe. Another organization formed under Quisling was the Norwegian State Police, which modeled itself after the Gestapo and even called itself "Stapo." Notorious leaders of the Stapo and Hird were Karl Marthinsen and later Jonas Lie. All these groups were archenemies of the Norwegian resistance.

The Gestapo and its homely stepbrother, the Stapo, set out in a relentless effort to infiltrate the Norwegian resistance and arrest its members. At the village of Ålesünd, on an island north of Bergen, a Norwegian infiltrator named Henry Oliver Rinnan reported on locals who were aiding the Shetland Bus runs. On February 23, 1942, the Gestapo burst on the scene just in time to intercept a fishing smack setting out with 23 people aboard, en route to the Shetland Islands. Brutal interrogations yielded 20 more Norwegians involved. The leader was executed under the provisions of the notorious *Nacht-und-Nebel* order—the directive that certain resisters were to be dragged into the night (*Nacht*) and made to disappear in the fog (*Nebel*).

Soon after the Ålesünd incident came a more vicious visit by the Gestapo to Tælevåg, a small coastal village in the rolling terrain outside Bergen. Since Bergen was the nearest major city to the Shetland Islands, the area had been a natural landing place often used since the beginning. Numerous boats bound back and forth from the Shetlands had placed transmitters and weapons in Tælevåg, which the Gestapo discovered. As Simon Ovretviet, a resident of Tælevåg, later explained, "There was no betrayal. Norwegians weren't used to being at war. People simply talked and the wrong person found out." The wrong person, in this case, was the local police chief, an NS member, who reported the information to the Gestapo in Bergen.

On Sunday morning, April 26, 1942, the Germans came in force to Tælevåg. Converging on the peaceful fishing village were 12 Gestapo and Norwegian NS men, along with about 50 SS troops. They went directly to a small farm where the weapons, ammunition, and radios were known to be hidden.

The farm was owned by the local Milorg leader, Lauritz Telle. Not only was equipment stashed there, but also in the barn were two SOE-trained Norwegian agents, Arne Verum and Emil Hvaal. Asleep, the two agents were surprised by the Gestapo and SS troops.

Verum seized the Luger out of the hands of a Gestapo officer and killed him with it; Hvaal did the same to another. Then the two opened fire in a futile attempt to escape. Both Norwegians were shot—Verum died quickly on the scene and Hvaal survived only long enough for interrogation.

By the next day, others had been identified as having a part in either resistance activities on land or the ferrying service on sea. "My father and my uncle Mikkel both owned fishing boats and had made the trip to the Shetland Islands," Ovretviet explained. "On Monday, they were both arrested and taken away. Tuesday and Wednesday were quiet."

By then, word had reached *Reichskommissar* Terboven, and Tælevåg would not remain "quiet." Terboven ordered the little village razed to the ground in reprisal. In stark contrast to the secret killings of the *Nacht-und-Neben* order, Tælevåg was to be an example for all the rest of the country to see.

"On Thursday morning, the Germans burned the first three houses," recalled Ovretviet. "One of them was my parents' home. I had gone into hiding at my Uncle Lars' house, but that morning all men aged 16 to 60 were rounded up and arrested. All 68 of us were herded into a barn and dynamite was placed all around it. I didn't know what would become of my wife and son, 16 months old. I didn't know what would become of me." The SS troops then set about setting fire to more of the 70 houses that dotted Tælevåg's once tranquil hillside. About 260 women, children, and elderly people were forcibly taken away to be interned. "Instead of detonating the dynamite, they marched us out of the barn on down to the dock and we watched there as all the houses were burning. Barns and boat houses, too."

Explosions rocked the countryside and fires consumed the last structures, until nothing remained standing. Tælevåg was wiped off the map in the style of Lidice, Poland. The difference was that the male population was "spared," not killed outright as at Lidice. Instead, the men of Tælevåg were transported first by boat to Sandvik, then by train to Grini Concentration Camp, where many eventually died. Simon Ovretviet's father, Joseph, remained at Grini for the rest of the war. Simon Ovretviet eventually was sent to Sachsenhausen labor camp, where many prisoners contracted dysentery and died in 1942. (Both Simon Ovretviet and his father returned to rebuild Tælevåg after the war.)

The local Milorg leader, Lauritz Telle, was soon executed, but Terboven wanted more: 18 other young resisters arrested in Ålesünd were executed after torture that yielded the names of Milorg leaders throughout Norway. In May and June 1942, the Gestapo and Stapo went on a rampage of arrests, dragging off Milorg leaders in Oslo, Bergen, Drammen, and Stavanger. In those two months, organized resistance in Norway's southern half was decimated.

One Milorg leader, Trygve Freyer, recounted his experience:

> *Germans hit and whipped their way to information. . . . Bernt Skeie, arrested ahead of me, died under German torture. Rieber-Hohn cut his arteries at the wrist with a pocket knife, but was 'saved.' He died as an NS prisoner at Natzweiler. We were all severely tortured. . . . Four of us were deported with the tag 'MUST NOT RETURN,' probably since our bodies were so badly damaged that we might eventually be used as witnesses against the Gestapo.*[17]
>
> *The Gestapo leader, Hartung, told me that he knew that the leadership of the resistance in Bergen was among the six of us arrested. . . . It was probably my knowledge of languages that saved me. I understood what the Germans said and reacted adequately. I also had mastered French and had good contact with a French doctor who twice saved my life.*

By the fall of 1942, resistance in Norway's northern half would suffer a succession of blows that nearly put it down for the count. Churchill's obvious interest in the area, as shown by two landings on the Lofoten Islands and persistent naval activity off its coasts, alarmed Hitler.

Churchill also had become obsessed with Operation *Jupiter*, a plan for massive landings at the northernmost parts of Norway where Luftwaffe airfields launched sorties against the Allied convoys. Although he didn't know *Jupiter* by name, Hitler's paranoia about such an invasion led him to prioritize Norway over even the offensive against the Soviet Union. Consequently, Hitler kept an inordinate number of troops in Norway. (By mid-1944, Hitler would increase occupation forces to 17 divisions.)

Vast numbers of occupation forces and heightened alert meant that SOE and Milorg's resistance groups had painfully little chance of success, and, as it turned out, little chance to exist. In October 1942, the Gestapo and Stapo launched another all-out offensive to scour resistance clean out of northern Norway. Hundreds were arrested and 24

SOE agents and Milorg leaders were executed. Ten citizens also were executed as part of the terror tactics. By the end of 1942, the Nazis had purged Norway of organized resistance.

The disasters that crippled the Norwegian resistance happened under German order and independent of Quisling. As they were happening, Quisling lusted to assert his power and attract favorable notice from Hitler, so he launched an effort to Nazify the schools. The Germans knew how important it was for the future of the thousand-year Reich to reach young students, so they made every effort to plant Nazi ideology in textbooks and teaching.

The same month he settled into the post of prime minister for the second time, Quisling tried to force all history teachers to include what today might be called "revisionist history"—specifically, that there was a "Jewish world conspiracy" in which Jews had been scheming for world domination for years through monopolies of international economic markets. No teacher accepted this. He followed up by imposing on instructors compulsory membership in the Nazi Teachers' Union, which required loyalty to Nazi authorities. As a result, more than 12,000 of Norway's 14,000 teachers resigned. On March 20, 1942, Quisling ordered 1,000 of them arrested; 500 of these were sent on a torturous 1,600-mile voyage, crammed in a ship's hold with 250 berths and two toilets, from Trondheim north to Kirkenes. Their sentence: hard labor on the docks in the Arctic, indefinitely. A ticket home was as easy as joining the union. Only 50 joined under the coercion. When the rest would not agree after six months, Quisling relented and brought them back. The teachers received a hero's welcome at home and schools were reopened.

Having failed in coercing teachers, Quisling turned his attention to what would surely bring approval from Hitler: a round-up of the Jews.

Minor Jewish persecution began early in the German occupation. During the first month, the Germans desecrated the synagogue at Trondheim and seized some Jewish businesses. As in Denmark, when the Norwegians threatened revolt, the Nazis decided to table the issue for the time being. Their only action at the time was a decree that forbade any Jew from leaving the country.

Quisling used the judicial bodies of the puppet government to persecute the Jews—all done within the law. He resurrected a defunct provision of the Norwegian Constitution of 1814 that barred Jews and Jesuits from Norway. (The provision had been struck from the books in 1851.) When the provision was reinstituted, it made all Jews inside Norway's borders illegal aliens. This set them up for deportation and subject to the "final solution."

The Norwegian people stood up to protect their own. From the ashes of the Norwegian resistance rose the Home Front, which issued false identification documents and worked with villagers and farmers along land routes to Sweden to create an escape line. By the time the process of deportations began in November 1942, 935 Jews of Norway's 1,720 Jews had been shuttled to safety.

The unfortunate ones remaining became complacent, confident in the protection of their sympathetic countrymen like the few caught in Denmark. Or they simply understood Nazi motives too late. The remaining 759 were deported and only 25 survived the war.

Just when it seemed the Germans could rest on their laurels, confident that they had liquidated the resistance in Norway, saboteurs struck, depriving them of what could have been their most devastating weapon. The Norsk Hydrogen Electrolysis plant, largest producer of heavy water in the world, was the target.

"Heavy water" looks like water, but is a variation in which hydrogen is replaced by atoms of heavy hydrogen (called deuterium). It serves as a nuclear "moderator" for a nuclear reactor built around a chain-reacting uranium pile. The production of heavy water requires tremendous amounts of electricity. During World War II, this electricity was amply available at the Norsk Hydro in Vemork, near Rjukan and Hardanger Fjord in the southern province of Telemarken.

Hitler had not invaded Norway with the strategic thought in mind to capture the heavy water plant, any more than he had seized Czechoslovakia for its rich uranium deposits. With both, however, Hitler casually came into possession of the basic ingredients for an atomic bomb.

The race for the first atom bomb was on. The mere possession of such a facility as Norsk Hydro caught the attention of Allied scientists, and the fact that Germany ordered increased production to 3,000 pounds of heavy water a year in 1940 alarmed them. When the Germans upped production demands to 10,000 pounds a year in 1942, the Allies went into action. A strike against the threat became a top Allied priority.

The first step was to select and train a team of saboteurs. Candidates for the mission included both local Milorg resisters and commandos of Company Linge. The plan became to land an advance party of saboteurs by parachute. The rest would come later by glider.

It was well known that a glider landing would not be easy. The terrain offered no suitable landing field within miles of the plant. Even once on firm ground, the approach to the target was difficult. Heavily guarded, the plant was perched on a mountain girded by almost sheer cliffs. The raiders would have no alternative but to make a hair-raising descent into a deep valley, traverse it, then scale difficult slopes to approach the plant from the rear.

The four-man advance team, all chosen from Company Linge, was code-named *Swallow*. The four parachuted through the frigid darkness in the hills of the Sogne Valley, just before midnight on October 18, 1942. They gathered their supplies, and traveled through deep snow to a prechosen, isolated cabin. Because they had to make several trips on skis to shuttle their provisions, it wasn't until November 9 that they were able to begin making daily transmissions of information about the plant provided by local resisters. Based on Swallow's intelligence, along with photographs and information provided by physicist Leif Tronstad, a consultant for the plant's construction, and Dr. Jomar Brun, a former Norsk Hydro engineer, a scale model of the plant was created down to the last known detail. The model helped the demolition team train for almost any eventuality. Key equipment was targeted and the right explosives chosen to destroy it. Location within the plant was pinpointed and the right entry door was identified, as was the position of guard shacks and number of guards.

By November 19, the saboteurs were ready. Thirty-four men, all highly trained, divided into two gliders, which were towed by RAF bombers to Telemarken. They took off from an airfield in northern Scotland, but they didn't make it to Telemarken. Terrible weather caused both gliders to crash 100 miles from their destination. Some of the men were killed on impact. Survivors were captured and executed.

It took three more months for a second team of saboteurs—code-named *Gunnerside*—to be trained. The approach was different this time. Rather than a commando assault with 34 men, only six Norwegians would approach in a stealthful hit and run.

Gunnerside left England on January 23, 1943, and actually flew over Norway, but cloud cover and fog prevented them from finding the signal lights set up by Swallow. Not wanting to repeat the experience of the previous group, they turned back.

On February 10, 1943, Gunnerside, under the command of Joachim Rönneberg, landed successfully on the frozen Lake Skryken as planned. After 13 days, they made contact with the advance group who had been there for months—much longer than expected. Nearly frozen and starved, they had survived by eating reindeer moss. Over the following four days, they finalized details of the raid, the newcomers learning all they could from the veterans who had spoken with local resisters familiar with the plant.

On February 27, 1943, they skied cross-country, up and down hills, scaled the cliffs, and finally reached a railroad track that led to

Norsk Hydro. There they divided into two groups—some men serving as a covering team and the other a demolition team. Rönneberg led the demolition team; Knut Haukelid led the covering team.

Their plan of attack included a contingency: If capture was imminent, they would commit suicide without hesitation. Each carried a cyanide capsule.

At 12:30 A.M. Haukelid's team found its way to the plant's railroad gates and clipped a chain locking it, then they took concealed positions to keep watch on the guard hut. Meanwhile, Rönneberg's team slipped through the gate. "I stopped and listened," Rönneberg recounted. "So far we had not been detected. The hum of machinery was steady and normal. There was a good light from the moon with no one in sight except our own men." He and the three others of his team crept to the plant's cellar door. It was locked.

They looked at one another, their anxious expressions visible in the bright moonlight. The guards would pass here in seconds. They split up into pairs to search for a cable tunnel, which they knew from endless study of the model based on Brun's and Tronstad's knowledge. Rönneberg and Fredrik Kayser found it and shimmied inside through a spaghetti of cables. As they moved forward under the plant floor, they heard the humming of machinery growing louder above them. Finally they emerged into a room and found an open door.

Once inside, they overpowered a Norwegian security guard. Then, Rönneberg began placing explosive charges as Kayser covered him with a Colt .45. All was going well when suddenly a heart-stopping shattering of glass startled them nearly off their feet. Kayser wheeled around and thrust his pistol forward, but the "intruder" climbing through the window was one of their own. Kayser said later, "I almost killed him. If there had been a bullet in the chamber of my gun, I probably would have. I recognized him just in time."

The later arrivals helped place the remaining explosives. Fuses were coupled then lit. They told the Norwegian security guard to run for his life. Then they crashed through the cellar door and sprinted just 20 yards outside when the explosives went off. Now the objective was reduced to the most basic human instinct: "We just wanted more than ever, now that the mission was accomplished, to save our lives as well," Rönneberg said. They succeeded, scrambling down the gorge and disappearing into the rugged landscape before the search lights snapped on.

The raid was perfect. Mission accomplished, with no lives lost.

The raiders fled to Sweden, leaving behind a two-man team to provide continuing intelligence by radio. They sent one immediate message:

> GUNNERSIDE OPERATION CARRIED OUT WITH COMPLETE SUCCESS ON NIGHT OF 27TH-28TH FEBRUARY STOP HIGH CONCENTRATION PLANT COMPLETELY DESTROYED STOP NO SUSPICIONS AROUSED AND NO SHOTS EXCHANGED STOP GREETINGS

A year's production of heavy water had been destroyed. The British estimated that Germany's atomic bomb program had been set back two years. Nine Norwegians turned the course of the war.

Pulitzer-Prize-winning author Sigrid Undset, who fled Norway in 1940 because of her anti-Nazi writings, had written wistfully from America in 1942: "Some day—maybe soon—we will be able to unfurl our flag . . . over the ruins of homes to be rebuilt."

German forces retreating from Norway *could* have left a smoldering wasteland in their wake—as they did in the Baltic States, Poland, Yugoslavia, and to some extent Holland. Even though much of the German forces had capitulated, rumors flew that the still-powerful Wehrmacht in Norway would continue the fight.

Milorg/Home Front had risen like a phoenix from the ashes and grown through 1943 and 1944 to nearly 40,000 members by spring 1945. They were put on alert by the BBC (in the open) for May 6 and 7 to prevent destruction. In particular, they were to protect power stations and bridges from German parting shots, and also seize records that Quisling and his henchmen would want destroyed. It was already known that resisters had in their possession the incriminating archives of treacherous Stapo police chief, Jonas Lie.

When General Jodl signed the surrender papers in the early hours of May 7 at Rheims, whether or not the occupation forces in Norway would surrender was still unknown. Later on May 7, the commander of the Norwegian-based Wehrmacht, General Böhme, broadcast his intention *not* to surrender.

Allied forces were prepared for the worst: Operation *Doomsday*—the invasion of Norway. That operation relied on the forces of Milorg. On May 9, elements of the 1st Allied Airborne Division took off from England for Oslo. Out of 35 aircraft sent, 27 turned back, but 8 landed near Oslo as planned—and were welcomed in the Norwegian capital.

As it turned out, Undset's worst fears didn't come to pass. No major battle with the Allies took place there and the Germans surrendered where they stood, leaving Norway intact. The 1st Allied Airborne found Norwegian sentries armed and standing guard at all key points in the capital.

Later, Norwegians pursued the matter of Nazi collaborators. Police files were opened on about 90,000 Norwegians suspected of collaboration—a figure that should be compared with the total population of 3,000,000. Jonas Lie committed suicide. Among the few executed was Vidkun Quisling, after being convicted for treason.

On June 7, 1945, five years to the day after leaving Norway in exile, Norway's original resister, King Haakon VII, returned to the warm welcome of flag-waving, cheering crowds in a free Norway.

## CHAPTER 5

# The Netherlands

In five days it was over. Germany's invasion of the Netherlands was a veritable showcase for the arsenal of modern warfare. The Wehrmacht's integrated air and ground attack sent Panzers roaring into the Lowlands under a top cover of Messerschmitts. Crack German paratroopers floated down into "Fortress Holland," where the "Soldiers of Orange" fought bravely, although outnumbered and vastly outgunned. In the Zeeland, Dutch forces fought side-by-side with French troops. In desperation to prevent the German advance, the Dutch blew up their age-old dikes to flood hard-won farmland. It was all to no avail.

The invasion began on May 10, 1940. Three days later, Queen Wilhelmina, her family, and Dutch government officials escaped across the North Sea on a British destroyer bound for the safe harbor of Harwich. On May 14, Holland's second largest city of Rotterdam was bombed mercilessly, its center blasted and burned into ruins. On May 15, the Dutch commander in chief, General H.G. Winkelman, ordered his troops to lay down their weapons. Despite Winkelman's orders, thousands of Dutch troops kept their weapons and went underground, awaiting the day when the Netherlands could rise up again.

Their homeland was now clenched in Hitler's fist, and occupation was a fact. Luxembourg, Belgium, and finally France fell, too. It was painfully clear that liberation wouldn't come anytime soon. Resistance started small and slowly, with the usual minor actions designed to perturb the Germans. For the Dutch, this meant capers by nighttime artists who splashed the large *V* for Victory in Holland's trademark vivid orange on walls everywhere. Another graffiti favorite was *OZO*, abbreviation for the Dutch words for "orange will conquer." Citizens grew orange flowers and displayed them prominently in their window boxes until the Germans realized their symbolism and forbade them. Dutch audiences walked out of theaters when Nazi propaganda short subjects were shown, again, until forbidden to do so.

The Roman Catholic and Protestant churches began their own, very public spiritual resistance. Both church bodies objected to the tactics of the Nazis. Catholic bishops focused on the Nazi leadership, writing letters and meeting with members of the administration on Dutch soil. Protestant pastors focused on the victims, writing letters of encouragement to those who had abandoned hope and religion.

A few weeks after occupation was complete, a public demonstration celebrated the June 29 birthday of a member of the royal family, Crown Princess Juliana's husband, Prince Bernhard. The celebration served as a perfect opportunity to get under the skin of the occupier. The prince was a pureblooded German who, as Queen Wilhelmina's only son-in-law, had declared loyalty to the Netherlands from the very beginning. Despite a very thick German accent (or perhaps *because* of it), the prince had won over an approving Dutch public. The mayor of The Hague joined the celebration by signing birthday wishes for the prince, which resulted in the mayor's prompt expulsion from office. Another small-town mayor was forced out of office because he named his daughter Juliana, after the crown princess. (Many babies born during the occupation were named after members of the royal family.)

Queen Wilhelmina in particular was exalted as a symbol of freedom and hope. Dutch coinage—silver 10- and 25-cent pieces bearing her likeness—were cut into pins, pendants, bracelets, and brooches until the practice was strictly outlawed following the recall of Dutch coinage at the end of 1940. Widespread loyalty to the royal family irritated the Germans, who did all they could to stomp it out. But, like stomping around in a patch of orange wildflowers, all it did was scatter more seeds of Dutch patriotism.

An early order forbade any reference to the royal family (and negative accounts of Germany's role in World War I) in school textbooks. Such references were masked out with pasted-on paper. As Juliette Marres, a schoolgirl at the time, later wrote: "School children being what they are . . . the forbidden items were more often read and better retained than the permitted parts."

Organized resistance began cautiously in the summer of 1940. Initially, as with most resistance groups throughout Europe, it formed around the nucleus of an existing organization. In Holland's case, it happened not around political parties[18] per se, but instead along social lines, such as church bodies and among students, former military officers, and so on. Three of the most prominent such groups were the *Orde Dienst, Raad van Verzet*, and *Knokploegen*.

*Orde Dienst*, or Law and Order Service, usually called by its abbreviation OD, emerged that summer as a resistance organization with the solid, long-range goal of equipping its members to rise up and fight alongside Allied troops after their return to the Continent. Once the occupier was driven out, OD planned to handle government administration until the government-in-exile could return. In the meantime, sabotage, assisting evaders/escapees (many of them Allied fliers), and intelligence work became the plan of the day. Founded by officers of the former Netherlands army, OD was organized in a military-like structure and tended toward the right wing. *Raad van Verzet*, or Resistance Council, was left wing but not communist. The *Knokploegen* was mainly Calvinist- and Catholic-led.

As in all the occupied countries, geography dictated much about resistance operations, as well as the actions of the occupier. Nine million citizens crammed into 33,000 square kilometers meant dense population concentrations in urban areas—among the densest on the Continent. And a thick mesh of roads throughout the country meant few inaccessible regions, which enabled the highly mobile German army to race to virtually any location in the country in a short time.

The Netherlands' flat, mostly treeless terrain made guerrilla warfare impossible. There were no mountains and only seven percent of the land was forested, not nearly enough to give safe sanctuary for guerrilla redoubts. Resistance in the Netherlands needed to take other forms more suited to its environment, such as intelligence gathering, escape routes, and sabotage.

Because the Netherlands is located close to Great Britain (only France and Belgium are closer), the Germans heavily fortified the Dutch coast and massed troops there as part of the "Atlantic Wall" against Allied invasion. After the first year, access to the coast by the general population was forbidden. The heavy concentration of troops and relatively short, open coastline made regular sea routes, like Norway's Shetland Bus, impossible. Many Dutchmen tried to reach England by boat, but only 200 were known to have succeeded during all five years of war. In addition, the German radar network, antiaircraft guns, searchlights, and numerous Luftwaffe fighter units made safe air travel impossible, except by nighttime parachute drop. And finally, unlike more geographically fortunate countries, the Netherlands shared no common border with a neutral country. Escaping by land through Belgium and France to either Switzerland or Spain required crossing three heavily patrolled borders. All this served to hem in Holland.

Occupation policies for Holland also steered the Dutch resistance. As with Denmark, Hitler made a concerted effort to win the favor of Holland's general population. To begin with, he ordered the release of some 20,000 Dutch prisoners of war held in German POW camps, as an act of good will. (This would not last, but initially all were allowed to return home.) Other Dutch troops not shipped to POW camps had been held under "house arrest" at their own duty stations; these were gradually demobilized as the Dutch military was dissolved. Epko Weert, a 21-year-old sergeant stationed in northern Holland, had been among them. He said, "When we surrendered after five days of war, I was a prisoner in my own barracks. Germans told us that we had been doublecrossed by the British, but they said: 'We are your friends, your brothers. Look at us—the same blond hair and blue eyes. All of you go home and pick up your work again.'"

The fact was that the Germans wanted and needed to keep Dutch industries going. They needed workers and production. About a third of Dutch industrial production was harnessed directly for Germany, including the forced production of weapons. Holland's principal industries, including steel, cement, ammunition, and textiles, were the stuff of armament and fortifications, all needed for the German war machine.

One Dutch industry benefited resisters, not the occupier. Holland's printing industry with its abundance of presses soon began producing underground newspapers. First efforts were crude, stenciled sheets sent weekly or monthly, most simply recounting the BBC's news and debunking German propaganda. Within the first three months, there were four major papers. (By 1941, the number would grow to 120, and by 1943 an additional 150 were in regular circulation.)

Radio broadcasts were another lifeline of communication. Some nationalities needed underground newspapers to translate the BBC's news, but many Dutch people spoke English, enabling them to understand broadcasts throughout the day. There were also Dutch broadcasts by "Radio Oranje," on which Queen Wilhelmina regularly offered words of encouragement.

More active resistance took form in helping Allied airmen and soldiers escape. In the summer of 1940, a small forerunner of a soon-to-be substantial group banded together in Amsterdam and developed an escape line to cross the border into Belgium, which linked up with other lines to the south. (More on this in chapter 6.) The line continued through France and on to Switzerland or Spain, ultimately for return to England. The first such escape group was apprehended by the Gestapo in the fall of 1941, but its work was continued by others.

In Holland, aiding in escape and evasion was called *pilotenhulp*, meaning "help to pilots." On the many days and nights when Allied bombers bound for target-area Germany flew over, the escape-line scouts went into action, searching out injured and lost crash victims, and those already hidden by local resisters. Actually, many of those helped in *pilotenhulp* were not downed aircrews of the RAF or USAAF; they were escaped prisoners of war wandering aimlessly.[19]

The occupiers commandeered a large proportion of Dutch-grown food to feed the German soldiers in the Netherlands and elsewhere. The Germans demanded 50 percent of the vegetables and fruits for direct transport to Germany; another 25 percent was reserved for occupation troops inside Dutch borders, leaving a mere 25 percent for the Dutch.

# THE LOW COUNTRIES

0    50    100 miles

0    160 kilometers

*North Sea*

IJssel-meer

Amsterdam

The Hague

HOLLAND

Rotterdam

GERMANY

Antwerp

Albert Canal

Dunkirk

Ypres

Calais

Brussels    Maastricht    Aachen    Cologne

Lille    BELGIUM    Liége

Namur

LUX.    Trier

Sedan    Luxembourg

Metz

Demands were heavy and disproportionate, but—in sharp contrast to less fortunate countries, like Yugoslavia and others in the east—the Germans *paid* the Dutch for their exports. It benefited the Reich to keep the Dutch economy intact.

Responsible for the smooth operation of Holland was the new *Reichskommissar*, Dr. Arthur Seyss-Inquart, a mild-mannered Austrian and a lawyer by trade. Seyss-Inquart tried to charm the Dutch with visions of a place of honor in Europe's "new order" if only they would accept the tenets of national socialism. But the Netherlands, among the oldest democracies, rejected this without hesitation or compromise. Most people saw it for what it was and flatly rejected attempts to Nazify them.

Government on the local level remained in place, now overseen by *Reichskommissar* Seyss-Inquart and his four assistant commissioners. Civil servants who remained in their posts felt they were obligated or at least justified to remain in their work by a Dutch Cabinet directive of 1937 that said even in enemy occupation they "must try in the public interest to carry on the administration as well as possible under the circumstances." In order for them to remain in their jobs, however, they were reduced to a state of impotent obedience. The court system also carried on, handling all cases except crimes against the occupiers. Those crimes were tried in Nazi military tribunals, in rough accordance with laws of the Geneva Convention that gave an occupier jurisdiction over only "emergencies," not an occupied country's internal matters. It was all very proper.

Occupation troops were under strict orders to behave properly, too. This was a pleasant surprise to the general population and, like in Denmark and Norway, may have slowed the rise of organized resistance.

The 2,000 communists of Holland were well organized, had seasoned leaders, and already operated with the habit of secrecy. They hated the Nazis, but faced the same dilemma as their communist brethren throughout Europe because of the German-Soviet Nonaggression Pact. Direction for behavior toward the Nazi occupier was clear and concise: "Be neutral to the Germans." Leadership in Moscow continued to preach a steady gospel that the British and French had been the warmongers. On the surface, communists in Holland supported this line in their underground newspaper, *De Waarheid* (The Truth), with words condemning past exploitations by the British and French. But like the vast majority of Dutch, they didn't want fascism to infect their homeland. Against Moscow's orders, several months before Operation *Barbarossa*, they embarked on some of the first open resistance in the Netherlands when, on February 17, 1941, the German regime ordered 3,000 metalworkers in Amsterdam to forced labor in Germany. The communists called for a strike that brought out a moderate number of protesters. The Germans surprised everyone by listening to the protest and backing down from the demand. The 3,000 metalworkers were not forced to go.

A far larger strike followed a week later, after the arrest of 425 Jews in Amsterdam on February 22 and 23. The Jews, men under the age of 35, were rounded up for deportation to a concentration camp in Austria. Even before being taken away, they were treated brutally in full view of many in Amsterdam. Word of it spread quickly. The communists again instigated a strike by cranking off thousands of mimeographed pamphlets calling for a

*continued on page 113*

Wholesale murder in the east. Two unknown resisters breathe their last before being shot by German officers over a pit where many already lie. *National Archives*

Danish saboteurs caused this train wreck between Denmark's village of Herning and Karup Airfield. Saboteur Kaj Christensen remarked, "I saw the train the following day. It was a perfect blow-up, with railcar after railcar lying in layers like layers in a layer cake. Talk about destruction. And on the very top of this pile of destroyed carriages stood a brand-new—at least it looked like it—big German truck. They could only get it down one way, namely by pushing it, and then it was smashed anyway." *Nationalmuseet (The Museum of Danish Resistance)*

Royal symbol of defiance. King Christian rode the streets of Copenhagen daily, greeting all Danish people, but shunning German soldiers even when they saluted.
*National Archives*

The synonym for traitor: Quisling. The self-proclaimed prime minister of Norway, Vidkun Quisling, was hated by Norwegians for betraying his country and for his very willing devotion to Hitler and Nazism. His administration created the notorious Stapo and Hird, archenemies of Norwegian resistance. At ceremonies in Oslo, Quisling (right) salutes and spouts "Heil Hitler!" in unison with a German official.
*National Archives*

The October 22, 1940, edition of *Fritt Folk* (*Free People*), the Norwegian Nazi party's official mouthpiece, trumpets "Quisling Saves Oslo and Southern Norway." The boxed headline at left refers to "Councilman Jonas Lie," a Quisling lackey later appointed chief of police and commander of the Hird. Although the Norwegian resistance did not, as a matter of course, assassinate collaborationist leaders as did the resistance of some countries, it did assassinate Lie's predecessor, Karl Marthinsen, resulting in an even more brutal regime under Lie. After being captured at the end of the war, Quisling was executed for treason and Lie committed suicide. *Author's collection*

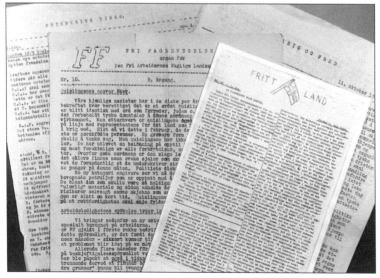

Underground newspapers reached millions of readers in virtually every occupied country of Europe. These Norwegian papers recounted news heard on BBC broadcasts and also published editorials, cartoons, and words of encouragement. *Norges Hjemmefrontmuseum (Norway's Resistance Museum), Oslo*

*Våpentransport*

Translation: "Weapon transport." Norwegians used humor to help them cope with the occupation. In their own native humor called "Kjua-gutt" wit, Norwegians also had many wartime jokes. For example: A German soldier saw a Norwegian boy resting on his bike. The Nazi smiled and said: "I'm planning a long bike ride around the German Reich when I've returned from the war." The boy smiled and asked: "What are you going to do in the afternoon?" *Copyright: Norges Hjemmefrontmuseum (Norway's Resistance Museum), Oslo*

Norwegians of Company Linge prime grenades aboard a Royal Navy ship en route to the Lofoten Islands, off Norway's coast. This photo is dated December 27, 1941, the same day they landed, along with British commandos, to raid the German garrison stationed on the islands. The raid quickly overpowered the Germans, but the Norwegian commander and namesake for the company, actor Martin Linge, was killed in action that day. The raiders withdrew back aboard ship before the German occupation forces massed for counterattack. *National Archives*

Queen Wilhelmina of the Netherlands speaks to her people from the BBC studios in London, during the early years of the occupation. On May 13, 1940, she and government officials fled to England (as did the leadership of most Nazi-occupied countries) to lead the fight from there. *National Archives*

Nazi propaganda preached anti-Semitism throughout occupied Europe. This piece, directed toward the Dutch, hoped to see *De Joden* (Jews) "cut down to size." In the Netherlands, it failed to impress or motivate the general population: More Jews were hidden for the duration there than anywhere in Europe. *Verzetmuseum Amsterdam (Dutch Resistance Museum)*

This poster was created early in the war by Belgium's government-in-exile to inform the British population that Belgians continued the fight against the Nazi occupier, and to encourage the British to support its resistance activities. *Author's collection*

In Brussels, weapons and explosives were smuggled via this novel means of transport, which bears the name of a local laundry. *Belgian Center for Research and Historical Studies*

On this fence in Verviers, Belgium, is a collection of the war's most popular defiance graffiti, including "RAF," "de Gaulle," and "V." *Belgian Center for Research and Historical Studies*

Intelligence-gathering operations notified the Allies about troop movements, arms shipments, resistance activity, location of war industries, etc. All the occupied countries had such operations; some of the more effective ones were in Belgium, Denmark, France, Czechoslovakia, and Poland. Here, two Belgian resisters transmit messages to London from Brussels. *Belgian Center for Research and Historical Studies*

Fraternizing with German soldiers brought certain benefits during the austerity of occupation, like occasional exemption from curfew, dinners in nicer restaurants, and perhaps extra ration coupons. But it also carried with it the contempt of the resisting general population. *National Archives*

In August 1944, after four long years of occupation, two Parisians show their contempt for Hitler. Growing unrest had transformed *attentisme*, the French wait-and-see attitude, into a torrent of rebellion. By this time, the French Forces of the Interior (FFI) numbered 200,000. *National Archives*

Maquisards walk cautiously among the rubble of Cherbourg with rifles at the ready.
*National Archives*

Armed with grenades and an automatic weapon, 13-year-old resister Joseph Parachena was a combat veteran of the FFI in Carpentras, in southeastern France. When this photo was taken on August 26, 1944, a British flag (note background) already has been unfurled there. A wartime caption credits him with killing 13 Germans and wounding several others.
*National Archives*

The French resistance comes up from the underground, as the Allies battle through France in summer 1944. Resisters, carrying only small arms and grenades, engaged German tanks and infantry in city streets just before Paris was liberated. *National Archives*

In the town of Chateaudun, a member of the FFI holds an example of the Czech-designed Bren gun, supplied by the British. *U.S. Signal Corps via National Archives*

Many women served in the resistance. In France and Belgium, more served in escape-line roles than any other resistance activity, but some were maquisards as well, as shown here. *National Archives*

A resister shields himself from German sniper fire in street fighting at Dreux, near Paris, in early August 1944. *U.S. Signal Corps via National Archives*

Revenge after liberation: Head shorn and branded with a swastika on her forehead, this collaborator is prodded down a Paris street by resisters. *U.S. Signal Corps via National Archives*

Terror tactics. The Nazis have hung a man from a lamppost in Belgrade as a warning against other acts of defiance. Nazi brutality and murder precipitated a guerrilla campaign that seized back control of a large portion of Yugoslavia from occupation forces.
*National Archives*

The very charismatic Josip Broz, known the world over as Tito, at his mountain headquarters for the Partisans. He hoped to unite all Yugoslavians—Serbs, Croatians, and Slovenes—against the Axis occupiers, and strike a delicate balance that would make Yugoslavia sovereign, yet communist.
*National Archives*

*continued from page 96*

one-day work stoppage in protest. Impassioned wording included: "Demand the immediate release of all arrested Jews! Show solidarity with Jewish workers! Hide Jewish children from Nazi violence—take them into your home . . . STRIKE! STRIKE! STRIKE!" The pamphlets broadened the appeal by also urging wage increases and greater unemployment benefits. On Monday, February 24, the communists stationed themselves at key places like public transportation centers and busy street corners to hand out the pamphlets to every passerby.

For the first time, resistance against the occupier went beyond social groups or self-interest. Workers of all kinds, white and blue collar, joined together to walk off their jobs in Amsterdam and outlying areas. The great Dutch shipyards, normally bustling with activity, stood idle. Public transportation came to a halt as streetcar conductors joined in. Offices throughout the city were empty.

The largest number of protesters congregated at the center of Amsterdam, but demonstrations also took place across the city. German soldiers stood aghast. Such defiance seemed inconceivable to them, given the fact that German workers had not ventured a strike in all the years since Hitler took power in 1933. By Wednesday of that week, the strike continued and spread to Haarlem and Zaandam. Initially, Dutch police stood by passively, but eventually they were ordered to break up the strike.

The "one-day strike" incited by the pamphlets actually lasted several days. Communist resistance leaders must have been astonished at the overwhelming response their message had received, especially since the vast majority of workers who took part did not support communism. However, when the communists tried to instigate another strike a week later, it was met with no response.

The strikes of February 1941 aroused a public fervor that in some ways unified and strengthened resistance, which now broadened to include the hiding of Jews and others sought by the Nazis. These fugitives were called *onderduikers*, or "underdivers," because they had to dive under and hide within the folds of society—tucked away in attics, cellars, sheds, barns, and backrooms. The best account of life in hiding is the renowned *Diary of a Young Girl* written by Anne Frank while she and her family lived as *onderduikers* in an attic in Amsterdam.

The roundup of 425 Jews foreshadowed the far greater cataclysm to come. Approximately 165,000 Jews lived in Holland before the occupation. Of them, 115,000 were native Dutch; another 15,000 had fled from Germany and Austria in the previous years to find refuge; and an additional 25,000 newer arrivals had come, mostly from Poland, after invasions in 1939. All of them would be ruthlessly sought by the Nazis.

The incredible rescue of Jews in Denmark had been made possible by a water route to Sweden. Holland's geography left no such backdoor for escape. Exiting Holland became almost impossible once the clamp of Nazi tyranny closed down. Perhaps 2,000 *onderduikers* were spirited away via Spain, but the rest had to find a way to withdraw from all normal life and disappear.

German authorities gave the Dutch Nazi party a free hand to lash out at the Jewish citizens, which they did with evil delight, bullying and beating up Jews at random. By July 1942, local bullying had given way to deportation. Dutch records, which had fallen intact into Nazi hands after the occupation, gave the Gestapo the names, ages, occupations, and addresses of Jewish citizens across the land. As time went on, the Jews were segregated away from the Gentile population into ghettos, to await the fate of train shipment in cattle cars to concentration camps like Mauthausen. The Dutch had the same attitude as the Scandinavians: "Jews were Dutch citizens, pure and simple, accorded the same rights and privileges as any other," said Johtje Vos, an early resister. Their prosecution was an outrage in Holland. Almost the entire working class had joined in the strike over the mistreatment of Jews, but not all were willing to take the risk to hide them. The punishment for protecting Jews was well known, but many families risked their lives to do it. They were promised the same fate of the Jews themselves in concentration camps, which equated to almost certain death—odds for survival were 1 in 10. Since there were few remote forests and other secluded areas to hide, Jews had to be hidden in families' homes, businesses, or farms. For this massive mobilization to shelter its Jews, Holland became known for its "hiding places."

Johtje Vos lived in a small house in Laren, near Amsterdam, and took in 36 Jews at once. Years later, Johtje said: "I was at that time with my second husband, Aart, but my first husband had been German. When a Dutch girl marries a foreigner, she loses her nationality. I married a German, so I became a German myself. In a way I hated to be German, but on the other hand I liked it, because I could use it. As a German I could get double food stamps. I had my house full of Jewish people, so I needed to get food any way I could. But I had to go through terrible things in applying for this. I remember standing in line, and the Dutch people assumed I was German so sometimes spit on me. I didn't blame them and I knew I would do whatever was necessary in those days to get the food."

Johtje's *onderduikers* could move about the house freely, but all knew to move quickly to the escape tunnel in case of a German raid, and there were many. She remembered:

*The Germans came and pushed me aside from the front door. They walked in and opened all my drawers, all my cupboards, every door. They found nothing and no one. The tunnel Aart had built saved their lives. It started at the coal bin in our art studio, really a shed, attached to the back of the house. The coal bin had a false bottom that, when you looked on the top, all you saw was coal—not too much because that would not be good either, since coal was scarce. You lifted out that false bottom and climbed in, then followed the tunnel under our garden and into the backwoods behind our house.*

*Another day when the Germans came, a man was just in the entrance to the tunnel. I stepped up by the shed and stamped my feet and said to the Germans, "Oh, I'm cold. Aren't you?" It was a very warm day, and they must have thought I was crazy! But it bought precious seconds and tipped off the man to hurry down into the tunnel and out of there. It saved his life.*

No Jewish lives were ever lost in Johtje's hiding place.

Some viewed the German occupation as insurmountable and saw no point in resisting. That attitude of resignation led to the formation of some groups that cooperated in varying degrees with the Nazis. One non-Fascist group that argued for cooperation was called the *Nederlandse Unie*, or Netherlands Union. Akin to the French "wait-and-see attitude," the union's platform attracted a following of 800,000 members. The union's manifesto was delineated in five main points:

- Political cooperation
- Social justice
- Freedom of religion, including freedom for the Jews
- Economic strengthening
- Continued cultural ties with Belgium's Flemish-speaking areas and colonial South Africa

Union members saw their group's actions not as collaboration, but as a way to get *some* representation in a government where the Nazis had banned all political parties except for the homegrown Nazis of the NSB, an abbreviation for *Nationaal-Socialistische Beweging*, or Dutch National Socialist Party. The union's three founders—a provincial governor, a police commissioner, and a Catholic professor—were patriots with good intentions. They hoped to assert some influence over a bad situation in which only the voice of the Dutch Nazi Party now was heard by German authorities. A significant part of Holland's population joined with the same thoughts in mind.

The union's newspaper ran an editorial that said, "If we feel that the Germans are trying to force us to become like the German Nazis, then we will resist. We are peaceful but we are also stubborn." The German authorities promptly pulled that issue off the streets. The Netherlands Union was never taken very seriously, and the only reason it was tolerated at all was that Seyss-Inquart hoped it might ease the population toward an idea approaching fascism. The union lasted for about year, then the Nazis unceremoniously dissolved it.

In direct opposition to the Dutch resistance were native fascist groups. The most moderate of them was the National Front, founded by Arnold Meyer, who wanted to see a union between the Netherlands and Flemish-speaking parts of Belgium (in this way, like the Netherlands Union). A second group, the National Socialist *Nederlandse Arbeiders Partij* was extremist, and wanted complete outright integration of the Netherlands into the Third Reich. The third and most powerful was the NSB, founded by Anton Mussert in 1931.

The NSB had enjoyed eight percent of the vote in the 1935 election, but its popularity declined dramatically to half of that in the last prewar voting. Mussert, Holland's own Quisling, proposed to Seyss-Inquart that a self-governing Dutch government of NSB members should be formed, with Mussert himself as its head. Seyss-Inquart saw what had happened when Quisling installed himself into leadership after Norway's fall, and he was savvy enough to know that Mussert's NSB at the time had a following of only 30,000, a tiny percentage of the population.[20]

Elements of the NSB became the nemesis of the Dutch resistance. The NSB had police and paramilitary groups, including the WA (*Weer Afdeelingen,* or "Defense Sections") and an all-Dutch unit of the SS, called at first the *Nederlandsche-SS* and later the *Germansche-SS en Nederland.* The unit was organized into a police regiment and five other regiments, some of which were sent to fight on the Russian front.

Unlike Poland and France, the Netherlands had made no advance plans for intelligence networks in the event of an invasion. Any skilled leadership from the military intelligence service left on the boat with the fleeing government in mid-May 1940. To top it off, those fleeing took the wireless transmitters and secret codes with them! There had been British intelligence operatives working in Holland before the war, but they also fled in such haste that a briefcase filled with secret documents was left behind and found by the Germans. This was only the beginning of the disasters involving transmissions of intelligence from the Netherlands to London.

Attempts to form the first intelligence network began in August 1940, when the SOE landed Dutch Navy Lieutenant L. Van Hamel near Leyden. Van Hamel brought with him one wireless set. His objective was to make contact with a number of groups who would gather intelligence and send reports to the SOE in England. The first groups he approached refused to cooperate, but he eventually found four that would. He equipped one group with his wireless set from England, and to equip the rest, three other radios were built following the first model. His mission complete, the lieutenant tried to return to England in October 1940, but the Germans tracked him down in Friesland and later executed him.

One of these four groups developed into the OD's intelligence service. It reliably transmitted reports to London until February 1942, when the Germans pulled a counterespionage coup and discovered a wireless set and its operator. A very competent Abwehr officer, Hermann Giskes, interrogated the operator, who eventually divulged some information on codes, but withheld information about security checks—unique phrasing or intentional mistakes embedded in the messages that informed the recipient that the message was secure. When Giskes forced him to transmit to London, the operator simply omitted his security checks and because of that there was no reply. The security system had worked as it was supposed to.

A few weeks later, in an independent operation, an OD branch in The Hague was infiltrated and SOE agents and Dutch resisters were arrested. Giskes uncovered yet another transmitter and its operator, Hubert Lauwers, as well as a complete secret code listing to decipher messages. Giskes saw the potential in this discovery, and he made sure that anyone who could know of the discovery was apprehended, so that no one could leak the news to London. Lauwers, who was forced to send a fake message to London requesting two additional SOE agents and equipment, thought he could safely send the messages by leaving out the security checks, because without them, the recipients in London would know he'd been compromised.

In an extraordinary lapse of security, the unthinkable happened: London replied.

Landing coordinates and a date of March 27 for a parachute drop were settled upon, and the two agents and their equipment literally fell directly into the hands of the Abwehr. Fifty-two more agents would be parachuted this way and would meet the same fate (only seven of them survived the war).

In a series of rogue operations, Giskes' Dutch collaborators set up red searchlights in a triangle to signal RAF aircraft to drop their loads of arms canisters. In time, guns enough to have outfitted 15,000 resisters were dropped. There were also untold thousands of canisters delivered with more radio equipment, sabotage materials, and currency to fund the Dutch resistance. In all, 12 RAF aircraft and their crews were shot down after the airdrops.

The Abwehr perpetuated the "game" by occasionally carrying out the orders of parachuted agents. Word would reach England that certain railroad lines (easily repaired or of little consequence) had been sabotaged. In Rotterdam harbor, a barge loaded with aircraft parts exploded in plain view of the public and sunk to the bottom—compliments of the Abwehr. Downed Allied fliers were even helped back to England after radio messages from London told of their whereabouts and requested assistance.

The operation would become known as *Englandspiel*, or England Game, and it began on March 12, 1941. It was also called Operation *Nordpol*, or North Pole, as written in Giskes' book titled *London Calling Northpole*. This represented one of the greatest successes ever recorded of "turning around" a wireless set. The effect of *Englandspiel* was far-reaching and went on for *two years*, until late 1943, when two arrested agents escaped from their Netherlands SS guards and made their way first to Switzerland and finally to England to tell the tale.

The Dutch resistance paid the biggest price: No fewer than 400 members were captured as a direct result. It devastated the OD and compromised resistance operations throughout Holland.

Another set of major strikes happened at the end of April 1943. German oppression in general had been increasing and reached a boiling point on April 29, when German authorities announced they would rescind their earlier act of good will and order the released servicemen of the Dutch armed forces back to internment in Germany. Without incitement from the communists or any other group, workers in the industrial district of Twente, near the German border, spontaneously walked off the job. The strike spread like wildfire to almost all industrial centers and the rural farming regions as well. The Germans dispatched their Dutch and Germanic police units and, as the strike continued into the first days of May, more than 150 Dutchmen were shot. The Germans threatened more violence, and eventually the strike ended.

As military veterans were forced back into German POW camps, some novel arrangements were struck. Epko Weert took part in the protection of Jews in a unique way that saved the life of one young man and also enabled Weert to continue in the resistance:

*Then they began to arrest a lot of the former soldiers. In my case, I gave all my papers to a 'middle man' so they could be passed along to someone who needed false identity. The documents were placed with a Jew. He became a Gentile named Epko Weert, who had been a sergeant in an antiaircraft battery. And with my name, he was arrested and sent to a POW camp—to which he didn't resist. Because of that he was able to live. My mother and sisters even sent parcels of food through the Dutch Red Cross to 'Epko Weert,' and he survived the war.*

Weert then became an *onderduiker*, benefiting from his resistance specialty of forging documents and creating food ration coupons.

Some historians believe that taking care of the *onderduikers* was the most impressive action carried out by the Dutch resistance. Thousands upon thousands of faked or falsified identity documents and ration coupons were created by the resistance. Families who had Jews living within their homes needed extra food for the extra mouths, and fake ration cards provided by the resistance made that possible.

Since this was such an enormous undertaking, care of *onderduikers* became a largely centralized responsibility of the *Landelijke Organisatie*, or National Organization. Its counterpart was *Knokploegen*, which sent small groups to raid food warehouses and offices that held public records. There were strong Calvinist and Catholic influences in both. *Landelijke Organisatie* needed funding for its work and got it via the *National Steunfonds*, or National Aid Fund—the "banker of the Dutch Resistance."

Given the vast number of *onderduikers* and the fact they were dispersed throughout Holland, other, smaller groups shouldered the same responsibilities as *Landelijke Organisatie*. Many operated on a local basis. These took it upon themselves to provide food and shelter to specified numbers of *onderduikers*, or simply all those within their district.

As the Dutch resistance movement became more proficient, so did its opposition. In 1943 a collaborationist security force sprang from the ranks of the NSB and the WA. Called the *Landwacht Corps*, they became the most hated of all—even more so than the Germans, because they were murderous, traitorous Dutch. Soon after, this group was retitled

*Landstorm Nederland,* and given over to direct German SS control, but an element of *Landwacht* was reestablished under NSB control. The *Landstorm*21 became the archenemy of the Dutch resistance.

Other enemies included the Henneicke Column, which focused especially on hunting down Jews in hiding, and a group called V-men, which was a treacherous collection of Dutchmen who infiltrated Dutch resistance groups. On the German side, there was also a labyrinth of security forces. Hanns Albin Rauter, an Austrian like Seyss-Inquart, headed the Gestapo and SD in Holland, along with the uniformed regular and military police.

With the many internal security forces at work, there was constant fear within the Dutch resistance. Weert recalled transporting weapons in a handcart through the streets of Amsterdam "20 or 25 times. I was sick with fear, but very nonchalantly whistled German tunes. I whistled 'Home Country of Your Stars' and other songs. I carried a gun with six bullets, always reserving one for myself. I didn't want to ever be captured. You always looked two blocks in advance for a roadblock. Once I went around a corner and came face-to-face with the Dutch Nazi Police. They took away my identity card, thinking that would force me to deliver myself for slave work in Germany. But later, I just opened my tin of false IDs."

After the devastation of *Englandspiel,* there were attempts at consolidating resistance groups, which was difficult to do and probably not wise anyway. *Orde Dienst, Landelijke Organisatie, Knokploegen,* and *Raad van Verzet* were brought together as *the Nederlandse Binnenlandse Strijdkrachten,* or Dutch Home Forces, under the ultimate leadership of Prince Bernhard. But the unified forces of the resistance became cumbersome and, always lacking enough weapons, struggled to become effective.

By the war's dark midpoint in 1943, even more *onderduikers* were hiding in the folds of Dutch society. Workers of all kinds were being ordered *en masse* for work in Germany, where the manpower shortage was now critical, which sent many more "diving under." Along with many soldiers who evaded the order for reinternment, these workers were now fugitives.

In April 1943, students at Holland's universities were coerced to sign a declaration of loyalty to the occupying powers. Coached by professors and clergy, few actually signed. Those who did sign went on with their studies; those who didn't were ousted from school and became prime candidates for forced labor in Germany. Reaction to those who signed was simply expressed by one disgusted former student: "That bastard has signed the loyalty declaration!" Most of the ex-students who did not allow themselves to be shipped off as part of the German labor force became *onderduikers,* too. Because of the nature of it, the total number of *onderduikers* was never known with any precision, but by 1944 may have peaked at an astonishing figure of 300,000.

There were other peaks, too, that showed the fire of Dutch defiance burned strong. The underground press was running full tilt. It is estimated that, throughout the Netherlands at this time, copies of some leading underground newspapers were being distributed in printings of more than 80,000 copies. Even through the worst of the famine and fuel shortages, when public transportation was shut down, most Dutch households received at least one underground newspaper each day. They had names like *I Shall Hold On, The Word,* and *Free Holland.* (The NSB also had a Nazi newspaper, titled *Folk and Fatherland,* with antiresistance propaganda.)

For most of Holland's war, sabotage and assassinations took a back seat to nonviolent resistance activities such as intelligence gathering, *pilotenhulp,* and hiding *onderduikers.* Had the Germans struck with the savagery of murder and destruction they committed in the east, the Dutch Resistance might have resorted to more violent measures. As it was, there were a few high-level assassinations, such as that of collaborationist Dutch General H.A. Seyffardt in February 1943. Seyffardt became a target after organizing the Dutch Waffen SS that accompanied German troops to the Russian front. There also was a failed assassination attempt on the German chief of all internal security forces, General Hanns Rauter. But in general, acts of this nature were condemned by the Dutch government-in-exile in London and by some resistance leaders, as expressed in underground newspapers.

Before D-Day, most sabotage in Holland was individual, spontaneous, and small-time, like sugaring the gas tanks of Nazi staff cars or cutting telephone wires. Railway sabotage did not have long-lasting effects, since most of it had been easily repaired and hampered nothing serious. Skilled communist resisters in particular carried out the more violent sabotage. In March 1943, 750 communist members took part in targeting the population registers in Amsterdam and other cities in preemptive strikes to destroy the excellent documentation about citizens that the Dutch government inadvertently left to the occupiers. In all, about 400 raids hit registration offices housing records about thousands of Dutch about to be deported for forced labor. In November 1943, the same saboteurs assaulted a police headquarters in Hertogenbosch, where 900 handguns were captured. Not long after, communist elements unified with the *Raad van Verzet.*

After the D-Day landings, sabotage was stepped up like never before in Holland. Beginning in October 1944 and lasting until April 1945, the Dutch Home Forces launched a campaign to disrupt German transportation, particularly during the last two months of occupation. Equipped through increasing Allied airdrops, some

1,000 resisters fanned out over western Holland, concentrating on transportation lines. At least 400 German vehicles were destroyed. Roads were made impassable.

On September 17, 1944, the First Allied Airborne Army landed at Arnhem and Eindhoven. The Dutch were eager to do their part in the liberation, so a third and final major strike began. A few hours after the first paratroopers landed, the BBC broadcast the Dutch government's order to all Dutch State Railway workers to shut down. It was part of General Eisenhower's strategy, based on a hopeful timetable that the Netherlands would be liberated in at most a few weeks. Field Marshal Montgomery was to cross the Meuse, Waal, and Lower Rhine rivers. Depriving the Wehrmacht of rail transport at this key time might have great effect.

When British paratroopers landed and fighting broke out near Arnhem, elements of the *Knokploegen* wanted to join the fighting, but it fizzled quickly. Through mix-ups, many were not able to rendezvous as hoped. Those who made it were not equipped with weapons, in the wake of *Englandspiel*.

Hoping for help in the advancing front, the Allies dropped the Dutch Resistance some 30,000 weapons during fall 1944. Weert recounted a typical drop:

> *One of us had wired a secret code word to London—quite simple things, like "Elsie had the flu." When you heard those words spoken twice in the evening on the BBC, you know the night of the next day there would be a drop. Before the drop could be made, the dropping field had to be checked by 2,500 feet by 2,500 feet. It was done in reclaimed lake land. We stood in reversed Ls with hand lamps and two red lamps for the wind directions. The drop zone had to be 10 miles away from anti-aircraft guns and 4 miles away from the nearest German post. They dropped Sten guns, Enfields, Bren guns, bazookas, grenades, and hand grenades and ammunitions. They dropped them in large containers of 550 pounds with four grips so four men could carry them away.*

The German security forces naturally made the tracing of those weapons a high priority. The Germans are said to have found a full third before they could be used.

Although geography did not favor this, the Dutch resistance tried guerrilla operations in the final two years of the war. The numerous professional military officers who had founded OD attempted to establish military-like training camps during 1944 and early 1945. All were discovered by the Germans and efforts were abandoned.

In theory, the Dutch Home Forces' function was yet to come. Following the original charge of *Orde Dienst* to rise up as the Allies invaded, resisters attacked the retreating Germany army from the rear. They were especially effective in eastern Holland, which was liberated in March and April 1945. The Dutch Home Forces did not have the firepower to take on the greater numbers of transient German units moving out of Holland back to Germany.

Weapon shortages were still a problem. In the northwestern part of Holland, 4,100 resisters had only 1,575 Sten guns and a handful of other weapons. In the area were still 17,000 well-equipped German troops. So the plan was scaled down to smaller support operations for advancing troops. For instance in Rotterdam, resisters seized the offices of the water-supply agency. In the ancient village-fortress of Axel, on the Belgian-Dutch border, resisters stormed a German garrison and hundreds of soldiers surrendered. In cities and villages across the land, resisters captured collaborationist Dutch officials as they tried to bolt, including the police commissioner of Wolfheze (west of Arnhem) when he tried to get away in his car.

Ill-equipped as they were, men and women of the Dutch resistance were on alert everywhere, prepared for battle as the Germans began to retreat and the Allies approached. Suddenly, all became moot when *Reichskommissar* Seyss-Inquart declared a halt to the fighting, and all German forces in Holland surrendered in mid-April 1945.

## CHAPTER 6

# Belgium and Luxembourg

In his BBC program that aired January 14, 1941, a Belgian resistance veteran of World War I uttered a simple idea that would fire the imagination of millions and become ubiquitous among the Allies in every theater of war. Pointing out that his first initial *V* also was the first letter of *vrijeid*, or "liberty," in his native tongue of Flemish, and the first letter of "victory" in English and *victoire* in French, Victor De Laveleye unwittingly inspired the V-campaign.

"It was a typically Belgian idea, a product of the spiritual heritage of a grand little nation that has never learned to accept defeat," wrote author René Kraus during the war.

*V* was taken further by BBC radio personality "Colonel Britton," who challenged his many listeners on the Continent to defiantly scrawl a *V* on every fence and wall of occupied Europe. *V* was also cleverly set to music—the first measure of Beethoven's Fifth Symphony, matching the staccato of the dot-dot-dot-dash of *V* in Morse Code. The same rhythm could be easily tapped on a window or door.

Not to be outdone, Dr. Joseph Goebbels, the German minister of propaganda, countered with an attempt to commandeer the symbol for the Nazi propaganda machine. He created flyers emblazoned with a bold *V*, declaring that it stood for *German* victory. But by then, V-for-Victory had already taken hold staunchly for the Allied cause.

What began as light commentary on a Belgian radio program would take on epic proportions when it became closely identified with Winston Churchill. Among the most famous images of World War II is Churchill, cigar pressed between his lips, thrusting his hand upward with fingers forming V-for-Victory.

The symbol *V* served a practical purpose, too: Resisters in Belgium and the other Low Countries had been painting the relatively time-consuming letters "RAF" as graffiti. Once *V* became the popular symbol, it was surreptitiously painted throughout the land to taunt the occupier and cast a ray of hope on the dismal occupation. Its simple shape offered the advantage of a deft swipe or two of a brush, then the artist could run. But at this time, Belgium was still a long way from victory and *vrijeid*, and so was its tiny neighbor, Luxembourg.

The Germans attacked both countries early in the morning of May 10, 1940. Both were invaded by Germany for the second time in 25 years, although this time the method was more swift and brutally efficient. The countries succumbed to an abrupt aerial assault that thrust airborne troops and paratroops into important strategic points like crossroads and communications centers, followed by the crushing advance of mechanized armor.

Defended by little more than a zigzag of barbed wire and radio posts manned by gendarmes, Luxembourg yielded quickly. "But at this point in time, we trusted that Germany was soon to be defeated," said Aloyse Raths, who would later become a leader in the Luxembourg resistance. "We were very sure that the German army would be stopped at France's Maginot Line and soon move back through our country going the opposite direction. Unfortunately, that was not the case."

Belgium had been among the better militarily prepared countries in western Europe, already bolstering its defenses in October 1936, when it adopted the stance of armed neutrality. It had disbanded its navy before the outbreak of war, but increased its land army numbers. Plus, it maintained a respectable air force of 157 aircraft. However, with superior numbers and performance, the Luftwaffe's Messerschmitt Bf 109s swooped in during the first days of the invasion and decimated the assortment of Belgian interceptors that included Gloster Gladiators, Hawker Hurricanes, and others.

Fort Eben-Emael, the "invincible" sentinel over the Albert Canal and its critical bridges, was breached by German airborne forces. The fort's 1,000-man garrison surrendered in less than a day. The remaining Belgian troops fought on bravely for 18 days, but at 4 A.M. on May 28, King Leopold III announced Belgium's capitulation.

The fall of the two countries paralleled that of their Scandinavian neighbors. Luxembourg, like Denmark, gave no pretense of armed preparation; Belgium, like Norway, fought on, grimly hoping for Allied deliverance.

Meanwhile, the governments of both conquered countries slipped away to England. Charlotte, the grand duchess of Luxembourg, and her family went with them, but Belgium's king stayed to share the fate of his 8.4 million people. The little grand duchy of Luxembourg had a population of only 300,000 on a land area of 999 square miles. Despite Luxembourg's small size, it ranked as the sixth-largest steel-producing country in the world which, aside from its vulnerable location near Germany, made it particularly appealing for conquest. Belgium offered similar benefits to feed the German war machine.

"The Germans took away everything that could be taken," said Raths. The Germans immediately requisitioned food, fuel, and other commodities. They seized the steel works, then brought in seasoned German industrialists to run operations. They took away long-time institutions, like the Catholic Boy Scouts association, whose members would re-form as a resistance cell under the leadership of Raths in 1941.

The Germans even took away the very *names* of Luxembourgers. By order of Gustav Simon, chief of the German Civil Administration, those who did not have German surnames were required to take the equivalent German name or, if there was no corresponding German name, they had to choose a German surname. Family names of German origin that had been shortened or changed into a non-German form had to be changed back to the original form. The order came on August 6, 1940, and each person was given a deadline of February 15, 1941, to make the change. Otherwise, the German administration chose a name for him or her.

Along with the order to change surnames came a requirement for all street names to be changed from French to German. The Germans took away foreign languages as well. Luxembourgers spoke French, Letzeburgesch, and German, but by German decree, the language became exclusively German. French as a language could no longer be taught in schools. Adults were prohibited from reading anything written in French, writing in French, or speaking in French. Even wearing a beret was forbidden.

During the war, an official publication of Luxembourg's government-in-exile defiantly asserted: "French and German are spoken in Luxembourg. The bilingual situation is as old as the Grand Duchy itself. The influences of the two big neighbor countries are apparent in all the branches of Luxembourg life. But the inhabitants of this small country have always made it clear that they wish neither to become French nor German. . . . We do not discuss our German origins."

The Germans took away all the multicultural and material things they could. What could *not* be taken by the Germans were the gold reserves of both countries, which were deposited in Paris before the invasion, and Belgium's merchant shipping fleet and its colony of the Belgian Congo. Both the Belgian fleet and the African colony would provide considerable money and manpower for the war effort. The governments-in-exile gladly offered remaining resources not in German hands to the Allies without reservation, and then set about continuing resistance from London.

In the chaos left by the blitzkrieg, circumstances did not seem to promote the will or the means to resist. Two million Belgians and Luxembourgers had taken to the roads, hoping for refuge in France. But the same devastation was happening there, where *10 million* French people jammed the roads. When it became clear everyone was impossibly bottled up, submission to the occupier was the only recourse.

Yet, resisters in Belgium and Luxembourg started with one advantage: experience. Of all the freshly overrun countries of Europe, Belgians and Luxembourgers were the only ones who were experiencing a second occupation within a single generation. The first occupation lasted four long years during World War I, so they knew active resistance well. That helps explain why, after just a month, the first underground newspapers began reaching readers. (By 1944, there would be 300 in regular circulation in the two countries.) Some newspapers carried the same masthead names as their World War I predecessors, such as the resurrected *La Libre Belgique* (*Free Belgium*). Papers were printed in French and Flemish, as well as German—and, in defiance, Letzeburgesch.

Belgium had two distinct national communities: the Walloons, who spoke French, and the Flemings, who spoke Flemish. The two had contrasting views—a fact that the Germans capitalized on in World War I, when they played the two sides against each other. That would not be their strategy in this war. This time, the Germans welcomed anyone who would cooperate with them.

Experienced resistance veterans of World War I, like Victor De Laveleye, immediately stepped forward. In some cases, they picked up where they'd left off in 1918. Camille Joset, a resistance veteran in the earlier war, led the *Mouvement National Belge* that became a national force engaged in intelligence, sabotage, and propaganda. The Clarence-Cleveland intelligence network was led by a World War I resistance veteran, Walthere Dewe.

For the veteran resisters, it was *déjà vu*: Parallels of the two wars quickly became evident during twin four-year occupations. Not only was a German regime installed, but the military governor of Belgium and Luxembourg, as well as northern France, was German General Alexander von Falkenhausen—the nephew of General Ludwig von Falkenhausen, who had been military governor there from 1914 through 1918.

The youth of the two countries became involved. "Young people felt strong and ready to defy the Germans," according to Raths, age 19 in 1940. One young Belgian girl, Yvonne de Ridder Files, offered a lesson on how someone could find and join the resistance:

*Nine months after the German invasion of Belgium, I had a conversation with an acquaintance while coming home on the streetcar. We were on the platform, and our exchanges were, of course, in double talk when they had anything to do with the war or the army of occupation. But I had a funny feeling, like a sixth sense, that was telling me that this man was involved in the resistance movement. This prompted me, as I was getting ready to get off the streetcar, to remark to him, "If I can help you in any way, let me know."*

*This was perfectly innocent. If it were overhead by enemy ears, I had many an explanation to justify this remark. I could have meant, "If I can help you with one of my rations when you are short" or "If your wife is not feeling well, give me a call, I'll come and help," etc.*

*The peculiar look he gave me in return to my remark gave me a feeling I had struck gold! Then one evening, less than two weeks later, the bell rang. This was always a reason for the adrenaline to shoot up. If you didn't expect anyone, a doorbell was quite often an unwanted "enemy" visitor, either for your arrest, or to search your dwelling.*

*My caller was the acquaintance from the streetcar. The moment he entered my apartment he said: "You have been checked; you can start working."*

Gaston Vandermeerssche began his resistance work by producing additional copies of the underground newspaper *La Libre Belgique.* "I retyped the articles on my father's typewriter and ran off 20 or 30 copies on a mimeograph machine tucked away in the attic after my mother's teaching days," said Vandermeerssche. "Then I'd distribute them secretly at school and in people's doors."

Many resistance groups were formed, some regional, some national. Some found certain "niches," while others were diversified in any type of activity that could hamper or frustrate the Germans. At first, there was little if any direction from the government-in-exile. But after the fall of 1942, the Belgian resistance was controlled by two distinct departments of government responsible for coordinating activities that they termed "military" and "civil," much like Norway's two categories of resistance. The Belgium Ministry of Defense directed military resistance (this kept close liaison with SOE), while the Ministry of Justice, Information and Propaganda directed civil resistance—mainly intelligence-gathering and escape lines.

Groups that concentrated on military resistance were numerous. Some of the more active included *Mouvement National Belge*, under Joset mentioned earlier; Group G, which specialized in sabotage; *Légion Belge* composed mainly of former army officers and led by Colonel Bastin, a high-ranking official in the government-in-exile; and

*Armée Belge des Partisans du Front de l'Independence et de la Liberation,* an active communist group that killed 500 Germans and more than 1,000 Belgian collaborators during the course of the war. There was also a profusion of regional groups, like *Les Insoumis* in Hainault, the *Armée de la Liberation* in Liege, and *Witte Brigade* in Antwerp. The government-in-exile referred to all of these collectively (and wishfully) as *Armée Secrète,* but the fact was they were not integrated together. Adding to the confusion was the fact that the name *Légion Belge* later was changed to *Armée Secrète* when Colonel Bastin attempted to combine his *Légion Belge* with the *Armée de la Liberation,* the *Witte Brigade,* and others. His charge from the government-in-exile was to raise a secret army numbering 50,000 that eventually would come under Allied command.[22]

In Luxembourg, there were also numerous military resistance organizations, including *Letzeburger Partiote Liga* (Luxembourg Patriots League), *Letzeburger Volleks Legioun* (Luxembourg Peoples Legion), *Letzeburger Freihétskämpfer* (Luxembourg Freedom Fighters), *Patriotes Independants* (Independent Patriots), and *Unioun vun de Resistenzmouvementer* (Union of Resistance Movements) that unified most cells of the Luxembourg resistance in March 1944.

Except for the Ardennes, the terrain of Belgium and Luxembourg was mostly flat and treeless and did not support guerrilla warfare. Worse still for guerrilla-style combat was the fact that a highly concentrated population was readily accessible for reprisals. Guerrilla groups did exist (termed maquis, like the French), but their activity was severely limited. Since guerrilla activity is best conducted in remote and less accessible areas, the geography of the Low Countries made poor grounds for it. However, some SOE-trained Luxembourgers were parachuted back into their homeland to form French-like maquis bands. Some 400 Luxembourgers volunteered with the SOE for such assignments, but only 10 Luxembourgers could be chosen to parachute back into occupied Luxembourg. (Many of the rest enlisted in the Belgian army.)

The SOE-trained Luxembourgers went to the Belgian Ardennes and began gathering groups of maquisards from Belgium and Luxembourg, along with escaped Russian POWs and deserters. Using a mishmash of weapons, including .50-caliber machine guns scavenged from crashed Allied bombers, the groups targeted German patrols, communications, and railways with deadly success. Military resistance took other forms, like extensive sabotage and intelligence work.

So-called civil resistance was highly successful. Both escape lines and intelligence activities grew to incredible proportions. Belgium boasted the largest escape line of World War II in the "Comet Line" (which will be covered in greater detail later).

Resisters, here, as everywhere, came from all walks of life—teachers, miners, factory workers, and clergy. There were also combat veterans who had volunteered for the Spanish Civil War in the 1930s.

Starting in October 1942 in Belgium, all men between the ages of 19 and 50 and all unmarried women between 18 and 35 were required to register for forced labor in Germany. Before it was over, a quarter-million Belgians would go to Germany to work under slavery conditions. Many others avoided conscription and joined the ranks of the resistance.

Similarly prompting many Luxembourgers to join the resistance was a German order for compulsory service in the Wehrmacht. Starting in August 1942, all Luxembourg men between the ages of 18 and 24 were forced to enlist. (Just after the D-Day landings, the draft age was lowered to 17.) Luxembourg labor launched mass strikes in protest on August 31, 1942. Workers in the mines, steel mills, and factories, mainly in the south, walked off the job and into protest lines. Students joined in. Resistance in general stepped up. The Nazis responded with 21 executions of Luxembourgers decreed after court-martial, and several hundred deportations. The compulsory service order still stood.

In all, 11,160 young Luxembourgers were forced to enlist. Among them was Aloyse Raths, drafted on November 7, 1943. He was sent into combat in Russia, where he and many others deserted the German army.

"I was found and arrested in Russia," Raths said. "Two German guards took me from Barawucha, through Lithuania, with a stop in Berlin and finally to Luxembourg. There, I was brought in front of the Gestapo, which was going to take me to the concentration camp at Hinzert. Thank God in a last minute attempt, I was able to flee and went into hiding."

Raths remained in hiding nearly a year, until the U.S. Seventh Army liberated the region—not an easy place to hide since locals knew each other well and isolated places were hard to find. Refugees had to move into barns, cellars, attics, and abandoned mines. About 500 Luxembourgers facing Raths' predicament crossed the border to join the maquis in France. Others stayed to join the resistance in Luxembourg or across the border in Belgium. Some made it all the way to Spain and across the Channel to join Allied forces. About 220 Luxembourgers joined *Brigade Piron*, a Belgian volunteer unit under the command of the British.

As soon as the German military administration passed over to a civil administration under the leadership of a *Gauleiter* named

Gustav Simon, several intelligence networks began sending information to London. The nets were active and the information valuable. One of the earliest effective nets was established by Walthere Dewe, previously mentioned, who had operated an intelligence network called *La Dame Blanche* during World War I. During the World War II occupation Dewe transmitted information or sent it by courier through the newly established Clarence-Cleveland network. His messages were directed to both his government-in-exile and Britain's MI6. Many of the transmissions concerned the railways—schedules and locations of freight and troop transport—because so much had to pass through Belgium on the way to German ports in the northwest and U-boat pens of Biscay.

The Belgians did not segregate their communications into intelligence nets and military nets. Transmissions to London all went through the same wireless operators and equipment. The SOE discouraged this practice for security reasons, and it may have contributed to Dewe's capture and death. Although he knew well the dangers of the work from his experience in World War I, Dewe was captured on January 14, 1944, in Ixelles. During an attempted escape, eight months before the liberation, he was gunned down as he ran. Dewe was known as a deeply religious man, and as he lay in the street on the brink of death, his Gestapo pursuers forbade help from passersby, including a Catholic clergyman who wanted to give him absolution.

Ten intelligence nets had been established in Belgium by the end of 1941. By early 1942, 25 were operating. That year, Belgian intelligence sources supplied 80 percent of all information sent to England from occupied Europe, according to Winston Churchill's own words. Especially helpful to the British was information on German radar stations and Luftwaffe night fighters that were proving a formidable defense against Allied bombing missions over Germany.

Some intelligence groups were regularly fed mail from Germany, diverted by Belgian postal workers. The letters were sent mostly from the Russian front, where some 8,000 Belgians served in the Waffen SS. The purpose was twofold: It dampened the troops' fighting spirit by severing communications with home and gathered tidbits of information that might be helpful to the Allies.

By D-Day in June 1944, there were 40 nets run by Belgians, sending information from both French and Belgian locations. In Luxembourg, three nets were supplying information to London by the time of the Allied invasion of 1944. One of these pulled the intelligence coup that first alerted the Allies to the Germans' top secret facility for V-1s at Peenemünde. A conscripted Luxembourger had returned home on leave and reported the site. Allied bombing raids quickly followed as a result.

Much of the intelligence information, like the Luxembourger's scrawled diagram of the Peenemünde facility, could not be communicated via radio transmissions and had to be hand-delivered in the form of paper or microfilm. Couriers risked their lives traveling with the items to and from the Belgian consulate in Barcelona, Spain, for delivery to London. Gaston Vandermeerssche began as a courier in the Belgian resistance, operating as part of what came to be called the Raymond-Ramon line, which ran through France. Later he was appointed to establish courier routes for the Netherlands, which he himself named the WIM network,[23] at the behest of Queen Wilhelmina. At the age of 21, he found himself in charge of nearly 2,000 underground agents. He later explained:

*Even if resistance groups had radio transmitters, they still needed maps, microfilms, and other documents delivered in person. There was so much information—military, economic, and political—to deliver. For six months I traveled from Belgium through France and over the Pyrenees to Spain. Along the way, I stayed at safe houses, or what we called "letterboxes." I was very careful where I stayed—never in a letterbox used by another courier or if the owners looked fearful. Fearful people attracted the attention of the Gestapo. Despite the well-publicized threats of the Gestapo that anyone hiding an agent like myself would be shot, people all along the way didn't hesitate to take me in. After many months, I was becoming too familiar to the Germans along that route, so I was pulled out of there and rather than actually delivering messages, it became my job to figure out which courier lines had been infiltrated.*

*Later, I was asked to set up an underground network for Holland, and I traveled for one year between Holland and Spain. [For my personal missions,] it went like this: Intelligence [agents of the Dutch resistance] would bring microfilms to a butcher shop in Antwerp. Couriers, including myself, would pick them up there. We'd take a train from Antwerp to Brussels and on to the French border, where we knew customs officials who could tell us which German guards might be bribed so that we could get through.*

*Once we made it to the Vichy border, we had a man named Orset who managed several stone quarries in the area. The Nazis had given him a paperwork that let him pass freely between occupied France and Vichy France. Orset had made a secret compartment behind the back seat of his car. He'd pull out the backrest of the seat, have me get in and then he folded my legs and arms just so, and put the seat back into place. I barely fit. He*

132 | RESISTANCE!

*had shown me a short strand of rope inside the back seat cushion that ended up dangling right in front of my face when he put it all back together. Orset said, "If a German border guard pulls on that seat, hang on to that rope with everything you've got!" Several times in crossings, border guards did stop us and checked inside the car. It was a quite a feeling knowing the hand of a German was passing within an inch of your face as they checked that seat. Your heart would beat so loud, you would think the German could hear it!*

*Once in Vichy, we continued by tram and train to the Pyrenees. I made 14 passes across the Pyrenees, but the 15th time I was captured at the French border just when I was going to cross.*

During the devastation of *Englandspiel*, Vandermeerssche and 51 other couriers of his WIM network were discovered and captured by the Gestapo in mid-1943. All were condemned to die. The Germans had not yet carried out his sentence when American soldiers liberated his prison in May 1945.

Escape lines followed roughly the same routes as courier lines. Because of their strategic location, both Belgium and Luxembourg stood at a critical junction for escape of downed Allied aviators and isolated soldiers on the run. Among the largest and best known of the escape lines was the Belgian-based *Comète*, the Comet Line, established by 24-year-old Andrée (Dédée) de Jongh and her schoolmaster father, Frederick. There was also the "Pat O'Leary" Line, run by a Belgian named Albert-Marie Guérisse in close association with MI9, Britain's secret escape service. Central operations for the Patrick O'Leary Line were actually in the southern coastal city Marseilles, France, but its northernmost reach was all the way to the Belgian border at Lille. In Luxembourg, resistance groups also originated very active escape lines, among them the *Roude Léif,* or Red Lion (after the Luxembourg symbol), which dovetailed into Belgian and French lines to help spirit hundreds to safety.

Andrée de Jongh had been inspired to establish her escape line by a heroine of childhood named Edith Cavell, who was killed by the Germans in Belgium during World War I for aiding in the escape of 600 Allied soldiers across the border to neutral Holland. Dédée delivered her first evaders, a British soldier and two Belgians—the first of 100 she personally brought across the Pyrenees—safely to Bilbao, Spain, in August 1941. Initially, her operation was headquartered in Brussels, but it moved to Paris in May 1942 and a Belgian baron, Jean (Nemo) Greindl, took responsibility for operations in Belgium. The line became so large that it extended its network into Luxembourg and Holland. Unlike the O'Leary Line, which meandered in a more cautious route through Vichy

France to reach Spain, the Comet Line cut a swath straight through occupied France where checkpoints and borders were heavily guarded.

At the time, most of its "passengers" didn't know the Comet Line by name. They knew nothing more than the people who guided them, the next guides mysteriously appearing soon after the previous ones left. George Watt was one of those who didn't know until years later what organization had brought him to safety and freedom. Watt was a B-17 waist gunner in the England-based U.S. Eighth Air Force. Flying a mission to the Ruhr Valley on November 5, 1943, his aircraft was shot down near the Belgian villages of Zele and Hamme.

From the moment he parachuted to earth, Watt was among friendly natives. He had landed in an open farm field, which immediately drew the Nazi attention. When authorities arrived on the scene, the bystanders pointed in the opposite direction from where he fled.

Watt hid in a ditch and determined his "next problem was to figure out how to connect with the underground." He didn't have to worry about it for long, because members of the underground quickly *found him* and joined him in the ditch. One named Raymond said, "Tonight, after dark, I will bring you some clothes, and I will buy a railroad ticket for you."

Later, he was taken to a rural homestead where he was given civilian clothes and some good food. From Raymond, he heard what disruption his arrival brought. "[Raymond] had gone home to find his wife in tears. Their house was in a shambles. The Germans had been there and had torn everything out of closets, ripped beds, and destroyed furniture. They had searched for me in houses throughout the village, leaving utter devastation in their wake."

Watt's next destination would be Brussels, into the heart of Comet Line country. Here he was taken to a group who interrogated him to ensure he wasn't a spy. He passed the test. "From here on my escape was no longer a stab in the dark, a hit-or-miss proposition. I no longer had any decisions to make. Everything was planned for me." Watt was now aboard the Comet Line.

"The spontaneity was gone but not the hazards," Watt wrote. "The underground was well organized, but it was up against a well-oiled and ruthless machine."

He began his journey with Comet Line members Octave and Thérèse Malfait. "The Malfaits were a gentle couple who didn't fit any preconceived stereotype of the heroic resistance fighter. Octave Malfait was an accountant."

By Watt's eighth day in occupied Europe, he had been handed off in Paris and was on his way to the French border by train. "We got off at Rumes and followed our guide to the end of the station platform. We stepped into a shadow behind a large structure. She told us to wait there while she disappeared into the blackness." In a moment she reappeared with more evaders. Suddenly, a flush came over him when he realized one of them was from his own B-17 crew, Technical Sergeant "Tennessee" Johnson. Between the two of them, they figured out that two of their crew had been killed in flight, eight had parachuted, and all but three of them had been captured.

From the station platform, they were led on foot to a farmhouse in the woods of northeastern France. "We settled down for a long stay. We had no idea how long, but we knew from our guide that there was trouble. The day after we arrived in Paris, the Gestapo had penetrated an entire chain in the underground. Many people were arrested, and the line was broken."

Watt understood the consequences. "For us, the escapees, it was an inconvenience; it delayed our departure from Paris . . . but for the resistance fighters who were arrested, it was the ultimate tragedy. I knew they faced imprisonment, torture, and possible execution. . . . I could not help thinking of the Malfaits, the Thibauts, and the beautiful people in Zele and Hamme."[24]

After three weeks, another member of the Comet Line came to the farmhouse and took them back to Paris. There, he was given a false identity—as a *clerc* being transferred to southern France—and put on a train for Bordeaux.

As it turned out, those false papers were critical. "Just outside Bordeaux the train came to a halt in a wide clearing. Through the window I saw a cluster of German officers, standing on the ground below. They split up in pairs and boarded the train at several different points. One pair boarded at the opposite end of the car behind me, and I watched with mounting nervousness as they examined papers, occasionally asking questions, working their way slowly through a mass of flesh toward my car. Then the rear door of my car opened, and I stood face to face with the enemy. He was a short mousy guy wearing high polished boots and a peaked officer's cap that made him look tall and forbidding."

At the officer's demand, Watt handed him the papers. The German studied them carefully, paying careful attention to the photo. "He looked up at me. I looked straight into his eyes. I was quaking with fear inside. He looked down at the picture again, then glanced up at me once more. He looked down at the letter a third time. My stomach dropped. I was bracing myself . . . '*Merci.*' That's all he said. He handed the letter back to me and turned to the next passenger."

Once in Bordeaux, a new guide waited with a new means of transport: Bicycles. The group, numbering six, rode until early evening across the back roads of the countryside until they reached a country inn. The bikes were quickly hidden by a man and woman there.

The evaders were fed and given a place to sleep upstairs. Unexpectedly that night, the inn became crowded with German soldiers who stayed until 2 A.M. playing German music and talking loudly.

The next morning, they started off again by bicycle through back roads until they reached the foothills of the Pyrenees at the threshold of Spain. Watt had crossed them once before, as a volunteer during the 1930's Spanish Civil War. He was 24 then, and now at 30, he was the oldest of the group who would make the crossing that day. "The ancient smugglers' trails along which we trudged single file were steep and rocky—and never ending. Every time we reached a summit, thinking it was the last, there rose another hill above us. We tackled that one, and there was another, on and on . . . we spent four days and three nights, hiking by day and resting in shelters at night. But this was mid-December, not August [the month he had crossed before], and the thin coat I was wearing was no protection against those strong blustery winds blowing right through me. The old paper-thin shoes . . . given me in Hamme were disintegrating. When the sole of my left shoe tore loose, I tied it on with a handkerchief. But snow caked inside, and I kept tripping over it. I tore the dangling sole off the shoe and walked the rest of the way with nothing between the snow and my wet stockinged foot. Why I didn't get frostbite, I still don't know."

As Watt and the rest approached civilization in Spain, he thought about how he'd been cautioned in his intelligence briefing "about a peculiar quirk in international law: the legal distinction between 'escapee' and 'evadee.' If you had been captured by the enemy and managed to escape, you were an 'escapee.' If you had never been apprehended, you were an 'evadee.' The Franco government was obliged to return all escapees to their own governments, but evadees could be interned in Spain for the duration of the war. Our intelligence officers had instructed us, if we were caught, to claim we were escapees and to back up their claim by inventing an escape story—even one in which we killed a guard."

Watt tensed up once more, because in the Spanish Civil War he had fought on the side against Franco. "Safe at last? Franco's Fascist Spain could never be neutral for me—I was still in enemy territory." Again, however, Watt made it through, even restraining himself while talking with a captain of the Spanish Internal Security Police, "undoubtedly a supporter of Hitler and Mussolini." His Comet Line guide brought him to the British Embassy in Barcelona. From there he went to Gibraltar, where he boarded a B-24 Liberator for London. He immediately cabled his family a Merry Christmas (arriving just one day late) to say he was safe—the best Christmas present they could have received that December 1943.

The Comet Line persevered for three years, rescuing more than 1,000 grateful people like Watt. Dédée would not see it through to the end. In June 1943, she and her father, along with many others working along the line, were arrested after two German spies, posing as downed American airmen, infiltrated the line. (Dédée endured concentration camps for the duration and survived.) Others resisters stepped in to take her place, and the line continued. From its founding until Belgium's liberation in September 1944, 1,300 escape line workers were arrested. Most were killed—meaning that more than one resister lost his or her life for each airman or soldier spirited to safety by the line.

Helping Jews escape was even more difficult and dangerous than helping downed airmen and isolated soldiers. The Nazis went after Jews in Belgium, as elsewhere, with unbridled viciousness. Belgians who harbored Jews faced the same fate as the Jews themselves. In effect, it was a capital offense, because the sentence was deportation to a death camp. "We truly gave no thought to that whatsoever at the time," said resister Mary Sigillo Barraco. "These were human beings hunted down like animals, and we went to whatever lengths were necessary to protect them."

When the Jews could no longer leave Continental Europe through legitimate channels, the only thing left to do was to hide or cross the borders secretly. Aspiring to the incredible coup in Denmark, Belgians in all places and stations of society helped their Jewish neighbors in any way they could. King Leopold, along with the dowager Queen Elizabeth, did their part on an official level by pleading with German authorities not to deport Belgian Jews. In addition, Belgium's highest cardinal, Joseph-Ernest van Roey, directed Catholic agencies at every level—schools, individual churches, convents—to secretly give refuge to Jews. A Jewish faction of the underground also took part in the rescue and long-term concealment.

Approximately 90,000 Jews resided in Belgium at the outset of the war. The Germans deported 28,000, most of whom were held briefly at the ancient fortress of Breendonck outside of Antwerp. Breendonck had been turned into a transitory camp in the first months of occupation. Belgian Jews then went on to concentration camps in Poland and Germany, most to Auschwitz. Only 1,200 Belgian Jews survived the camps, according to the testimonies of four German generals after the war; 26,800 perished. But about

25,000 were never captured and survived by being hidden in Belgium's rural area, or smuggled across to southern France and on to safety in neutral countries.

Luxembourg, on the other hand, was homogenous—almost all Roman Catholic peasants and steel mill workers. An official census in Luxembourg during 1935 numbered Jews at 3,144, and of these only 840 were Luxembourgers and 2,274 were foreign. Numbers no doubt shifted by May 10, 1940, when many fled *from* Luxembourg to France and America, and many fled *to* Luxembourg from Germany. One estimate places the number at 3,700. Most of them were deported to the Ghetto of Lodz-Litzmannstadt, and later concentration camps. Few survived the Holocaust.

When Hitler seized Luxembourg, he assumed that there was willing support in the country for the Third Reich. After all, citizens of the little grand duchy had a strong dose of German in their speech and in their blood. Instead, Hitler found complete rejection—more complete than in any other occupied country of Europe. *Gauleiter* Simon had organized a plebiscite on October 10, 1940, to prove where Luxembourg's loyalties lay. Results embarrassed him: More than 97 percent of the population gave Nazi Germany the thumbs down. Fewer than 3 percent of the Luxembourgers were pro-German.

While Luxembourg earned the distinction of having almost no collaborators, Belgium had a troubling share of them, most residing in Flanders. A pocket of collaborators living in Flanders made for the highest concentration of pro-German sympathizers in western Europe. From the start of the occupation, rumors persisted in the cities and towns about fifth column movements and sinister betrayals that were helping the conquering Germans. This was based primarily on the fact that a large separatist party in Flanders, the *Vlaamsch Nationaal Verond* (Flemish National Party), or VNV, had welcomed the occupation troops, although they were not known to have taken an active role in the invasion. The VNV later formed an Anti-Bolshevik League to fight against the Soviet Union. From willing groups like this, the Waffen SS drew some 3,500 recruits. Some in Flanders even called for annexation into the Reich.

The region of Wallonia also had collaborators. A party called the Rex, led by Léon Degrelle, was fascist and collaborated willingly. Rexists formed a uniformed militia, called the *Formations de Combat*, in August 1940, and many of its members eventually enlisted in the Wehrmacht. Other unique *Gendarmerie* forces were formed with both

Walloons and Flemings (in separate sections) to fight the resistance, preventing sabotage and maintaining order. Across Belgium's large population of 8.4 million, support for the Nazis in Belgium was proportionately very small.

The Belgian resistance became very active in sabotage. It reached a peak in 1943, when German records documented 8,000 separate acts of sabotage.

The resistance organization achieving the greatest successes was Group G, made up of 3,000 resisters, many of them engineering school students. The group targeted industry. On January 15, 1944, Group G pulled off a masterpiece of sabotage that knocked out high-tension lines across the entire width and breadth of Belgium, costing the Germans untold man-hours of work to repair.

Yvonne de Ridder Files hid explosives for Group G in the cellar of her apartment house. At first, she tucked into her broom closet cases of grenades that had belonged to the Belgian army. "But the activities of Group G grew quickly in scope due to the advent of the marvelous [British] air-drops," she explained. "Instead of painstakingly homemade sabotage devices, there now came from England magnificent twenty-five and fifty-pound metal drums filled with all sorts of material to be used for sabotage: PE2, the putty-like substance used for our explosive charges; fuse cord; delay pencils; Sten guns; ammunition; and more. They came to depots in Brussels and Malines. . . . The sabotage missions increased. Our main targets were still railroads, marshaling yards, and communication centers."

Just after the D-Day invasion, sabotage in Belgium focused on the rail lines leading to France and the Normandy coast. On June 8, 1944, the Brussels-to-Paris line, along with the Aix-la-Chapelle-Liége line, was struck repeatedly to prevent the dispatching of Holland-based troops to France. Rails were not restored until September 1. Delays cost the Germans precious time that could not be redeemed.

As the Allies turned the tide of war, momentum built among resistance groups. There was palpable excitement for liberation among resisters, and gloom among the occupation troops. Yvonne de Ridder Files remembered:

> *Group G's activity was on the increase again. Although I no longer had the big cache of explosives in my cellar, I still had smaller quantities of munitions hidden in paper bags behind a sofa in my study, and in my kitchen broom closet, behind the pails and cleaning supplies. They were always ready for immediate delivery, and they were in great demand.*

*There was something in the air, a feeling of something about to happen. There was a tension, not exactly visible, but manifested in various ways more felt than seen.*

*The German military did not give the appearance of victorious masters anymore. Now the air of the victor was replaced by a subdued, even downtrodden composure. Their physical appearance, too, had taken a complete turn. Their uniforms looked tired; their walk, once proud and determined, was now forlorn; the songs they sang while marching didn't have the rhythmic, forceful cadence of the early occupation days, but was now forlorn and weak.*

*That evening, I was glued to the radio, listening to the forbidden BBC, as the invasion was announced. . . . Liberation was coming! I left the house, and followed my regular route down the long block, then left on Avenue Elizabeth, right past the German command post. I practically danced as I passed in front of them, unable—in fact not wanting—to hide my elation! I felt like thumbing my nose at them!*

Since June 1944, the Allied armies had been pushing their way eastward across France. As in several other occupied countries, Belgium's *l'Armée Secrete*—a secret army of maquisards, many of whom were ex-soldiers drawn together by SOE agents—lay in wait for the right moment to rise up and attack the Germans. Despite an elaborate plan, a widespread uprising wasn't needed.

As it turned out, the Allied advance was so fast that by mid-September[25] Luxembourg and most of Belgium was liberated. The Germans withdrew quickly and didn't have time to leave "scorched earth"—that is, except for the all-important port facilities of Antwerp. Here, the Belgian resistance played a key role that would have strategic ramifications.

Well aware of the value of Antwerp's port, the Germans had given priority to destruction even above the urgency of retreat. With the Allied approach imminent, the Germans made Antwerp a powder keg. To delay the Allied advance, the Germans cluttered the open fields just outside the city with obstacles of all kinds, and flooded other fields, to prevent aircraft landings. They blocked vehicle and pedestrian tunnels, and prepared bridges for demolition, all to buy time so that Antwerp's docks could be rigged with great amounts of dynamite. Five block ships loaded with 1,000 tons of explosives were positioned to blow the quay faces into the water. After a succession of withdrawals lately, the Germans had experience in demolishing port facilities.

Different aspects of the Belgian resistance worked hand in hand. On September 3, when word reached the resistance that the

Allies were within a few miles of Antwerp, resisters went into action. Intelligence sources had tipped off resistance leaders about German plans. Belgian maquisards then seized key areas, and engineers went to work defusing the charges. Among the Belgian resistance groups taking part were *l'Armée Secrete* with its many military officers, *les Milices Patriotiques, le Mouvement National Royaliste,* and *les Partisans Armées.* A local Antwerp group called *la Brigade Blanche Fidelio* also took part. In all, the groups fielded about 600 resisters.

In a masterful plan of attack, the resisters slashed through defenses to capture the Kattendijk and Bonapart basins the next day. Within two days, they had secured strategic bridges on the Albert Canal as the British army moved in to take the port. In the end, Antwerp's port remained intact. In the hands of the Allies, it was used extensively to supply Montgomery's continued advance into Germany.


Hazards of resistance work claimed thousands of lives in both Belgium and Luxembourg during World War II—as many as 6,000 Luxembourg resisters and 16,000 Belgian resisters. Among them were 65 Belgians in SOE service, out of 250 Belgian agents trained. About 240 Belgians were killed as a result of reprisals for resistance activity.

Also among the dead were more than 3,000 young Luxembourgers who had been forced into the Wehrmacht to fight on the Russian front. Another 3,000 had tried to escape, and many had succeeded. Today, men of that age are called the "Sacrificed Generation."

Of the Luxembourgers who joined the French maquis, 69 were killed in action or died in captivity. Within Luxembourg, 23 patriots who took part in the escape lines were captured and executed.

Grand Duchess Charlotte of Luxembourg returned to the welcoming citizenry of her country on April 14, 1945. It was not so simple for King Leopold III of Belgium, however. Political crisis loomed, as the greater part of the Belgian resistance demanded that the king abdicate. The king's brother, Charles, who had been active in the resistance, was commissioned as regent in the meantime. Some of the king's disfavor among his subjects stemmed from an incident in November 1940, when he traveled to Berchtesgaden to meet with Hitler. The general population learned about the trip, but not the reason for it—to negotiate a solution for his country's food shortage. The king was already unpopular among some parts of Belgian society, and this resulted in more misunderstanding and mistrust. The king had also approached Hitler in the winter of 1942 to protest forced labor of Belgian citizens in German factories. As a result, Hitler made some grudging concessions for certain women, young girls, and children of POWs. These exemptions may have prevented the deportation of a half-million Belgians. Again, this was largely unknown or misunderstood. Complicating the situation further was the fact that the Germans had forced the king and his family to move to Germany on June 7, 1944 (the day after the D-Day landings), and later to Strobl, Austria. He wasn't freed until the day of German surrender, May 7, 1945.

Adding to the tension in Belgium were renewed struggles between the Walloons and Flemings. The Walloons accused the Flemish of collaboration, focusing on the small percentage of extremists who had wanted full absorption of Flanders into the Third Reich as the so-called "State of Thiel" envisioned by the Nazis.

At war's end, 77,000 Belgians were accused of collaboration. Viewed alongside a population of 8.4 million, this means less than one percent of the total. Of these 77,000, about half were serious enough cases to warrant severe punishment. At least 4,000 were condemned to death, but only 146 were actually put to death. Another 28,000 lost their political rights. As in other liberated countries, resistance members are known to have carried out unofficial retribution in which many collaborators were executed.

Like France and other countries on the brink of civil war, there was much healing necessary. Time, in this case, did heal some wounds, and King Leopold eventually returned to the throne.

## CHAPTER 7

# France

The defining moment for the French resistance came on the evening of June 18, 1940, when "a huge man with highly-polished boots, who walked with long strides, talking in a very deep voice" stepped up to a microphone in a fourth-floor studio of the BBC in London. Wearing a French army uniform with the rank of general, he placed his typed notes (extensively revised with handwritten scrawls) on the podium before him. Responding to the obligatory voice-check for the BBC's production crew, he uttered two words: "*la France.*" A BBC staffer raised the microphone to accommodate the general's six-foot, five-inch frame. And with that, at 8:15 P.M., according to the official *History of Broadcasting in the UK*, everything was ready for the first wartime address of Charles de Gaulle.

A virtual unknown at this moment, de Gaulle stood on the brink of destiny—France's and his own. "He stared at the microphone as though it were France," recounted Elizabeth Barker, a BBC associate working in the studio that day. He received his cue and began speaking in a voice that was "clear, firm, and rather loud, the voice of a man speaking to his troops before a battle. He did not seem nervous but extremely tense, as though he were concentrating all his power in one single moment."

He began by simply stating that the new French leadership had ordered the army to stop fighting, avoiding tones of judgment. Then he paused and his words grew impassioned: "We certainly have been, and still are, submerged by the mechanical strength of the enemy, both on land and in the air. The tanks, the aeroplanes, the tactics of the Germans far more than their numbers were responsible for our retirement. The tanks, the aeroplanes, the tactics of the Germans astounded our generals to such an extent that they have been brought to the pass which they are in today. But has the last word been said? Has all hope disappeared? Is the defeat final? No!"[26]

He concluded with firm conviction: "Whatever happens, the flame of French resistance must not and shall not go out."

De Gaulle's address emphasized the *method* of the German invasion, and implied the shortcomings of his own country's defenses. This was perhaps a subtle "I told you so," because de Gaulle himself had been a long-time proponent of armored forces working in unison with air power. In fact, some people attribute the Germans' well-coordinated air and ground attack to de Gaulle's own thesis as expressed in his book *Toward a Professional Army*, published in 1933. It was a forward-thinking book that preceded one written along the same line by another little-known contemporary, Erwin Rommel, who published *Infantry Attacks* in 1937. Despite the opinions of some, many German generals read the latter, and none are known to have read the former.

Instead of preparing for technologically advanced warfare, France had placed all of its eggs in one basket, with staunch faith in a colossal failure called the Maginot Line. Formidable as it was, the Maginot Line was a static defense in a new world of highly mobile warfare. The Germans simply skirted it on May 12 and within six weeks blitzed all the way to the Atlantic coast. France's greatest living soldier, the World War I hero of Verdun, Marshal Henri Philippe Pétain, ordered the humiliated French army to stand down. Furthermore, after meetings with Hitler during the first weeks of the armistice, Pétain ordered—in no uncertain terms—collaboration with the occupier.

Few people heard de Gaulle's broadcast. Most of the intended audience was indisposed—being marched to a prisoner of war camp or on the run in retreat. At that moment, it has been estimated that 10 million French civilians were fleeing by road and rail to escape the invasion.

Considering the circumstances, the message was inordinately bold and seemed, in a word, wistful. But the fact was that the "flame of resistance" that de Gaulle exhorted into the BBC microphone *did* stoke the fires—beginning as a smoldering ember, then as a flickering flame, and finally as a roaring fire.

The first obstacle for the French resistance movement was breaking the hold of Pétainism. Marshal Pétain was universally known, and revered by the French. Supported by like-thinking defeatists, he became the legal head of government after Premier Paul Reynaud's resignation. Immediately after taking office, Pétain broadcast to his devastated nation that he would seek an armistice. On June 16, 1940, he declared a cease-fire—a welcome relief to most French citizens. He became a hero all over again, this time not for making war, but for making peace, thereby saving France from the recurring nightmare of bloody battle on home ground.

For the French, there would have been no comparing Pétain and de Gaulle at this point. De Gaulle was an upstart—France's most junior general appointed just three weeks before. Furthermore, de Gaulle did not enjoy the usually implicit advantage of being an upstart—that is, starting with a clean slate. He had already alienated many senior French officials. He did not hold a humble view of himself or his country, and considered himself the embodiment of French honor. By sheer force of character, de Gaulle thrust himself onto the scene, albeit somewhat presumptuously. But in order for France to break the Nazi yoke, he and his vision of a "Free French" movement were what France needed, even though the majority of the French population would have disagreed at the time.

In contrast, Pétain was almost a saintly figure. In many French churches, his portrait was hung behind the altar. In schools, his name was placed alongside that of Joan of Arc.

Pétain had requested no terms from the Germans. He asked only for an armistice—honorable peace, "as between soldiers after the battle." At 84 years of age, Pétain spoke the language of a chivalrous time long past. Since Pétain asked for no conditions, Hitler was happy to draft the terms of the armistice from scratch, alone. Hitler delivered those terms in the same railroad car where the German generals of the Great War had accepted the armistice terms of Marshal Foch on November 11, 1918.

The armistice divided France into two zones—one occupied and the other, surprisingly, unoccupied. The Alsace and Lorraine regions were annexed to Germany outright. The occupied zone included the northern two-thirds of the country, along with the Channel and Atlantic ports on the western coast. Control of the rest, the so-called Free Zone, along with France's colonial empire, was given to Pétain's government. Pétain established the seat of his new government at Vichy, a resort town 175 miles south of Paris.

Other conditions and concessions of the armistice: France would be required to pay the staggering, unlimited cost of the German occupation forces, both government administration and military. French prisoners of war, numbering some two million, would remain in captivity until the war's end. The considerable French navy fleet, however, was to remain in French hands. Finally, Vichy was allowed a standing army of 100,000 soldiers, precisely matching what Germany had been granted by the Treaty of Versailles. (This army was *not* used as an instrument to combat the resistance, until the maquis rose up in open battle around D-Day.)

The Vichy government was a paradox. It never did declare war on Great Britain and, in many regards, it muddled through ambiguously with an attitude the French called *attentisme*, "wait and see." Yet Marshal Pétain stated unmistakably, "Today I enter upon the path of collaboration." What he meant by "collaboration" was not entirely clear, at least not at first. The French soon found out it meant complete submission to their Nazi overlords. The

Vichy government performed subserviently to their bidding and sometimes even acted in anticipation of it.

A telling example of Vichy initiative was the establishment of a French version of the Gestapo, called the *Service d'Ordre Légionnaire* (which would later evolve into the fearsome *Milice Française*, numbering 30,000 members). Like the Gestapo, its members relished in the capture, torture, and murder of French resisters. This organization also took responsibility for hunting down Jews, thereby reflecting Vichy's full support of the "final solution." The Jews of France tried to organize their own resistance to protect themselves, but they were targeted so savagely by the Nazis and their own government that few groups could stand for long.

Vichy's justice system was another example of partnership with Nazism. Among its earliest rulings: Condemnation of Charles de Gaulle for his aforementioned radio address. In absentia, de Gaulle was sentenced to death for treason.

After the fall of France, the Wehrmacht continued winning victory after victory, next overrunning Greece, Yugoslavia, and the Baltic States. With each victory, the Vichy government strengthened its resolve that Germany would win the war. It was all proof that Pétain and his stance of defeatism was correct.

Pétain, as an individual, continued to be revered, but his ministers were ignored or scorned. Pierre Laval, France's new premier, was among those violently hated and in fact targeted by early, unsuccessful assassination attempts. Somehow, Pétain remained apart from the rest, even though he was the centerpiece of Vichy France—Germany's lackey, which submitted so willingly to self-exploitation, embraced anti-Semitic tenets, and slaughtered thousands of its own sons and daughters in the resistance.

A hated government administration with an adored leader . . . it was all part of the French paradox.

Despite their adoration of Pétain, people began to reject the ideas of armistice and collaboration. They began to reject policies of government that supported labor conscription and fascist principles. French resistance began to take hold. But before people could fully come to the fold, they needed to reject the saintly status of Pétain.

"Think Pétain" were the watchwords of the day, ingraining an acceptance of German domination into all citizens. To overcome this, French resistance not only had to fight to liberate the country; it first had to fight to liberate the minds of the people. Even a pioneer in the French resistance, Henri Frenay, struggled to overcome it. Frenay later wrote:

*Public opinion was divided over Marshal Pétain. In fact, it continued to be so well after the end of the war. . . . Despite growing and indisputable proofs, I felt a sort of repugnance to admit to myself that the old Marshal, whatever his intentions, was actually serving the enemy. My judgment was muddied, my initiative constrained, by the powerful influence of my own social background.*

Eventually, he and many others would "abandon the *Pétainiste* myth" and reject "earlier hope that de Gaulle could be France's sword while Pétain remained her shield."

The Pétain myth started to break down because of Vichy's actions. "Pétain made fundamental mistakes that people witnessed," Gaston Vandermeerssche said. "In France, we learned that even Jewish children were being rounded up into camps and then sent to Germany. The real face of Vichy was exposed. It was de Gaulle who emerged as a clear leader whom people could look up to. He was inspiration to me even as a Belgian [resister] working in France. By radio, we heard de Gaulle speak in such a sensitive way and he had a great impact on us."

The focus of resistance in the "Free Zone" was more anti-Vichy than anti-Nazi, simply due to the absence of Germans. Pulling volunteers together into organized resistance groups was relatively easy, because Vichy did not initially have the infrastructure of professionals to police against it (but that *would* happen later).

There were three major movements in the south: *Francs-Tireur et Partisans* had left-wing radical leadership in the person of Jacques Duclos. *Libération Sud* drew together a combination of trade union members and socialists, all under the leadership of Emmanuel d'Astier de la Vigerie.

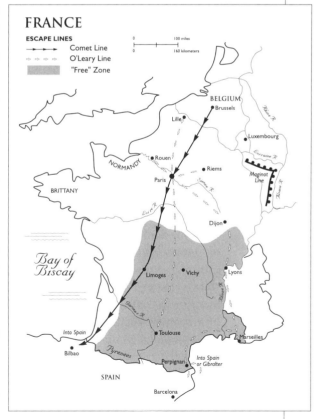

FRANCE
ESCAPE LINES
→→→ Comet Line
⇦⇦⇦⇦ O'Leary Line
"Free" Zone

*France au Combat* comprised a Catholic and Protestant mix, mostly from the professional classes. *Combat's* leader, Henri Frenay, broke ground impressively to make structure where there had been none. He organized his underground forces by task: intelligence, propaganda, parachute-drop rendezvous, document forgery, and so on. There was also a secret resistance within the Vichy's Armistice Army, called the *Organisation de Resistance de l'Armée*. Smaller groups included *Libérer et Fédérer*, *France d'Abord*, and *Le Coq Enchainé*.

Conditions were different in the northern (occupied) zone, and so was the resistance. Here, the German presence brought the conflict to the fore. Resistance didn't require a "liberation of the mind" before feelings of defiance began. It was plain to see who the enemy was. This was much less complicated, but naturally more dangerous, because the Germans installed a full complement of Gestapo and occupation forces in the region.

Resistance in the north had more, separate groups. The area was larger and more populated, plus the Nazi presence gave provocation to join. Fledgling resistance groups included *Ceux de la Libération, Ceux de la Résistance, Valmy, Arc,* and *Pantagruel*. Groups that grew quickly were the *Armée des Volontaires, l'Organisation Civile et Militaire*, the *Mouvement Nationale Révolutionnaire, Bataillons de la Mort,* and *Libération Nord*. These movements developed concurrently with those in the south, but remained autonomous and separate from them.

Early resistance took form in the usual way, as underground newspapers. Among them were *Résistance*, published as early as mid-December 1940 by a youthful group from the *Musée de l'Homme*, and *Défense de la France*, the product of university students. These papers drew content of hard news from the ubiquitous BBC, and also Radio Switzerland and Moscow, and later from France's North African colonies. The largest distribution and readership was naturally in the urban areas, where occupation forces also had the largest concentration. The most famous of all underground newspapers was *Combat*, edited by Albert Camus. It had a long list of distinguished contributing writers that included Jean-Paul Sartre, Simone de Beauvoir, and André Gide.

Labor strikes were another early form of resistance and were sometimes sparked by the urging of underground papers. In May 1941, miners in the occupied zone walked off the job in protest against exploitation by both the mining companies and Germans. The Vichy government soon enacted legislation that abolished or otherwise crippled the unions, which made later strikes more difficult. It also cast the Nazi spotlight on union members, after strikes disrupted delivery of resources needed by the German war machine. Many union members banded together in *Liberation Nord* because of the persecution against them.

Union members were joined underground by many who fled deportation for forced labor. Early in the occupation, many French men and women had *volunteered* for the labor service, especially when Premier Laval negotiated a release program for French soldiers being held as POWs. The deal was this: For every three volunteers, one POW would be released; 200,000 patriotic citizens quickly signed up. After word reached the population through underground newspapers that life in the labor service was little better than slavery—deplorable working conditions, mistreatment, little food, 12-hour work days, and barracks quarters—the pool of labor volunteers dried up. That resulted in compulsory labor, which sent many French citizens into hiding.

A large share of resistance effort was then directed toward caring for these fugitives, who needed false travel and identity papers, food, and clothing. Resistance organizations did their best to provide for them, much in the way the Dutch resistance did for their *onderduikers*. As more and more French citizens became fugitives of the regime for various reasons, the resistance enjoyed a windfall of volunteers. With that came increased activity, including violent acts such as sabotage.

Resistance in the north attracted the attention of the Gestapo and nearly all groups suffered setbacks through infiltration by French collaborators and sudden arrests. Unlike their more experienced Belgian neighbors, the French had little actual practice in clandestine warfare. They didn't know how dangerous careless talk or a haphazard notation of a name and address in a notebook could be, when operating right under the noses of the enemy. Resistance actions had been branded "terrorism" by the legally appointed government. Inexperience and youthful exuberance accounted for some resisters being caught and paying the ultimate price.

"One night, seven of us tried to blow up a train," said Elisabeth Sevier, a teenage resister in Paris. "We were captured by the Germans and they pushed us all together at gunpoint. I was the only girl there. We were put down on our knees with our hands in the air. I thought for certain I was going to die. Gunfire rang out and all of us dropped with our faces to the ground. I fell down like everybody else, so certain that I was shot. To this day, I can feel the sensation as if a bullet had struck me. But the Germans came over and pulled me to my feet. I had *not* been shot. I, alone. They deliberately did not shoot me. Instead they dragged me off to prison." (Sevier later escaped and rejoined the resistance.)

Inexperience was not a problem for one segment of the French resistance: the powerful communist faction. Its members were already skillful in stealth and subversion. These resisters not only had experience but a preexisting underground structure in place. Contrary to Moscow's orders, the French communists had never accepted the coexistence of fascist and communist ideologies, or even a neutral stand, before the German invasion of Russia. In May 1941, a month before Operation *Barbarossa*, French communist cells banded together in what they called *Front National*, a movement intended to unify Frenchmen from all backgrounds, *and* bridge resistance of the north and the south. For the first two years of the occupation, this was the only movement that had a hand in both zones.

This changed with Operation *Torch*. On November 11, 1942, the Allies invaded Vichy North Africa, and French forces on the coast failed to put up much of a fight. Most officers of the Armistice Army were loyal to Vichy, but they were shown to be averse, even openly hostile, to Germany. The bottom-line result of *Torch* was that the Germans became angry and distrustful, and occupied the rest of France. What this meant for the French resistance was that, after two years of being divided, movements in the north and south suddenly were on equal footing, and faced a common adversary. There was no longer any reason for separation.

Another byproduct of *Torch* was that Americans became embroiled in French affairs, ramifications for the resistance and its leadership. Lieutenant General Dwight D. Eisenhower and other Allied leaders had negotiated separately with French Admiral Darlan before the Allied landings. In fact, the admiral was invited to "jump ship"—abandon Vichy to join the Allies. He was chosen over General de Gaulle, who had evidently succeeded in alienating yet another high-level politician—*the* most powerful one in the world, President Franklin Roosevelt. Admiral Darlan accepted the offer to become leader of the Free French Forces, but within a month he was dead—assassinated by a young member of a Royalist *corps franc* on Christmas Day 1942.

In early 1943, the United States revisited the other candidates they'd considered among Frenchmen in the regime, such as General Maxime Weygand and General de la Laurencie. None had the will or nerve to lead the Free French Forces. The Americans spirited General Henri Giraud out of France and tried to press him on the resistance, but the match wasn't right. By default, and sheer strength of will, General de Gaulle remained in the fore, now officially commanding what he had been unofficially commanding already. He would head the French National Committee, and thereby the French resistance.

De Gaulle had already formed his own secret service, called the BCRA, or *Bureau Central de Renseignements et d'Action* (Central Information and Action Bureau), in late 1941. With agents in the field, this bureau had overlap, as well as inevitable conflicts, with the French section of SOE. Established in London, the BCRA moved to Algiers when the French provisional government was set up there after Operation *Torch*.

After full Nazi occupation of France, the Germans became more oppressive. Campaigns in North Africa and Russia had sapped German energies, forcing them to demand conscripted workers and volunteers for its army. Premier Laval was given the unenviable task of drawing manpower from France's population to send to German factories. From February 1943 on, forced labor quotas sent more fugitives-turned-resisters into the forests of France. From 1940 to 1942, resistance had been mostly urban. The years 1943 and 1944 saw a marked increase in the maquis, the guerrilla forces in remote areas of France.

*Maquis* is actually the French word for Corsican underbrush, where bandits could hide out from police. So the maquis, in the resistance sense, took to the wild, bushy land common to Brittany and the mountain ranges of the Vosges, extending 120 miles along the Rhine, and the Jura, extending 200 miles along the French-Swiss border and throughout southern regions of France. These regions were ideal habitat for guerrilla bands.

The secret army of maquis, as well as other parts of the resistance, received supplies and weapons dropped by parachute from both the SOE and BCRA (although the BCRA received most of its allotments from the other Allies). A group responsible strictly for airdrops, formed under Jean Moulin's leadership, expanded on Henri Frenay's excellent compartmentalization of duties. Moulin organized the country into six regions to receive supplies and distribute them appropriately. Compared with most of the occupied countries, France received much material assistance, but less than it could have used.

As the maquis reached full fighting trim, other aspects of the resistance developed. Escape lines grew in volume and efficiency. From the earliest days after the blitzkrieg, *passeurs* (volunteers or paid help) had been smuggling fliers and other refugees from the occupied zone to the free zone, and on to Switzerland or Spain. By the war's midpoint, when Allied round-the-clock bombing hit its stride, France's escape lines filled their queues with evaders. French resisters worked hand-in-hand with those in neighboring countries, especially Belgium, where many Allied airmen fell to earth, virtually on Germany's doorstep. With support from MI9, Albert-Marie Guérisse ran the Patrick O'Leary Line, based in Marseilles (as noted in the previous chapter). And Andrée de Jongh's Comet Line, originally based in Belgium, eventually moved its "headquarters" to a more central location in Paris.

Intelligence networks provided a steady stream of information about the massive coastal defenses and internal troop locations and movements. The most active intelligence network was *Confrérie Notre-Dame*, established by de Gaulle's BCRA. One of the network's members, a house painter named René Duchez, made off with the plans for Atlantic Wall defenses from an office used by the Germans in Caen in May 1942.

Sabotage also became a major activity of the French resistance. One of the more notable sabotage operations in France was a raid on the Peugeot factory, which manufactured German tanks. Aerial bombing had been tried with mediocre results; raids demolished many warehouses and workshops but production continued. Then French SOE agents took a direct approach: They simply asked the owners, the Peugeot family, to disable production lines. The family turned out to be very willing and pro-Allied. They knew exactly where to place explosive charges to destroy key machinery without totally destroying their factory or endangering French workers.

Combating and undermining the German war machine was only one side of the struggle for the French resistance. Confronting the massive body of French collaboration could be as treacherous, or even more so. "I hated the collaborators even more, because they were French," said Elisabeth Sevier, expressing the sentiment of most French resisters.

It was an enemy as strong as any faced by the resistance in any occupied country. France's internal police forces had risen up in opposition to the burgeoning, better equipped, and increasingly effective resistance.

While still under Vichy, specialized police units operated in the free zone. The *Police de Sûreté*, or Security Police, was part of what came to be called the National Police after full occupation; it was responsible for investigating "political crimes." Some police units had names pointed enough to be self-explanatory, among them the Police for Jewish Affairs and the Anti-Communist Police Service. Other highly specialized police services included the *Gardes Méssiers*, or Harvest Guards, and the *Garde des Voies et des Communications*, for protection of Roads and Communications. These worked in conjunction with the German SD, and most eventually had jurisdiction nationally.

There were 10,000 Frenchmen in the *Groupes Mobiles de Reserve*, the GMR, directly responsible for antiresistance operations. Along the same lines was the *Legion Française des Combatants* composed exclusively of war veterans who followed the model set by their hero, Pétain. This group had several divisions, one of which was the *Service d'Ordre Légionnaire*, which would evolve into the much-feared *Milice Française*—the most ruthless and effective internal security created by Vichy. Led by Joseph Darnand,[27] the

*Milice Française* had a main branch called the *Franc Garde* with 5,000 permanent men and women, and 8,000 reserve or part-time. The *Franc Garde* waged a bloody war on the resistance—in effect, an undeclared civil war. The *Franc Garde*'s first action was in the spring of 1943 at Haut Savoie; before the end of the year operations expanded into the north as well.

The *Franc Garde*, the GMR, and the Wehrmacht[28] combined forces in February 1944 to cordon the Glières plateau, where a maquis battalion numbering 458 had taken refuge. Nearly 12,000 men of the combined collaborationist and German forces attacked the resistance redoubt, suffering losses of 150 collaborators and 700 German troops. The maquis had taken a gallant stand, but a third were killed—42 in combat and 83 after capture and torture.

Julien Helfgott was a 24-year-old maquisard who witnessed the slaughter:

> *The* Boche[29] *fired without ceasing. Never in my life have I witnessed such a sustained fusillade. For over an hour they held us pinned down with their machine guns and mortars while, split into small groups, we defended ourselves as best we could. Finally we could stand the hammering no longer and in wild confusion we scrambled to our feet and ran, some one way and some another but most toward the sanctuary of the rockfalls and trees at the base of the mountain. . . . Our panic only made us easier targets for the Germans. Most of my comrades were shot down before they had gone three or four metres, some reached the rocks but got no further. Miraculously, a few of us survived.*

If collaborationist forces had entirely won out over the French resistance, France in effect would have become a partner in the Axis. But incidences like Glières were catalysts that inspired more resistance, and more French men and women to join the maquis. Glières Battalion saw a surge of more than 3,000 fresh recruits come into its ranks as a result.

With their *Front National* movement, the communists tried to bring together all Frenchmen against the Germans from the earliest days of occupation. Unifying the French on *anything* would have been difficult. France was a country that had suffered many divisions during the decades of the Third Republic.

It became General de Gaulle's ultimate goal to unify the various resistance groups and bring their considerable strength to bear on the

Germans. De Gaulle hand-picked Jean Moulin, a former préfect, for that critical mission.

What Moulin achieved exceeded de Gaulle's wildest hopes. By mid-1942, Moulin had successfully created the *Mouvements Unis de la Résistance*, or United Resistance Movements, in the old southern zone. All of its volunteer groups were consolidated into *l'Armée Secrète*, a single secret army under the command of General Charles Delestraint, who reported directly to de Gaulle. In March 1943, Moulin drew together leaders from across all the fragmented movements into the *Conseil National de la Résistance*, or National Resistance Council, to steer resistance on a national level. These included socialists and communists, too.

Moulin served as chairman of this council, until his arrest by the Gestapo. He was apprehended in Lyons on June 21, 1943. Although tortured to death, he divulged no secrets of his secret army—and he knew them all. Moulin's most remarkable legacy is that all these groups accepted and supported de Gaulle's leadership of the resistance. Thanks in part to Jean Moulin's efforts, de Gaulle became known among the rank and file of the resistance and "Gaullism" gathered strength in France, whereas previously, "the resistance, a full year after its birth, was unaware of de Gaulle's supposed leadership—even his moral leadership," according to Henri Frenay. What had seemed impossible in 1941 and 1942, during Pétain's spell of defeatism, was coming to be: Pétain's popularity was waning and de Gaulle's was rising exponentially.

Since Allied leaders planned to invade Continental Europe on the coast of France, the French resistance began to receive the weaponry and supplies demanded for so long. In preparation for Operation *Overlord*, a profusion of airdrops came from SOE, as well as the BCRA in Algiers, in the spring of 1944. Many "Jedbergh" teams—SOE liaisons—parachuted into France to help coordinate and train resistance fighters.

De Gaulle's National Resistance Council directed the massive buildup. Within the council, military committees were established, one for each region of France. Correspondingly, liberation committees were established in France on the local level, so that all resistance throughout the country had direct ties to leadership.

On February 1, 1944, the FFI—the *Forces Françaises de l'Interieur*, or the French Forces of the Interior—was formed, unifying the whole width and breadth of French resistance as it had never been. It drew together Delestraint's *l'Armée Secrète*, the communist *Franc-Tireurs et Partisans*, and Giraud's Army Resistance Organization. De Gaulle gave

General Pierre Koenig and General Jacques Leclerc joint leadership of the FFI, or what also came to be known as France's "Home Army."

On the eve of D-Day, all national energies had been focused in support of the landings on the widest scale possible. Forces were united internally (even more than externally—notification of the invasion went out generally to France's resistance, but de Gaulle was never actually informed of D-Day's date of invasion). Communists were ready to fight alongside moderates, and the strongest Gaullists would fight alongside former Vichyists.

By June 6, 1944, the FFI had received arms enough through air-drops to fully equip 20,000 resisters, and partially equip another 50,000. Resistance leaders pulled out all the stops, issuing weapons from the French army arsenal that had been hidden since 1940. Large stocks of guns, ammunition, and explosives were in the hands of the resistance, for a do-or-die effort.

On D-Day, resisters would be ready to take action when the pre-arranged signal came. Targets for sabotage were encrypted: Code *Bleu* for electric power stations and lines; Code *Violet* for communication lines; and Code *Vert* or green for railroads. And there was Code *Bibendum* to launch delaying actions to hamper German reinforcement on roadways taking them to the landing beaches; this meant attacking convoys, sabotaging bridges, and felling trees across roads—anything that would put an obstacle in the Germans' path.

When the first waves of Allied troops hit the Normandy beaches, the French resistance began a flurry of subversive activity. Sabotage hit simultaneously across the country: canals were flooded, trains ground to halt on mangled rails, fuel dumps exploded. And perhaps most important, resisters performed delaying actions to keep reinforcements from reaching Normandy, buying time for the Allies to gain a foothold on the beaches. The most notable delaying action was against the 2nd SS Panzer Division, *Das Reich*. The division needed to move northwest to the coast, but the maquis harassed it so badly that it was diverted for counterguerrilla operations in the Dordogne, instead of speeding north to meet the invasion. A tragic consequence was that the Germans became so frustrated they launched reprisals that massacred all men, women, and children in the village of Oradour-sur-Glane (near Limoges), then razed all village buildings—adding it to the growing list of obliterated places that began with Lidice in Czechoslovakia.

After D-Day there was a tremendous influx of citizens joining de Gaulle's forces. In February 1944, its first month, the FFI numbered 50,000. By midsummer, it had grown to 200,000. After the Normandy landings, the maquis fought innumerable small battles and some larger ones, expediting the liberation. Some were victories. Others ended in massacre.

In southern France, the plateau of Mont Mouchet was the scene of a large and victorious battle on June 11, 1944. The maquis, numbering 3,000, held off a succession of German forces numbering 10,000. By the end of the day, the Germans suffered losses of 1,400 killed and 2,000 wounded, compared to maquis losses of 160 killed and 200 wounded. But the Germans would not be denied. The next week, they brought in reinforcements that increased troop strength to 20,000, with artillery and aircraft in support. All were hurled against the maquis redoubt. The Germans began with a devastating artillery barrage and air assault that paved the way for the infantry to move ahead. The foot soldiers charged into the heart of the plateau and found—nothing. The maquis had vanished, dispersing and disappearing before the German charge had begun. It was the textbook-perfect guerrilla action.

The maquis would not be so fortunate the next time. On the plateau of Vercors, a natural fortress of rocky crests surrounding a high tableland, a huge maquis redoubt came under siege by German forces. Again, the Germans brought in artillery and aircraft to support a large number of Wehrmacht troops and the *Milice Française*. The OSS had sent in a 15-man team that tried to convince the Vercors maquis to avoid open combat; the team urged the maquis to follow the basic principles of guerrilla warfare with mobile hit-and-run attacks, then to disperse as they had done on the plateau of Mont Mouchet. But passions were strong for a showdown. They *wanted* a fight with the *Boche*. Plus, their boldness was fueled by their belief that they would be reinforced by Allied troops and heavy weapons after landings at the French Riviera—help that never came.

Fighting started on June 15 and lasted for five bloody weeks. The maquis' fate was sealed when seasoned SS and airborne troops landed by gliders and parachute amongst them. On July 23, the maquis leader finally gave the order to disperse, but by then it was too late. Defeat turned to slaughter when more than 700 maquisards were trapped. Many suffered torture and death after capture.

Following the Allied invasion, many units of the French Forces of the Interior were transformed into regular units of the French army. Responding to de Gaulle's invitation, more than 140,000 resisters donned the uniform by October 1944.

The French had endured four long years of occupation. Its resistance had accomplished much to aid the Allied war effort and, perhaps even more important to the people of France, kept alive the pride of the nation. In *The Complete War Memoirs of Charles de Gaulle*, the general praised them: "What an honor to France. . . . All voluntarily accepted the danger of the maquis . . . despite the number of young men who were *hors de combat* and the fact that the official Vichy machine, until its last hour, had hunted down and condemned all who resisted."

Even as France was liberated from the Nazi occupation, no one doubted the magnitude of challenges over the years ahead. Stemming from prewar conflicts, France had teetered on the brink of civil war, and could have gone the way of Greece and Yugoslavia after World War II.

To the end, even the leaders of the Vichy government had viewed themselves as patriots, doing what was right for France. In the postwar reckoning, as Pierre Laval was set before a French firing squad, he said, "You are accomplices in one of the great crimes of history. I die for having loved my country too much."

In the panic of invasion, the French had turned to Pétain, who so completely subjugated his nation to Hitler, and they followed him blindly. But the new leader would never settle for anything less than a free and united France. He had been the disembodied voice of that long-ago night of June 1940—an unknown, whose uncompromising "*Vive la France*" spoke as perfectly for war as it would for peace—Charles de Gaulle.

# Greece

Greece's resistance to Axis occupation was a story of extremes: high and low; left and right. The high point was a dazzling triumph in which the modern Greeks showed the mettle and fighting prowess of their ancient ancestors by winning the first clear victory over Axis powers on the European Continent, when they humiliated the Italian army. However, the lowest of lows came with the devastation of the German occupation, which was followed immediately by a bitter civil war between extreme left and right factions.

Before his military offensive, Hitler had launched a diplomatic offensive in the Balkans and given it teeth with the customary threat of force. Through these means, Greece's neighbors of Romania, Hungary, and Bulgaria were pressured to join the Axis order. Pressure continued on a vacillating Yugoslavia. Only Greece firmly dismissed the German diplomatic blitz.

Greece's resistance began with a rap on the door at 3 A.M. on October 28, 1940. Greek Dictator Ioannis Metaxas was roused from a sound sleep to find Italian Minister Emmanuel Grazzi standing on his doorstep in the brisk night air. Glancing down at the paper he held, Grazzi gravely informed Metaxas that he bore a message direct from *Il Duce*, Benito Mussolini.

"Can't it wait till the honest light of day?" Metaxas groused.

Thrust into his hands was the message that wouldn't wait. In the dim light, Metaxas' eyes followed along the lines of the page. Under the thin veneer of diplomatic language, with peaceful-sounding phrasing such as "assurance of neutrality," "protection," and "full respect of Greece's sovereignty," Metaxas discerned the implicit ultimatum: willingly accept occupation by Italian troops—or be invaded. This was much in the style of Hitler's preinvasion communication with the countries that became his "protectorates."

Without hesitation, Metaxas uttered, "*Oxi!*" "No!"

Grazzi exited the doorstep, perhaps a little amused in the way of a patronizing adult who has indulged a defiant toddler by letting him say "no." After all, this operation would be like taking candy from a baby: A nation of 43,000,000 Italians fielding a large modern and mechanized army pitted against a tiny country of 9,000,000 with an ill-equipped, rag-tag band that had no armor, few heavy weapons, and a few hundred obsolete aircraft. It was laughable.

While the Greeks continued their peaceful slumber, resistance in their nation had begun because of the utterance of that single word: "*Oxi!*" Two and a half hours later, at daybreak, Italian troops marched off intending to make short work of the Greeks.

Benito Mussolini's motivation was simple. He had jealously watched as the Nazis blitzkrieged across Europe, scoring resounding victory after resounding victory. The focus of the world was now riveted on Hitler, while Mussolini was second-page news. This was humbling to a man who hated to be humbled. Mussolini needed a quick, cheap victory to redeem himself.

The next day, the story of Metaxas' defiant response spread throughout Athens. Athenians were shouting "*Oxi, oxi, oxi!*" in the streets. British novelist Olivia Manning observed, "Everyone repeated '*Oxi*,' or 'No,' or 'Non,' and there were even those who, off guard, said '*Nein*,' but in the excitement this was overlooked. The sense of splendor was everywhere so it seemed that secretly everyone had wanted to enter the war instead of living uncertainly on the fringe of it."

Mussolini's conquering Roman legions moved *en masse*, 100,000 strong from Albania, Greece's small neighbor to the north, which had been forcibly occupied in April 1939. As the invaders slogged through the cold rain of late fall, over washed-out roads winding through mountain passes, the Greek defenders moved high into the rugged mountains to watch their enemy approach. Over three-fourths of Greece's land area is mountainous—a roller coaster of almost abysmal gorges and mile-high mountain peaks. It had been Metaxas' foresight that put defenders in the mountains of Epirus, near the Albanian border.[30] The fierce mountain warriors were mobilized as reserves and given only fragments of uniforms. They formed the core of the defense and the core of future resistance, as guerrillas who specialized in mountain warfare.

Metaxas ordered his forces to wait until the Italian columns were stretched like distended snakes in the narrow valleys, laying themselves open to attack. Then the Greeks let loose with all the firepower they had. Almost immediately they gained the upper hand. From unseen stations atop the jagged, rocky cliffs, mortar and artillery shells rained down on the surprised Italians. Time after time, the Italian columns were caught in the valleys and smashed where they stood.

Italian radio broadcasts whined that *Il Duce* had sent troops in good faith—in "a friendly, protective spirit" that would "begin a new period of Italo-Hellenic friendship and understanding." The Greeks, of course, paid no mind to this. By this time the world had become wise to the Hitler-like ploys.

Demoralized, hopelessly mired in mud, slipping on slick rocks, and routed at every turn, the Italians attempted an about-face. Some units had nowhere to go, cut off by the Greek mountain warriors who anticipated their moves. When the entire III Alpini Division was trapped in a gorge, 5,000 Italians surrendered.

After repulsing their adversaries, the Greeks abandoned their defensive positions and went into full pursuit. Italian units that could move back northward plunged into headlong, uncontrolled retreat. The counteroffensive hurled the would-be occupiers back to where they'd come from, and farther—a quarter of the way across Albania.

By November 21, three weeks after the ultimatum presented on Metaxas' doorstep, the Greeks wrestled away southern Albania's two most important cities, Koritsa and Argyrocastro. Outdistancing their supply lines, the Greeks halted their advance.

Between November 1940 and April 1941, Mussolini gradually increased the size of his invasion forces from 9 divisions to 28, but Greece's mountaineers—possessing the minimum in weaponry and an abundance of spirit—still held firm. No amount of men or material seemed able to open the northern door to Greece.

Mussolini had boasted that Greece would fall in 10 days, much like the timing of France's fall to the Germans. But after six months, Mussolini's troops were farther back than where they started.

Mussolini's move on Greece did not please Hitler. Hitler had not wanted to upset the apple cart in the Balkans—at least not yet. He needed stability in the region as he set about launching Operation *Barbarossa*. The last thing he wanted was his forces stretched thinner by the addition of another front. Additionally, Italy's aggression brought the British back to the Continent—as much a political move as military because of Winston Churchill's pledge to Greece to send help in the event of invasion. Great Britain had pulled four divisions badly needed in North Africa to occupy Crete and the Aegean island of Lemnos. The Royal Air Force sent squadrons to airfields in southern Greece, which introduced the threat of air attack on Romania's Ploesti oilfields, vital for fueling Hitler's Luftwaffe and Panzer units.

Hitler's original plan might have been to seize only strategic points in Greece (such as air bases from which the Luftwaffe would win air supremacy over the Aegean and eastern Mediterranean), but that was no longer adequate. Great Britain's infusion of troops and aircraft meant Germany now needed to seize all of Greece and eradicate the British. To further ensure a secure southern flank for Barbarossa, Hitler concluded that he must seize the whole of the Balkans. Operation *Marita*—invasion of both Yugoslavia and Greece—was drawn up.

The British knew about *Marita* because the month before it was to be launched, messages had been intercepted and decoded by *Ultra*, Britain's ultrasecret and ultraeffective counterintelligence operation. Without explicitly telling the Greeks of their foreknowledge, the British brought up battle-ready troops against the invasion they knew would come through Bulgaria and Yugoslavia, but they were far too few.

On April 6, 1941, an onslaught of German mechanized units swarmed into Greece from the north and east. Although the weather had not improved much and snowdrifts still blocked mountain passes, waiting until spring brought two benefits: General Metaxas died of complications after throat surgery in January 1941, and Bulgaria joined the Axis powers, offering a free-and-clear passageway for Germans to their staging areas.

After fierce fighting at Rupel Pass that briefly slowed the invasion, the Germans then steamrollered in an end-around sweep to attack the Metaxas Line from the rear. Like a mini-Maginot Line, the Metaxas Line was a static defensive wall with concrete blockhouses and a network of connecting passages. It formed a 125-mile crescent defending the border with Bulgaria. The same, simple outflanking maneuver that felled the Maginot Line was employed to crush the Greek defenders by April 9. Another German spearhead outflanked the 12 Greek divisions that continued to hold off the Italians in Albania. As usual, German strategy was superb and tactics were executed with precision. The Germans smashed through to begin movement toward Greece's interior. The rampaging Panzers pushed southward, through Monastir Gap, severing Greek and British forces.

Most British Commonwealth and Greek units fell back slowly across the flat Plain of Thessaly on the way toward Athens. Covering their retreat, small units of Greek and British troops fended off the Adolf Hitler SS Motorized Division at Thermopylae, buying time for others to retreat. There was little RAF air support, so the Luftwaffe was free to strafe fleeing units. By this time it was obvious there was no hope of reversals and that the British needed to evacuate from Greece. The Greek government cabled a message to the British commander, Lieutenant General Sir Henry Maitland Wilson: "You have done your best to save us. We are finished. But the war is not yet lost. Save as much as you can of your army to help win elsewhere."

In the panic of the ensuing German invasion, elements of the hearty Greek forces fell apart and into German hands. Many Greek regulars who were able to escape joined up with British Commonwealth troops—about 43,000 Englishmen, Australians, and New Zealanders. These troops were evacuated in what has been termed by some as the second Dunkirk. The Luftwaffe's Stuka dive bombers pummeled the Greek ports and ships laden with soldiers fleeing to Crete. Fortunately, the two evacuation nights were moonless and most ships slipped away under cover of darkness, but four merchant transports were lost.

The remaining defenders gradually moved south and within 21 days, the invaders reached Athens, where they found little but the blackened wreckage of equipment abandoned and destroyed at the last minute in the embarkation areas.

About half of the evacuees went to Crete and the other half to Egypt. The withdrawal was devastating to the Greeks, after previously winning a clear victory over the Italians. For the British, the operation was a complete debacle. They had done virtually nothing to help Greece, and had weakened their own forces in North Africa, opening up the possibility for the Desert Fox, General Erwin Rommel, to lunge at the Suez Canal.

Before Athens fell in April 1941, many members of the Greek government and its administrative staff fled from Athens to Cairo, as did King George II, Crown Prince Paul, and the royal family. There the government of Free Greece began to organize sizable armed forces from all those who had fled Greece, along with the Greeks living in Egypt and Cyprus—all told more than a half-million people. The Greek navy made Cairo its headquarters. Eventually, the government of Free Greece moved to London.

Following his plan, Hitler withdrew his powerful mechanized forces from Greece and sent them to Russia for Operation *Barbarossa* in June 1941. Consequently, Hitler never set up adequate forces to keep the whole of Greece firmly in his grip. There never was a serious effort to hold Greek territory outside the main lines of communication and the cities.

Hitler's occupation plan in Greece was to share control with his Axis partners, dividing the country into three zones. Germany took control of the areas around Athens, the ports of Salonika and Piraeus, and a few islands in the Aegean, including most of hard-won Crete;[31] Bulgaria was allowed to annex the land area from the Strymon River in eastern Macedonia through all of Thrace to the Turkish border; and Italy had the rest, which included the Ionian Islands, the provinces of Thesprotia, Ioannina, and Prenza that became attached to Italian satellite Albania.

As one conqueror to another, Hitler gave to Mussolini the overall role as the "great power" responsible for administration and defense of Greece. This was consistent with the prior understanding that Greece lay within the Italian sphere of control (along with Albania and Yugoslavia, while the inland region of Bulgaria,

Romania, and Hungary would be in Germany's). Italian control was only a façade, of course. The real power lay in the hands of Germany.

Some believe that, in his twisted ideology, Hitler had a soft spot for the modern-day Greeks because he identified them with their heroic ancestors, who defended Thermopylae in the famous battle of 480 B.C., when Leonidas and the Greeks prevailed over Xerxes and the Persians. Perhaps this is the reason he did not institute an invasion so brutal and occupation policies so destructive as those of neighboring Yugoslavia, where Hitler entered with nothing on his mind except destruction. Although the German occupation policies in Greece were less barbaric than in some countries, great economic damage was done to Greece.

As we've seen in all the occupied countries of Europe, the Nazis exploited the resources in whatever ways best served their interests. In western Europe, the economies were managed in a way that kept inflation in check. In Greece, however, inflation spiraled out of control almost immediately, making the Greek *drachma* worth almost nothing. Administration was left to an ineffective puppet government overseen by Italians, but the real devastation to the economy came as a result of Germans plundering anything of value—mainly ore and food—without offering anything in return or even attempting to keep industry solvent.

Additionally, the Germans commandeered the vital north-south railway without regard to the fact that it was the principal transport for food to Greece's cities. Even before the war in Greece's most productive years, 400,000 to 500,000 tons of grain had to be imported annually to sustain the population. So not only was food shipment cut off, but the scarce food found locally required literally wheelbarrowfuls of *drachmas*. Thousands of Greeks would starve as a result.

All these economic hardships were conducive to resistance. With guerrilla warfare briefly tabled, Greek resistance took the form of harboring Allied soldiers—thousands of British, Australians, and New Zealanders not able to get to the southern ports in time for evacuation. At the time of Nazi invasion, there had been 56,000 Allied soldiers in Greece, of which 43,000 escaped to Crete and Egypt. The rest who had not been captured or killed were now wandering across Greece. Common folk everywhere took them in, fed them despite the food shortage, and hid them. This was done spontaneously across the land, without formal organization of any kind.

Keeping the soldiers hidden was one thing; helping them escape from occupied Greece required organization on a large scale. Escape lines eventually formed to smuggle these soldiers to Egypt, Syria, or Palestine.

Entries in the wartime diary of Jeanne Tsatsos, resister and wife of a university professor, gave a representative account of this help. On

September 15, 1941, she wrote: "I saw the Englishman at noon as we agreed. In the evening we moved him to another address. I am glad about this every time I manage to help one of the British. I have the added satisfaction of feeling that in some small degree we are combating the violence of the conqueror. Because, whether by deceit or action, it is an absolute necessity for us somehow to oppose [them]." Later, she noted ominously: "The Germans have made a new law. 'Anyone who hides one of the Allies will be shot.'"

Once the shock of the invasion and occupation wore off, people began to unite into small groups, each one a little different in focus. Most became known only by their Greek initials, and in the beginning there were so many that they went all the way from "AAA" to simply "X" (*Archiyion Apeleftherotikou Agonos* to *Khi*). Two soon emerged as the most prevalent: the EAM (*Ethniko Apeleftherotiko Metopo* or National Liberation Front) and the EDES (*Ethnikos Draseos* or National Democratic Greek League).

By September 1941, aggressive resistance was beginning, first carried out by the National Liberation Front, known as EAM. EAM had smooth-talking leadership that, through shrewd ambiguousness, offered a platform that appealed to a wide range of Greeks. It attracted recruits by enticing them with promises of organized resistance against the hated occupiers, and free elections after the war. What it didn't mention was that it was communist led. Because it had been banned by Metaxas, the group already had years of practice operating in the style of clandestine resistance.

Many Greeks believed strongly in the church, family, and democracy, and were quite adamant against communism. So most of the recruits EAM welcomed into its ranks did not suspect its political drive. Recruitment was successful enough that EAM formed a guerrilla branch called ELAS (*Ethniko Laikos Apeleftherotiko Stratos* or the Army of Liberation).

ELAS was led by a man named Thanases Klaras, alias Aris Velouchiotis.[32] Aris was a Greek communist, physically imposing in his muscular frame, and sadistically brutal even by Moscow standards. He was also charismatic with his surprisingly soft-spoken rhetoric. He would march his guerrilla bands into mountain villages, holding the Greek flag high, singing the Greek anthem, then stand in the square to deliver recruitment speeches, eloquently and patriotically explaining how ELAS supported the struggle for national liberation. A one-time gendarme in central Greece described the response: "A spirit of revolution took hold in these regions, and many patriotic men gladly joined."

ELAS was well equipped compared to most irregular bands. This was due, in large part, to the fact that they had collected up the secret caches of arms and ammunition left in rural areas by the retreating British and Greek armies fleeing the Axis onslaught. Well armed and flush with new recruits, ELAS soon dominated the regions of northern and central Greece.

In Athens, a rival liberation group formed in the fall of 1941. Under the leadership of Napoleon Zervas, the National Democratic Greek League, called EDES, developed a strong following under the democratic bent of its leader. Like his ELAS counterpart, Zervas was also charismatic, but overweight and a hopeless hypochondriac. He was a colorful character, having been a colonel in the Greek army and later a professional gambler. Like many Greek republicans, Zervas hated communism as well as the monarchy. It was his hatred of the monarchy that had resulted in his expulsion from the Greek army's officer corps 16 years before.

As one of many strange-bedfellow relationships during the war, Britain's SOE had identified Zervas as valuable to its cause. Through contacts by clandestine radio in Athens in the spring of 1942, SOE tried to turn him into a mercenary, offering him 24,000 gold sovereigns (worth $200,000 at the time) to take to the mountains and begin active resistance as the leader of EDES. When he hesitated, SOE agents used coercion, suggesting they would turn him over to the Germans if he did not comply.

Zervas did move operations (mostly limited to talk and vague planning so far) to the mountains of Epirus—the victorious battlegrounds where the Italian army had been chased back into Albania. Joined by other prewar army officers, he recruited members from the mountain villages.

By the following summer, in June 1942, EDES launched its first raid—the first raid of consequence in occupied Greece. Using the same methods so successful in the Greek victories against the Italian invaders, Zervas positioned his group, numbering about 100, on the rocky cliffs of the Louros River Valley. They lay in wait for a 20-truck convoy and attacked, leaving the convoy in flaming wreckage, and successfully escaping with guns and ammunition.

EDES and ELAS grew slowly during the summer of 1942, each reaching about 100 full-time guerrillas. They operated in separate areas, using the Achelous River in northwestern Greece as an informal boundary. Without strategic direction, and using only hit-and-run techniques, their activity was so minor it was almost overlooked by the Germans, who chose not to station soldiers in the outlying districts. The occupation policy was simply to station a bare minimum of soldiers in-country and, if there was trouble, to send in SS execution squads to exact reprisals.

Just before midnight on November 25, 1942, an enormous explosion rocked a quiet valley in central Greece. That blast, followed quickly by another, ripped a huge gap in the Gorgopotamos viaduct, over which ran the railway line that connected Athens to the north. Two full spans plummeted into the deep gorge below, the sound of their impact providing an exclamation mark to the caper. Great, jagged stanchions stood mute and useless, supporting nothing. The vital railway—the main lifeline for shipments north and south to Piraeus (and on to Rommel's troops in North Africa)—was out of commission for weeks.

The British had asserted themselves again, this time as active participants.

Two months previous, in September 1942, a British demolition team led by Colonel Edmund Myers had parachuted into Greece for a joint sabotage mission with the help of local resisters. This might have been an isolated incident that barely warranted a footnote in the annals of the war, except for one thing: The British team stayed for years.

The original plan had been for Myers' demolition team to link up with Zervas' band to sabotage the viaduct. But a bad parachute drop had placed them at least 100 miles away from Zervas and unknowingly much closer to Aris. Talk of a British team looking to link up with the guerrillas spread among the mountain villages, and through the villagers, Myers found himself in touch with both Zervas and Aris. Both agreed to take part in the raid, so 150 men from EDES, ELAS, and the British team, led by Zervas, blew the viaduct.

The mission required experienced raiders in substantial enough number to neutralize the 80 Italians guarding the viaduct so that the British demolition experts could place their plastic explosives. It was not a textbook raid exemplifying stealth: The Greek guerrillas were pinned down by the Italians, but eventually the defenses were overcome and the viaduct reached.

The success of the raid and, more importantly, the coordination of the rival bands caused British HQ to order Myers to stay. The success of the mission did one more thing: When word spread about the British-Greek mission, thousands of Greek patriots joined EDES, ELAS, and other bands. New forces were formed as well, including a band of irregulars reestablished by Major Demetrios Psarros at Mount Parnassus.

As the Greeks were swelling the ranks of Aris' ELAS into a group five or six times the size of EDES, its communist control still remained a secret. Even the British team did not know for certain, although they began to suspect. However, no matter what, the British knew they needed ELAS.

With the influx of new members, EAM spun off an array of groups to support its purposes on many fronts. In addition to ELAS, the resistance's army, the group now included a tiny navy called ELAN, as well as a communist trade union organization (EEAM), a youth movement (EPON), a cooperative society (EA), a secret police squad (OPLA), and a civil guard (EP). They even had "ambassadors" responsible for relations with the communist parties of neighboring Albania, Bulgaria, and Yugoslavia.

ELAS had completely taken over large portions of Greece. EDES, with its smaller numbers, was limited to a small area of northwestern Greece, but more British support went to Zervas.

Myers' deputy, Major C.M. Woodhouse, eventually confirmed beyond all doubt that EAM, parent organization to ELAS, was communist run. The British made the decision not to support ELAS, but as long as the common aim was to drive out the occupier, the British continued coordinating activities with ELAS as much as possible. (Out of necessity, this was in direct contrast to the British policy in Yugoslavia, where Tito's communist guerrillas received extensive support. This will be covered in Chapter 9.)

Myers attempted to coordinate the Zervas' and Aris' groups, as well as other minor guerrilla bands. Zervas was agreeable, happy to support the British in exchange for money and arms. Aris resisted subservience to anyone, and the British were distressed to learn that ELAS was at work disrupting smaller rival guerrilla bands, even attacking, capturing, and executing them, in the bloodthirsty way for which Aris was known.

The Greek resistance endured several kaleidoscopic twists caused by the shifting of personal loyalties by two prominent leaders, Zervas and Colonel Stephanos Saraphis. Zervas had been an ardent proponent of a Greek republic and went as far as to take part in the attempted overthrow of the monarchy in 1935, but he now saw the monarchy as preferable to communism. He veered so far to the right that his men began wearing the royal insignia on their field caps. Saraphis, leader of the EKKA, began the war as a fervent nationalist, and was supported in his leadership by a confusing assortment of political figures that included George Papandreou, a former republican dictator and future liberal prime minister. In events that defy logic, Saraphis was captured by ELAS and became the man EAM's *communist* leaders would choose to head ELAS in March 1943, when they decided Aris was no longer the right leader. Saraphis refused the post at first, but through five weeks of captivity and public humiliation, in which he was labeled a traitor and pushed before jeering crowds of villagers, he had a change of heart. He concluded that ELAS, the largest and most powerful of the guerrilla bands, was Greece's best hope for liberation.

In May 1943, Myers facilitated a critical agreement in which ELAS, EDES, and EKKA united loosely in the "National Bands of Greek Guerrillas," which would take its orders from Allied command. Although EDES delayed signing and the agreement was soon to be dead, the unification led to very effective operations against the Germans.

Timing for this peak of effectiveness could not have been better, because in June and July 1943 the British launched a massive diversionary ploy. Code-named Operation *Animals*, the ploy had the objective of fooling the Axis into thinking that the inevitable Allied invasion was imminent and would take place at Greece. The British wisely told none of the guerrillas that Sicily was the actual target and that this was a diversion.

The deception began in a macabre way: A corpse, wearing a British officer uniform and bearing false documents, was set adrift at sea—intended to wash ashore on Spain's Mediterranean coast. The suboperation, code-named *Mincemeat*, placed in Spanish hands the dummy plan for an all-out Allied invasion at Greece, which was quickly reported to the Germans.

Fueled by hope that liberation was nigh, the guerrillas embarked a nationwide sabotage campaign that targeted supply and communications lines. In several weeks of well-coordinated attacks orchestrated by the British liaisons, they captured and held vital mountain passes, dynamited highways, and cut the oft-sabotaged north-south rail lifeline in 16 places.

The British also set up a ghostly "12th Army" poised to strike from Egypt, an elaborate ruse complete with fake displays of men and equipment, and false radio transmissions.

It made sense for Hitler to believe the ruse. If he were to put himself in Churchill's place, he would have chosen Greece for invasion. After all, when the British first invaded Greece, the Germans had made them look foolish—forcing the British to bring in much needed forces from North Africa, only to see them humiliated in a rout and evacuated. An invasion in the Balkans would be fitting redemption to wipe out the memory.

The Germans were duped into building up defenses in Greece. A mountain *Jaeger* (riflemen) division was brought from Yugoslavia as quickly as the north-south railway would permit. This was soon supplemented by another *Jaeger* division, along with a panzer division sent to the Peloponnese in June and a mountain division sent to northwest Greece in July. The Luftwaffe was also brought in force to the area of the Corinth Canal. All these might otherwise have been sent to Sicily.

While this was happening, the mood in Greece became increasingly frenzied. The Greeks, too, were convinced the British invasion was coming. With liberation seemingly on the horizon, both communist and anticommunist factions tried to position themselves to dominate postliberation Greece. At one point in a sabotage campaign, ELAS attacked EKKA and smaller separate guerrilla bands. Zervas and his EDES were becoming increasingly anticommunist as time passed. It was no longer clear even which was the greater enemy— ELAS or the German occupiers. Zervas was actually suspected of minor incidences of collaborating with the Germans in an attempt to gain the upper hand on ELAS. It was shaping up much like the ugly internal fighting in Yugoslavia, where the Chetniks and Partisans were at each others' throats.

ELAS now was becoming powerful to the degree that it fielded some 30,000 guerrillas. Most were ill equipped, but that would change when Italy surrendered. By September 1943, with Mussolini dead and Italy beaten, the Italian army in Greece put down its arms. Most of the 270,000 Italian troops there "surrendered" themselves to the Germans. But one anti-Nazi division commander approached the British liaison officers, offering to surrender to them *if* his 14,000 Italian troops could fight against the Germans. At the time, this division happened to be in Thessaly, where ELAS dominated. Before the British could do anything, ELAS swarmed the immobilized Italian division and seized its arms, which included thousands of rifles, no less than 20 light artillery pieces, mortars, and machine guns, along with trucks and other equipment.

This set up ELAS to confront EDES, which had received support from Great Britain in the form of arms. And the communists set up a personal confrontation by bringing Aris back into the picture. A month later, in mid-October 1943, EAM gave Aris a free hand to attack Zervas.

Aris led the ferocious attack on Zervas' forces. While the two sides battled it out, the British watched in dismay. Watching was *all* they could do. The Germans were watching, too, but marking time in a calculated way. After a week, they launched Operation *Panther*, inflicting 1,400 casualties through air attacks coordinated with a barrage of artillery and tanks. The three-way fighting went on throughout November. More antiguerrilla actions followed: Operation *Gemsbock* inflicted 2,500 casualties and Operation *Steinadler* inflicted

1,400 casualties. (The numbers do not distinguish between guerrillas and the civilians shot as hostages in reprisals.)

EDES was particularly hard-hit. Zervas had to retreat all the way to the Adriatic coast. Their backs against the wall, EDES might have been obliterated had the British not intervened once more with a large airdrop of arms in early December.

When the front between them had stabilized somewhat, the British (this time with Myers pulled and his deputy Woodhouse now in charge) negotiated a truce. Once the fighting had stopped, it was clear that ELAS' savage aggression had changed the attitude of some Greeks, alienating some supporters.

The ruse in Greece had helped Allied landings at Sicily succeed. The surrender of Italy left German forces in Greece's interior spread thin, so the Wehrmacht called upon Bulgaria to honor its Axis obligations by sending support. The Bulgarians were vicious in their attacks, and went after the Greek guerrillas of any political hue as well as villagers.

These attacks on innocent civilians were consistent with Hitler's shifting occupation policy, inflicting on Greece the same indiscriminate terror and reprisal tactics that had been launched on Yugoslavia from the very start. The Germans did not have occupying forces large enough to take full control of all areas, so terror unleashed against the civilian population was intended to discourage resistance.

The civilians in the cities and villages knew the cardinal rule for clandestine operations: Do not talk. They knew that in interrogation there would be "merciless beating, burning with hot rods and lighted cigarettes," as Tsatsos journaled. And that "dangers lie in wait in most unlikely places. In order to protect our friends from ourselves, we try to know as little as possible."

The church, headed by Archbishop Damaskinos, tried to intervene. On June 19, 1942, the archbishop met with Guenther Altenburg, the Reich plenipotentiary. He protested the executions of hostages, pointing out that reprisals were unjust for sabotage committed by unknown perpetrators. And Damaskinos added that Greeks expected better treatment from the Germans. After mass executions and reprisals, even pro-German Greeks looked upon the German occupation forces with hatred.

"They hunt us down without ceasing. Every day they kill," Tsatsos wrote. "This morning they executed hostages, 20 patriotic Greeks whose names they do not give out, nor do they turn over the bodies for burial. . . . Who, one wonders, are the slain? Each one trembles for his own."

Like the symbolic Czechoslovakian village of Lidice, many villages in Greece also were annihilated. All inhabitants of Dhistomon, near Osios

Loukas in Boeotia, were massacred because guerrillas had killed Germans. Perhaps the single most brutal reprisal was at Kalavrita, where more 696 men were taken to a hill overlooking their homes and forced to watch as the Germans burned the village to the ground. Then they were all machine gunned where they stood.

German records show that for the period of March 1943 to October 1944, 21,255 Greeks were killed by the Germans. Greek sources estimate that for the same period, the Bulgarians killed almost *twice* that many Greeks, mainly in reprisals. It's also estimated that guerrillas killed between 19,000 and 22,000 German and Italian troops.

During the first week of October 1944, the British launched Operation *Manna*, the invasion of Greece. A small force of 4,000 British troops landed unopposed at Patrai, a town in the northern Peloponnese. The Germans, under constant harassment by the guerrilla forces, had already withdrawn from the Peloponnese to the north of the Corinth Canal. The British forces set out for Athens, leaving behind the German stronghold of Crete.

Their fortunes of war steadily declining, the Germans saw no alternative but to abandon Greece. They pulled out of Athens on October 12 and the next day British troops moved in. On October 16, the Greek government returned to Athens.

Throughout the German withdrawal, ELAS scarcely fired a shot. Even though the Germans had done the usual upon retreating—destroying roads, railways, and bridges—ELAS saw no need to waste precious ammunition that would be needed for the attack they'd been long planning. Once the Germans were gone, they would seize control of the country.

Bulgarian troops still remained in Greece, but nothing significant came of it. In the face of strong Allied opposition, the Bulgarian troops were withdrawn from the eastern frontier. However, many Bulgarians deserted rather than return to Bulgaria, which in the meantime had been occupied by the Soviets.

The work of the Greek resistance was done. But guerrillas of neither side celebrated. Peace had not been won with the expulsion of Axis forces. All knew they now faced the civil war that had been hanging fire for the last three years.

Despite a defeat at the hands of the British at Christmas 1944, the ELAS guerrillas held on to remote bases in the north. In February 1946, the communists returned from those bases to again ignite a civil war that lasted until August 1949. The Communists were finally defeated, but not before some 80,000 Greeks were killed, and horrifying atrocities and massive destruction had devastated the land.

## CHAPTER 9

# Yugoslavia

Yugoslavia's strife was much like Greece's, but deadlier. As the largest Balkan state, Yugoslavia had 14 million people living in a land area three-fourths the size of Italy. The Serbs and Croatians had been poured like oil and water, along with a sprinkling of Slovenes, into the same pot. They'd been living in a cauldron on the verge of boiling over for years.

As a result, Yugoslavia's situation during World War II was as much about internal clashes that led to civil war as it was about resistance to German and other Axis occupiers.

Hitler turned his attention to Yugoslavia with no other intent than to destroy it. "We will burn out for good the festering sore in the Balkans," he sneered privately in Berlin.

Hitler groused about the Yugoslavians who taunted him by defiling his picture in public demonstrations in Belgrade as they vowed never to accept the Tripartite pact, even though Yugoslavian Prince Paul and his government officials had signed the pact on March 5, 1941. In fact, two days after the Tripartite pact had been signed in Yugoslavia, a *coup d'etat* forced Paul from the throne and led to the arrest of government officials. Paul's second cousin, 17-year-old Prince Peter, ascended to the throne, and a new government was formed from all the political parties, excluding those that supported the pact with the Nazis.

Hitler took the rebuff very personally, especially after Churchill made public statements quoted in *The Times* of London. Churchill proclaimed "Great news," saying "the Yugoslav nation found its soul." *Pravda*, the official Moscow journal, stopped just short of saying that the Soviet government actually congratulated Belgrade, but did state that "the Yugoslav people *deserved* congratulations" for their rejection of the pact.

Hitler groused most of all about Mussolini's half-cocked invasion of Greece, which started this whole ridiculous Balkan sideshow. Hitler thought it would affect his timetable for the main show—the invasion of Russia. Now, to ensure a quiet and secure southern flank, he was forced to squelch the noise in both Greece and Yugoslavia.

Early Palm Sunday morning, April 6, 1941, 20 German divisions with 650,000 soldiers stood poised on the Yugoslavian borders shared with Bulgaria, Hungary, and Romania. At 5:15 A.M., Hitler gave the order to commence the coordinated air and ground attack. Smacking of personal vengeance and with a name to match, Operation *Punishment* led off with a massive air assault that reduced the Terrazia to blackened rubble, incinerated medieval scrolls and artifacts precious to Serbian culture, and killed 17,000 people in Belgrade. Wehrmacht ground units tore into the whole of Yugoslavia with the swift fury of Judgment Day. Panzer units somehow traversed the rugged mountains believed to be impassable by armor. A spearhead thrust through the mountain passes common to Yugoslavia and Bulgaria in order to pierce through into Greece, and to link up with the Italians invading from Albania. Before the end of the morning, Yugoslavia was paralyzed. Communications were severed, there was no electricity, and the Germans had secured all critical airfields and bridges. Launched from Hungarian staging areas, German units reached the objective of Zagreb, which fell April 11; units launching from Romania captured Belgrade on April 12.

Then selective murder began, with suspected anti-Nazi civilians rounded up and machine-gunned where they stood. On April 17, military resistance shivered to a stop and Yugoslavia surrendered. Young Prince Peter fled to London to join the rest of Europe's royalty and governments-in-exile.

Because only 151 German soldiers were killed during the 11 days of invasion, the Germans were lulled into thinking Yugoslavia was a pushover. This gave them a false sense of security and caused them to pull a great majority of troops from the Balkans for Operation *Barbarossa*.


Yugoslavia's collapse was not so much a rout of overwhelming German military might as a masterstroke of German planning and exploitation.

Yugoslavia presented a unique scenario to an invader: No other European countries had preexisting internal ethnic dissension and political conflict like the Balkan states in general and Yugoslavia in particular. Hitler understood this very well, so German strategists capitalized on it by fanning the flames of racial hatred, religious antagonism, and political feuding. The Serbs were mostly Eastern Orthodox; the Croats were Roman Catholic. The Serbs wanted a central government; the Croats wanted a loose federation of provincial governments. Some members of both factions shared a racially based hatred.

The kingdom of Yugoslavia had been created after World War I when well-meaning peacemakers redrew the map of Europe in hopes of upholding ideals of freedom and self-determination among all the nations. They reasoned that the Slav nationalities in southern

# THE PARTITION OF YUGOSLAVIA

**April 1941**

| | |
|---|---|
| ① | "Independent" State of Croatia |
| ② | German government administration |
| ③ | Occupied by Germany |
| ④ | Annexed by Germany |
| ⑤ | Annexed by Italy |
| ⑥ | Italian government administration |
| ⑦ | Occupied by Italy |

| 0 | 50 | 100 miles |
|---|---|---|
| 0 | | 160 kilometers |

GERMANY

HUNGARY

Annexed by Hungary

ITALY

SLOVENIA ④

Occupied by Hungary

⑤ • Zagreb

BAKA

ROMANIA

①

CROATIA ②

• Jajce

• Belgrade

BOSNIA • Ravna Gora

DALMATIA

⑤ ⑥

Sarajevo • Uzice ③

SERBIA

⑦

MONTE-NEGRO

BULGARIA

⑦

Annexed by Bulgaria

*Adriatic Sea* ⑤

MACEDONIA

ALBANIA
(Italian occupation)

GREECE

Europe (Croats, Serbs, Bosnians, and Montenegrins) should join together to form this single, new country called Yugoslavia. However, from the beginning, the Slav nationalities ferociously sought individual sovereignty.

By the time World War II began, the Slavic disunion had become even more volatile and because of it, Yugoslavia and the other Balkan states would play right into Hitler's hands. He had tantalized four Balkan satellites—Bulgaria, Romania, Hungary, and Albania—with promised shares of Yugoslav territory. After the invasion, no time was wasted before hacking Yugoslavia into fragments divvied up among Germany, Italy, and the satellites. The northern half of

Slovenia was annexed to Germany; Austrian "settlers" moved in to take the place of the Slovenes who were killed or deported (those remaining were to be "Germanized"). Italy took the rest of Slovenia, where the repressed survivors were force-fed Fascism. Italy also took strategically important coastal areas, including many islands and the Dalmatian Littoral, featuring a ready-made naval base at Kotor. Responsibility for Montenegro was also left to Italy. The map of Albania, already Italy's satellite, was redrawn to include the western part of Macedonia and the plain of Kosovo. Kosovo's large Albanian population, finding itself suddenly with the upper hand, greeted the change by avenging old scores against their Serb neighbors. Hungary annexed Backa, a Danubian province, and smaller northern regions called Prekomurje and Medjumurje. Bulgaria annexed Macedonia and southern regions of Serbia.

The remaining central portion of Yugoslavia was to be a country of its own, absurdly dignified in name as the "Independent State of Croatia." It was allowed the fiction of its own army and police. The Germans and Italians shared responsibility for administration. Germany took the portion with Zagreb, Jajce, and Sarajevo. Although his field marshals advised against it, preferring martial law with German troops, Hitler let Mussolini install a puppet *Führer* (called a *poglavnik* in Croatia), a vicious Croat named Ante Pavelic. Pavelic unleashed a reign of terror through a group of Fascist thugs called *Ustachi*, who made it their primary mission to eliminate Jews and gypsies, and to neutralize the Serbs. Pavelic's plan for the Serb population from the outset, supported by his German and Italian masters, was to kill a third, deport a third, and convert a third to Roman Catholicism. The Ustachi took pleasure in the ethnic cleansing, beginning in Bjelovar and Kordun, where hundreds were indiscriminately shot. Stories of atrocities soon spread across the land: All male residents of the village of Glina were forced at gunpoint into the village's Orthodox church. The church was then set ablaze. The Ustachi encircled the burning structure with guns poised to kill any man or boy attempting to escape the flames.

"We are accustomed to dying," goes an age-old Serbian saying. All told, Serbs estimate the toll of the "cleansing" at 750,000.

After *Barbarossa* was under way, the Wehrmacht needed Yugoslavia to be a smooth-functioning slave state where a steady stream of food, raw materials, and manpower could be exploited for the German war machine. Once the Yugoslavs bowed dutifully to Hitler's New Order, the front-line invasion troops could be withdrawn. When unrest and defiance continued, the Germans concluded that the Ustachi atrocities against the Serbs did not support their objectives, and were actually contributing to the burgeoning ranks of the guerrillas. The atrocities even alarmed the SS, according to a Gestapo report of February 1942:

> *The atrocities perpetrated by the Ustachi units against the Orthodox in [the Independent State of Croatia] must be regarded as the most important factor for increasing guerrilla activities. The Ustachi units have carried out their atrocities not only against Orthodox males of military age, but in the most beastly fashion against unarmed old men, women and children.*

The Germans called for moderation from the Ustachi, but had no objection whatsoever to the persecution of the Jews and the gypsies. Those two groups didn't represent a serious threat, even if their survivors joined the guerrilla bands. Their extermination was in keeping with German ideologies. But already, Yugoslav men and women had taken to the forest and mountains in droves to join the guerrilla bands. The bands found ample arms left by the ruined army; the Germans had not been able to confiscate them because of the abruptness of the attack and surrender. These bands would form a considerable force capable of diverting military resources from the battlefront.

Many Serbs fell into ranks under Colonel Draza Mihailovich. As Yugoslavia fell, Colonel Mihailovich was serving in the regular Yugoslav army in Bosnia. He did not step forward with the Yugoslav units that surrendered; instead, he moved through German-occupied territory to the Ravna Gora area with 26 army officers, NCOs, and gendarmes. On May 11, 1941, he and his followers established a headquarters in the forested mountains 65 miles south of Belgrade. They formed the nucleus of the Chetnik resistance.

The name *Chetnik* (sometimes written *Cetnik* or *Tchetnik*) was used by the Serbs long before World War II. For centuries, the irregular mountain warriors who resisted the Turkish conquerors were called Chetniks. The term was used again later, just after the creation of Yugoslavia following World War I, for a Serbian nationalist organization. Led by army officers, the organization's mission was to encourage loyalty to Serbia in the face of adversity of any kind. The vague mission still fit.

Before the occupation, the leader of the Chetnik movement was not Mihailovich, but a Serb named Kosta Pecanac. Once at Ravna Gora, Mihailovich began to muster a patriotic movement, and he extended an opportunity of leadership to Pecanac. Pecanac declined, but in 1942 joined forces with a turncoat Serb general, Milan Nedic, along with his quislings *also* called Chetniks.

Initially, Mihailovich's goal was simple: restoration of the monarchy. His plan was to rise up when the time was right and take control of the country as the Allies invaded, in the same style of Poland, Czechoslovakia, Norway, and others. Until then, he preferred prudent restraint. He saw little value in sabotage or random attacks on the Axis, sure to provoke reprisals against innocent civilians. This was consistent with the philosophy of the government-in-exile, which implored Yugoslavians via BBC broadcasts to restrain themselves from armed resistance until the appointed time as dictated by the government. Mihailovich followed this government direction to a point, but did order some limited armed action on his own.

More active was a group led by a communist named Josip Broz. Broz became secretary-general of the Yugoslavian Communist Party in 1937. During World War II, he became known the world over as "Tito." After the Axis occupation, Tito immediately began to organize the 12,000 communist party members for a resistance movement. His followers became known as the Partisans,[33] taken from the Spanish word *partidas*—the name for guerrilla bands that opposed Napoleon's invasion. He sought Serbian-Croatian cooperation to combat the occupiers and the collaborating Ustachi.

Tito's policy for resistance was anything but restrained. His Partisan guerrillas attacked the occupiers unmercifully—tormenting the tormenters in kind. They were particularly merciless to the Italian soldiers, to the point that many of them were left wanting transfer to the relative safety of the front lines, where rules of the Geneva Convention applied.

Tito's aggressive resistance demanded strict coordination. This was in stark contrast to the much more relaxed organization of Mihailovich's resistance. Mihailovich wanted widespread patriotic bands with Chetnik members living a subdued life as part of local villages and farms, again, waiting for the right time to rise up in a major insurgence. Mihailovich sent out emissaries on recruiting missions, hoping to rally local patriots to organize local people into bands. During the first summer of occupation, recruiting was about the extent of Mihailovich's action.

The general lack of urgency did nothing to build cohesion among the Chetniks. Success of the isolated bands depended mostly on the ability of the local leader to drum up support and inspire loyalty to the cause. Consequently, loyalty went to the local leader, not the larger cause or Mihailovich. This cautious structure resulted in a slack collection of tiny fiefdoms in which leaders often disregarded orders from Mihailovich and acted on their own.

The Yugoslav people had lost their country and their freedom, and had suffered savage atrocities. They wanted *action now*. Tito offered it. In the July 4, 1941, issue of the newspaper *Politika* (the Yugoslavia's counterpart to *The Times*), Tito called for action from a unified front:

> *People of Yugoslavia: Serbs, Croats, Slovenes, Montenegrins, Macedonians, and others! Now is the time to rise like one man in battle against the invaders and collaborators, murderers of our peoples. Do not falter in the face of any enemy terror. Answer terror with savage blows at the most vital points of the Fascist occupation bandits. Destroy everything—everything of use to the Fascist invaders. Do not let our railways carry equipment and other things to serve the Fascist hordes in their struggle against the Soviet Union. Workers, peasants, citizens, and youth of Yugoslavia: . . . battle against the Fascist occupation hordes who are striving to dominate the world.*

Unlike Mihailovich's narrow Serb focus, Tito made it instantly clear that the Partisans welcomed any of the wide-ranging races of Yugoslavia, with the exception of monarchists. This appealed to many democrats, liberals, and progressives who delighted at the promise of action, including many in Mihailovich's camp.

Before Tito's appeal in *Politika*, resistance was isolated and fragmented, but afterward it became focused and intensified with all the makings of a major revolt. The very first confrontation is believed to have happened on July 7, three days after Tito's pronouncement. Communists fought openly with police in the Serbian village of Bela Crkva. Following that were flare-ups all over the country: Power stations were sabotaged, telephone wires cut, and small-scale ambushes were sprung on enemy troops.

A revolt began on July 15, 1941, in Montenegro, where resisters were well armed. A large cache of weapons had been hidden there as the Yugoslav army surrendered. For Montenegrins, resistance to invasion was an age-old point of pride—it had included battles with Napoleon's army early in the nineteenth century. Just after Montenegro had been declared a puppet independent principality, Partisans and Chetniks joined together there against the Italians and nearly drove them back into the Adriatic Sea. Four thousand Italian troops, their backs against the shore and with no place to escape, surrendered. This was most of the troops in the province. Their weapons were confiscated, but nearly all Italian prisoners were allowed to go, because the resisters were not able to keep prisoners. Five Italian divisions from Albania were rushed into Montenegro, but they struggled for a year before they would finally wrest back control.

More revolts followed in Slovenia on July 22, and in Bosnia and Croatia on July 27. Partisans also went on the offensive in Serbia, where most of the countryside and several towns were seized. The notable town of Uzice was held from September 24 to November 29. This was valuable time, because Uzice contained an arms factory that produced 400 rifles a day, which armed Partisans throughout Yugoslavia.

The revolt caught German attention on a high level. An order for brutal reprisals from the German High Command was written by Field Marshal Wilhelm Keitel:

> *In order to nip disorder in the bud, the harshest measures must be applied at the first signs of insurrection. It should also be taken into consideration that in the countries in question a human life is often valueless. . . . In reprisal for the life of a German soldier the general rule should be capital punishment for 50 – 100 communists. The manner of execution must have a frightening effect.*

Reprisals *did* have a frightening effect, as the Germans shot thousands during the fall of 1941 in places like Macva, Kraljevo, and Kragujebac. Instead of stabilizing a disintegrating situation and discouraging resistance, thousands of Yugoslavs streamed into the forested mountains to join the Partisans.

Marshaling this many new recruits into a military structure was a daunting task. Tito's first step was to summon his Partisan leaders at a Serbian town called Stolice. The leaders came from all parts of the country with the exception of Macedonia, where Partisans were fighting furiously against the Bulgarian Communists for control of the province. Tito told the leaders present what he expected of them and what his plan was for the future. A general headquarters would be set up for each region, and ultimate command would rest with supreme headquarters, where Tito would control all major activity and direct attacks against Axis-occupied towns and Axis-held countryside.

Tito knew that his Partisans were in a position to make major gains toward his goal of liberating Yugoslavia. The country is about one-third mountainous, wooded terrain—tailor-made for guerrilla activity. He knew the Germans could not hold all of it. Additionally, he knew that the Germans needed every soldier available for the Russian front. That was why they'd set up the Ustachi and other collaboration forces, supplemented by only scant German forces, to control key areas, towns, and main roadways.

A charismatic Tito told his local leaders that as general operational procedure, they must avoid full frontal assaults with an enemy known to have greater firepower, aircraft, and armor. Restraint was necessary, and Tito needed to be explicit about it, because he had many young and green local leaders who recklessly spoiled for a fight.

Tito's direction adhered to the strictest definition of guerrilla activity, characterized by hit-and-run activity with quick movement and dispersal, if necessary, to achieve the Allied ideals of resistance: To tie down as many enemy units as possible. Guerrillas were to pull out before superior enemy forces could be brought to bear. In this kind of warfare, victory was capped by rapid retreat (in classic guerrilla style), before German forces could encircle and obliterate them.

Mihailovich began to realize that Tito spoke to the mood of the people and their thirst for immediate action. During the summer and fall of 1941, Mihailovich grudgingly agreed to joint Chetnik-Partisan operations. For this short time, the two groups fought side-by-side with some success, liberating most of Serbia. It was to their great advantage that Operation *Barbarossa*, starting in June, took all but four German divisions out of Yugoslavia.

The Chetniks liberated Loznica on August 31 and Zajaca on September 1. Other Chetniks drove deep into German-held territory to Sabac, located 45 miles west of Belgrade. A priest named Vlado Zecevic, along with a regular army lieutenant named Ratko Martinovic, led a group of Chetniks in the successful capture of a long strip of the Drina Valley. The Partisans enjoyed triumphs elsewhere.

Considerable successes, even by his own guerrillas, had not excited Mihailovich. By mid-September, he ordered the Chetniks to halt the offensive. Disappointed, some Chetnik leaders, including Father Zecevic and Lieutenant Martinovic, crossed over to the Partisans, and their bands "defected" with them. They spoke for themselves and their followers when they complained of long, forced inaction with the Chetniks. Cross-overs like these meant that sizable Chetnik-held regions, liberated during the summer of 1941, changed hands over to Partisan control in the fall. The Partisans wasted no time in setting up "National Liberation Councils" to govern the liberated territory.

After ordering the Chetniks to stop, Mihailovich met with Tito in the village of Struganik, located in the Ravna Gora. This was the beginning of a troubled relationship. Tito came with the hope of unifying and sharing command with Mihailovich. Mihailovich came with an argument against revolution and violence. Mihailovich explained the rationale that such action would bring terrible reprisals and consequential withering of popular support from the people and, in the end, destruction of the country by the Germans. After establishing contact with the Yugoslav government-in-exile during the previous August, Mihailovich explained he needed time to consult with government leaders about Tito's ideas.

His contacts with London and the government-in-exile piqued the interest of the British. Later in September 1941, a British-Yugoslav mission was sent to talk. A British liaison officer, Major D.T. Hudson, and two Yugoslav representatives had landed by submarine on the Adriatic coast. The mission was given safe-conduct passage across Chetnik territory to reach Mihailovich's base of operations in the Ravna Gora.

In October, after several reports from Hudson and a recommendation from the Yugoslav government-in-exile, the British decided they would back the Chetniks and recognize Mihailovich as *the* leader of Yugoslav resistance. This meant prestige, money, and arms for Mihailovich. Major Hudson, like his counterpart in Greece, Colonel Myers, was ordered to stay with Mihailovich.

In late November, a second meeting was set for Tito and Mihailovich. This time, Mihailovich had the full support of the British government and the Yugoslav government-in-exile.

Tito assumed that the British liaison officer would be included in the meeting. When he wasn't, Tito requested his presence. He wanted the British to know about the Partisan strategies and objectives. Mihailovich refused, so the Briton was left sitting alone elsewhere in the camp, excluded from the talks.

Inevitably, differences between Tito, Mihailovich, and their diametrically opposed philosophies led to an impasse. Tito reiterated his desire for a unified Yugoslav resistance front, but Mihailovich fixated on Serbian nationalism. Tito was willing to accept the risk of reprisals in order to drive out the hated occupiers—Germany, Italy, Romania, Hungary, and Bulgaria—and in fact believed it served to drive more people into the ranks of the resistance. Mihailovich rejected all that flatly, fueled with resolve especially now that the British and Yugoslavian governments were backing him.

Through the summer and especially after contacts with the British in August 1941, the Chetniks' activities drew worldwide acclaim. In reality, it was the Partisans who carried out many of the operations against the Germans.

In 1941 word of any victory against Hitler was cause for celebration among the Allies and in a world that needed heroes so badly, the BBC and the press seized upon the Chetnik cause as its media darling. The picture that journalists painted was of a gallant band, staunchly loyal to the monarchy, facing overwhelming odds.

Newspaper wire-service articles in 1942 illustrate this: "After a punishing year of guerrilla warfare, the Chetniks hold more than two-thirds of their country. In enemy held territory, they've destroyed bridges by the score."

Mihailovich as an individual was held up as the Chetnik leader. The existence of other resistance groups was acknowledged, although sometimes confusingly called by the generic name "partisans," but explanations were left vague. The media looked for a hero and they found it in Mihailovich. Initially, the news services truly were not aware of the extent of the Partisan role and they did not know of a leader named Josip Broz or "Tito." The BBC monitoring service was not permitted to listen in on communiqués from a radio station called Free Yugoslavia, which originated from Soviet Georgia, and was the only source of information about the Partisans. Part of the misreporting resulted from the names "Partisans" and "Chetniks," which were loosely used for *any* guerrilla band. And "partisan" in particular (with no capital *P*) was applied to resistance fighters of almost any political hue, as long they opposed the Germans. It was not known that in the fall of 1941 the Chetniks numbered only about 5,000 and the Partisans numbered more than twice that. But even once the facts emerged, Tito's Partisans were played down in favor of building the reputation of Mihailovich's Chetniks.

Promoted to the rank of general, Mihailovich was appointed minister for the army and navy of Prince Peter's government-in-exile in January 1942. (Officially, Mihailovich became commander of the "Yugoslav Army in the Homeland," but the Chetnik name remained and the official name never caught on.) With his appointment came an even firmer commitment to the royalty's aversion to communism. The motto adopted for the Chetniks became "For King and Fatherland."

Meanwhile, Tito was largely oblivious to all this hubbub in the Allied press. His attention was on German offensives, the first major one being launched in mid-September 1941 against the Partisans in western Serbia. The Germans massed forces numbering 80,000 men. Units had been transferred from Greece, France, and the Russian Front. Along with them were collaborationist forces under Pavelic. The Germans' objective was to encircle the Partisan redoubt like a noose and squeeze the life out of it.

The Germans came close to succeeding, but the Partisan main body was able to slip away although losses mounted in retreat. The Germans won back control of Serbia, and sought to press their advantage. Two more offensives continued into 1942, causing the Partisans' further retreat.

Knowing the psychological value of even small victories, Tito lashed back with minor assaults that kept up morale and drew in more to his army of Partisans. By mid-1942, his forces had actually grown, despite losses in the German offensives.

Both Partisans and Chetniks were now fighting Axis forces, but they occasionally fought each other as well. British support in money and weapons continued to pour in for Mihailovich, even though there were suspicions and uncertainties. More than anything, it was a matter of politics: Mihailovich's allegiance was to Yugoslavia's royalty. Tito detested the monarchy and its unequal treatment of the Yugoslav people.

As the months went on, Mihailovich watched Tito from afar and was becoming anticommunist to the point of fanaticism. He developed a deep-seated hatred for Tito and everything he stood for. But was the hatred so all-consuming that Mihailovich would go so far as to *join forces with the Germans* to eliminate his enemy? That was a question now muttered in hushed tones in London. The question was soon answered.


Believing that the next Allied landings would take place in the Balkans, the Germans wanted firmer control of Yugoslavia and launched a renewed offensive against the Partisans. The Chetniks were now fighting side-by-side with the Germans. During January through March 1943, the Axis offensive included the first known major engagements where Chetniks fought openly in support of the German forces against the Partisans. All told, there were 150,000 troops, organized in five German divisions, three Italian Divisions, plus 18,000 Yugoslavs from both Chetnik and Pavelic's forces.

Against these overwhelming numbers, Tito sent 20,000 Partisans east toward the Neretva River, in hopes of moving closer to Serbia again. In tow were also roughly 3,000 wounded or sick with typhus, plus nearly 40,000 civilians, nearly all women and children, who refused to separate from the Partisans.

The Germans, along with Pavelic's troops, approached from the north and east, while the Italians came from the west and south. The Chetniks lay in wait on Mount Prenj on the other side of the Neretva, barring Tito's way. Tito knew the positions of all and made a desperate decision—the only one that seemed to have an even remote chance of success: He would charge through the Chetnik-held part of the enemy lines.

Confident in victory, Mihailovich himself came personally to oversee the rout. Instead, Tito's Partisans slashed through the Chetniks, regaining that portion of Montenegro. To catch their breath, the Chetniks took up precarious positions, knowing that overwhelming forces were still on the hunt for them. As expected, the Axis divisions moved in for the kill, now supplemented by Bulgarian troops to help encircle them.

In most battle zones, Yugoslavian terrain was ideal for Tito's brand of guerrilla warfare. But this terrain, Tito later wrote, "proved a disadvantage to us, and an advantage to the enemy. They restricted our maneuvering power and very nearly prevented our main striking force in Montenegro from breaking out of the enemy's encirclement. Great technical superiority, long-range guns, numerous aircraft and special units trained in mountain warfare gave the enemy for his part a definite advantage over us by helping him to surmount these difficulties."

The Germans had been outdone in the past by guerrilla surprise attacks and quick movement. This time they were ready to give the Partisans a dose of their own tactics. They avoided main roads and moved stealthily. Knowing that Partisans relied on the native civilians in the area, the Germans laid down the law: They made it known that if villagers were hostile to Germans and supportive of Partisans, whole villages would be obliterated. Most of the natives were simply cleared out of the area.

Simultaneous with the German offensive in May, the British sent three liaison officers. One was killed, but the other two lived to tell about the Partisan's ordeal: 16,000 Partisans faced 120,000 German, Italian, and Bulgarian soldiers. Aided by air support, the Axis soldiers encircled them in a pincer movement. This time the Axis was successful: The Partisans found themselves trapped in Montenegro.

Some say this was Tito's only major tactical mistake of the war. Axis forces trapped them, and the only way out was a nearly suicidal plunge into northeast Bosnia. In so doing, Tito lost 8,000 men and women.

Even in the darkest hour of catastrophic losses, help was coming— and from an unexpected source. The British, who all along had supported the Chetniks, realized which of the two groups was "doing the most harm to Germans," in Churchill's words.

Near the end of 1943, the Allies (both British and Americans) transferred their help from Mihailovich's Chetniks to Tito's Partisans *exclusively*. By May, even the British liaison officers, long attached to Mihailovich's forces (since August 1941) were withdrawn. Churchill explained to the House of Commons: "The reason why we have ceased to supply Mihailovich with arms and support is a simple one. He has not been fighting the enemy, and, moreover, some of his subordinates have made accommodations with the enemy, from which have arisen armed conflicts with the forces of Marshal Tito." With his assertion of "*subordinates* have made accommodations with the enemy," Churchill stopped just short of openly accusing Mihailovich of collaboration. Churchill concluded with: "We have proclaimed ourselves the strong supporters of Marshal Tito because of his heroic and massive struggle against the German armies."

With German forces all but disintegrated by October 20, the Partisans marched triumphantly into Belgrade. In this way, the Partisans were outfitted to support Russian troops as they approached Yugoslavia's eastern borders in the fall of 1944. From the capital, Tito hoped to transform Yugoslavia into his ideal of a united and independent—yet communist—nation.

Stalin had never trusted Tito, now undisputed leader of Yugoslavia. Yet Stalin fully anticipated that Tito would lead Yugoslavia into the awaiting arms of Communist Russia. All other Balkan states, except Greece, had already accepted that fate. However, on March 7, 1945, Tito christened a Marxist form of government and appointed himself its leader. And he managed the rarity of keeping his country independent of the Soviet Union. With that, his ideal was complete.

## CHAPTER 10

# The Baltic States

On June 22, 1941, the day Hitler launched Operation *Barbarossa* against Russia, Lithuanian resisters seized a radio station in the administrative capital of Kaunas and announced ecstatically: "Lithuania is independent again! The Red Terror is over!"

Much the same happened in Latvia's capital of Riga on June 28. Throughout the day, the national anthem and other patriotic songs were broadcast and spontaneous celebrations broke out in the streets. Latvian Arnolds Spekke later wrote: "Latvian flags were flying all over the city, Soviet emblems were burnt in a multitude of small fires . . . kindled in the streets which were crowded with people who felt an intense joy at being freed from the Bolshevik nightmare. . . . It is not surprising, then, that the German soldiers were greeted with flowers."

To the delight of Lithuanians, Latvians, and Estonians, the Germans were driving out the Soviet occupation troops practically as fast as their panzers could travel. With the help of 100,000 members of the Lithuanian resistance, the hated Bolsheviks were cast out of Lithuania in only three days. After fighting their way through Latvia, the Germans reached Estonia, the northernmost of the three Baltic States, by July 5.

In Kaunas, Riga, and other places, the Germans marched in to find throngs of cheering crowds. After suffering a brutal year of Soviet domination, the Balts welcomed the Germans as liberators. But as the cheering died down, the Balts realized things were not what they seemed. They gradually realized the abominable "Red Terror" had been replaced by an occupier every bit as cruel, and that one totalitarian regime had supplanted another.

With full Nazi occupation of Lithuania, Estonia, and Latvia in the summer of 1941, and the subsequent push for Stalingrad, Hitler's empire reached its zenith. The Baltics would be the last of the countries that Hitler wholly occupied and the last to begin mounting resistance movements against him.

Serious, organized resistance had begun in all three Baltic States, by happenstance, just before the German invasion. Although these fledgling underground organizations would become the core of anti-Nazi resistance, their beginnings were purely anti-Soviet.

June 1941 in particular had been an eventful month for Lithuania, Estonia, and Latvia. An ugly Soviet occupation had turned even worse when Stalin ordered mass, systematic deportations to begin the first week of June, just three weeks before Germany invaded. Arrests and deportations suddenly were no longer limited to political figures and intelligentsia; large, random cross-sections of the population now became targets. Baltic families were awakened abruptly by a knock on the door by the NKVD (the Soviet security police), arrested without explanation, taken by gunpoint into the night, and shipped to northern Russia or Siberia. Many perished en route in crowded boxcars. Survivors toiled in labor camps, most dying of disease, hunger, and maltreatment.

As a consequence, the numbers of resisters ballooned just prior to the German invasion. The threat of deportation sent waves of Balts scurrying to the forests, and simultaneously the proindependence partisan groups began to form. The numbers of forest brothers (Baltic partisans) grew even more when the Russians instituted a last-minute conscription of draft-age men as a stopgap measure to fight the invading Germans.

This was double the trouble for the Red Army. Not only did its troop strength not increase with fresh Baltic recruits, but the Balts fleeing Russian conscription joined the partisan groups and harassed the Russians as they fled desperately from the chomping teeth of the Nazi blitzkrieg.

Realizing he was not prepared for such a large, technologically advanced foe as the Germans, Stalin ordered his troops to retreat from the Baltics. In the same breath, he ordered a "scorched earth" policy for the land he was abandoning. Specially designated destruction battalions (*hävituspataljonid*) were unleashed to wreak undiscriminating ruin in the Baltic States, so that nothing of value would be left for the Germans. The first major combat actions of the partisan resistance groups were against these battalions to prevent destruction of their homeland.

In Lithuania, action against the destruction battalions had probably the most widespread success. Partisans liberated groups of political prisoners before the fleeing Russians could execute them; industries were largely saved from destruction; and partisan leadership dispatched its bands to communities as the front moved east to avert atrocities and material destruction. About 2,000 resistance fighters were lost while defending against the hated *hävituspataljonid*. The number of people saved—undoubtedly in the thousands—would be impossible to tally.

In Estonia, the assault of the Soviet destruction battalions was probably the worst, because the northernmost areas were the last to be "liberated," allowing the Soviet occupiers more time to linger. The Estonian forest brothers, numbering about 50,000, inflicted heavy casualties on the remaining Russians—as many as 4,800 Russians were killed and 14,000 captured—with comparable losses to their own numbers. With the way partially cleared by partisans, German spearheads reached the Estonian cities of Pärnu and Viljandi by July 8.

As German troops approached Tartu on July 10 and prepared for another battle with the Russians, they realized that the forest brothers were making headway against the common foe. The Wehrmacht stopped its advance and hung back, leaving the Estonians to do the fighting. The battle of Tartu lasted two weeks, and destroyed much of the city, but under the leadership of Friedrich Kurg, the partisans drove out the Russians mostly on their own. The Russians had been in the process of murdering citizens held in Tartu Prison and had killed 192 before the forest brothers captured the city.

At the end of July, the Germans resumed their advance in Estonia, now working in tandem with the forest brothers. Both German troops and Estonian partisans went on to take Narva on August 17, followed by the Estonian capital of Tallinn on August 28.

Before the invasion, about 33,000 Estonians had been coerced into Soviet conscription, fearing reprisals on their families if they refused. As it became clear the Soviets would be driven out of the Baltics and such reprisals were no longer a threat, several thousand deserted the Red Army and joined the German side. The now-large Estonian forces could have been converted into regular Estonian army units to fight alongside the Wehrmacht at this juncture, as could have the irregulars of Lithuania and Latvia. Germany might have secured three new allies to join forces against Russia, the way Finland joined the Axis, but Hitler would not allow it. He wanted slaves and Baltic land, not allies. German troops disarmed all the partisan groups they found, except for small bands temporarily placed in a role of the Home Guard (*Omakaitse*) to eradicate any remaining remnants of the Red Army and *hävituspataljonid* in the rear areas.

Leaders of Lithuanian political parties, in a gesture of infinite hope for independence, formed a provisional government. This government lasted only six weeks, during which the Nazis placed every conceivable obstacle in its way and finally suppressed it out of existence.

The Latvians attempted a provisional government, too. One of its leaders, a finance minister named Alfreds Valdmanis, even formally proposed restoration of a Latvian army that would join in the fight against Russian forces, in exchange for state independence under German direction. Others supported a satellite arrangement like Slovakia's.

Estonians also set up a government administration, led by Jüri Uluots, as soon as the Soviet regime toppled and before German troops arrived. Estonian guerrillas who drove the Red Army from Tartu and other places made possible this window of time, albeit brief. But all was for naught, because the Germans disbanded these provisional governments quickly and installed puppet governments in the three states.

The *Zivilverwaltung*, or German-controlled administration, came under jurisdiction of a Baltic German named Alfred Rosenberg, who was appointed reich minister for the occupied eastern territories in mid-July 1941. Despite being born and raised in Tallinn, Rosenberg was an "Aryan race philosopher," who viewed the Baltic States as prime *Lebensraum*—the perfect testing ground for German settlement and experiments in colonization. Rosenberg appointed a deputy as *Reichskommissar* for the "Ostland," which included the three Baltic States and Belorussia. But given his personal ties, Rosenberg retained much of the power and made many of the decisions that would most affect the Nazi-occupied Baltics.

In much the same ruinous style as Yugoslavia, Poland, and Czechoslovakia, the Germans seized complete control of the economy in the Baltics. Here, it was even simpler because the Soviet regime had already centralized all economic administration during the yearlong plunder. Adhering to ironclad conquerors' logic, the Germans regarded the Baltic States simply as former Soviet territory, not acknowledging them as ever being the Baltic *Republics* they had been only a year earlier. Given this, the Germans justified their own actions involving the Baltic economy by saying Baltic "Sovietization" had been legitimate. It was convenient for Germany to recognize the Baltics' annexation to Russia as perfectly legitimate, whereas the Western Allies had never recognized the annexation.

Colonization of the Baltics by German citizens began promptly. There had been Germans living in the Baltics prior to the Soviet takeover, but most had been quietly encouraged to return to the safety of Germany on the eve of Russian takeover. Now, at the expense of Baltic citizens, mostly farmers, German settlers moved in to take the land. One example of this was in the Memel and Suvalki regions, where 30,000 Lithuanian farmers were evicted and forced to move to eastern Lithuania, while German farmers took their places. Aryans in Baltic society were usually not subject to the confiscation.

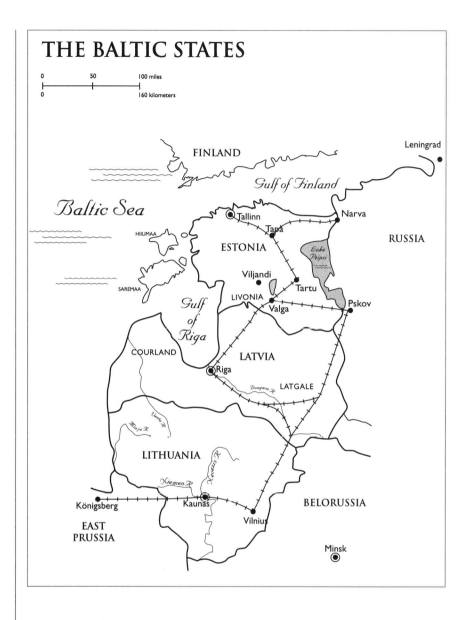

# THE BALTIC STATES

The disillusionment over government, and the very palpable commandeering of Baltic goods and land, brought many Balts back into the resistance. Even more joined when the Gestapo picked up precisely where the NKVD left off—with a reign of systematic terror and deportations against average citizens.

The Baltic resistance faced a unique and unenviable dilemma: How could they resist the Nazis *without aiding the equally feared and hated enemy, Russia?*[34] Still clinging to the hope for independence, the Balts put their faith in the Atlantic Charter, with its provisions for restoring sovereign rights to occupied countries. The charter was timely, coming in August 1941, within weeks of Nazi occupation. They understood that Great Britain and the United States did not want to jeopardize the Western-Soviet alliance against Nazi Germany, but they counted on the Western Allies upholding the words of the charter at postwar conferences. (The Atlantic Charter would be entirely moot for the Baltic States, as it would turn out.)

Even so, it was clear that the Balts needed a particular succession of events to occur, and that timing was everything. The best scenario was *not* a rising up of a home army at the most opportune moment, as planned by so many occupied countries in the Polish pattern. That would probably mean prolonged fighting against the Germans, which would have given the Soviets time to encroach again while the home forces were busy fighting. In a way, the Baltics already *had* their "rising" at the start of the German invasion. The resistance had fought well, but the outcome was dismal—an exchange of one totalitarian regime for another. The same would likely result in an internal uprising timed with a Russian invasion, only in reverse.

The best scenario possible would be the sudden collapse of the Third Reich, in which Berlin itself capitulated, leaving occupation troops to surrender where they stood. In the vacuum of the surrender, the Balts could then seize control once again and maintain it—*with* political intervention by the Western Powers. This, more than anything, probably drove the strategy of the central committees for the Baltic resistance. Instead of gearing up and stockpiling weapons for a major insurgence (à la Warsaw) they would maintain a widespread, paced, continuous resistance to wear down the Germans in any way they could.

This strategy relied not only on armed resistance, which became highly active and helpful to the Allies, but on the passive resistance of farmers and citizens everywhere. Every laborer could play a part in the effort to thwart the occupier. As Rita Cavalouski, daughter of a Lithuanian resister, later wrote: "Gradually the whole country became part of the underground movement, bent on outlasting the enemy."

The Germans' primary aim was to exploit Baltic resources for the war effort. As they did everywhere, the Germans set quotas for food and industry critical to their needs. Throughout the Baltics, workers slowed their pace at work and hampered production in any way they could. A whole consortium of Balts, beginning with farmers, worked to slow the process, produce less than dictated, confuse deliveries, tamper with records, poison grain in railroad cars, bribe officials—anything to deprive the occupier.[35]

Any sort of tampering was done at great personal risk. Like reprisals for armed resistance, the penalties for such acts were severe—most likely execution, and certainly nothing short of deportation for perpetrators and their entire families. Whole villages were sent to labor camps or even concentration camps. In 1943 the Nazis executed 40 peasants at Vilnius, Lithuania, for sabotaging a shipment of food. Reprisals, again, only drove more men and women into the arms of the resistance.

Conditions in the Baltic States were not as ideal for partisan activity as in Yugoslavia, although some Baltic regions were forested and remote enough to hide groups. Some of the forest brothers had lived in the Baltic forests since the earliest anti-Soviet resistance.

The Lithuanian Activist Front, or LAF, began in October 1940. Through rigorous recruiting, it had some 36,000 members by January 1941. (It had been the LAF that laid the groundwork for the failed provisional government in Lithuania.) Early on, the LAF established contact with leadership in the form of a one-time Lithuanian minister, Colonel Kazys Skirpa, who had fled, ironically, to Berlin to escape Soviet deportation. Already disdaining the Soviet Alliance, the Germans knew about the contact between the Lithuanian resistance and Skirpa, and quietly approved of it at that time.

On September 20, 1941, the LAF was still operating in the open and sent a memorandum to Hitler asserting the right of Lithuanian independence. It pointed out the *Zivilverwaltung* was no different from the Soviet administration that the LAF had helped vanquish. It was signed by many of LAF's members, with the name of its "on-site" leader, Leonas Prapuolenis, prominently at the top.

The memo impressed no one in Germany, and the next day, September 21, the customary knee-jerk reaction sent Prapuolenis to the concentration camp at Dachau. (Prapuolenis would later be released through Skirpa's appeal, but would remain exiled from the Baltics.) In addition, with the stroke of a pen, the Nazis banned the LAF. For a while, Lithuanian resistance was without central leadership. However, it would emerge later in different cells and under different names.

In Estonia, resistance groups without weapons had formed in numerous areas and these began to band together by March 1941. By the time the Soviets began deportations the following June, the Estonians were armed and active. In the northern region, the forest brothers numbered more than 5,000 men, 1,500 of them together in a single forest stronghold northeast of Tallinn.

In Latvia, the earliest resistance groups were made up of mostly former soldiers from the Latvian army and home guard units who had taken to the woods. They, too, were known as forest brothers. There were many such groups of partisans, usually named for the region or forest where they operated.

Help from the Western Allies, in the form of British arms drops or any other aid, was almost nil. This was partly because of perilous or unreachable distances by air, and partly because of political uncertainties with Mother Russia. Russia parceled out very limited help, and only when it suited a specific Russian aim. So forest brothers carried motley arms—mostly the old rifles of their dead national armies, and German and Russian weapons captured in battle. They sustained themselves by raiding German units and German road convoys and, as always in guerrilla territory, with the support of the local population.

The underground press flourished in the Baltics during the Nazi occupation. The early issues focused on the undying Baltic determination to win back independence and the *real* objectives of the Nazi occupation. Some of its commentary was in direct response to the German-controlled rump press that endlessly reminded readers of the gratitude due Germany for liberating them from the Red Terror.

Creating and distributing underground newspapers was especially dangerous business in the Baltic States. There were dangers in that large quantities of paper and other supplies were not readily available in the free market, and the Gestapo remained on the look-out for any clue that would lead them to the sources of the underground newspapers. There was lots of work to be done to produce the papers but no shortage of willing people. Balts went to work cultivating information sources, funding ongoing press operations, and delivering hard copy to audiences. The larger papers, like Lithuania's *Nepriklausoma Lietuva* and Latvia's *Neatkariga Latvija (Independent Latvia)*, were printed in numbers ranging up to 20,000 copies, which were passed along from person-to-person. There were risks every step of the way.

The Baltic underground press became known for its resiliency. Sources for all three states cite instances when the Gestapo discovered and destroyed presses, arrested and murdered the staff. Without missing a beat, the same newspaper appeared the next day—printed in the same format and with the same masthead by another press operated by an entirely different group—to the astonishment of the Gestapo.

Content ranged anywhere from satire to timely war news and patriotic editorials. Newspapers like *Nepriklausoma Lietuva* did more than plant rhetorical questions in readers' minds. They offered direction, based on "inside information" if available, as they did when the Germans attempted to mobilize all officers and some enlisted ranks of the former Lithuanian army in April 1944. The April 28 issue urged the men to resist for clearly stated reasons:

> *The Germans intend to use our men in the West, in dangerous areas and cities of Germany where the Allied bombing is going on. In fact, they demand that we should fight not against Bolshevism but against the English and Americans. In this way our nation would be placed in danger of becoming an enemy of England and America.*

Like in many of the other occupied countries, organized resistance in the Baltics slowly matured. There were many setbacks and many dangers for inexperienced people opposing the professionals of the Axis.

In Lithuania, fragmented resistance groups acted on their own for a time without the central leadership of the LAF. New groups sprang up in communities, their members sometimes united for no other reason than a common desire for independence. Political parties also transformed themselves into resistance organizations. Among them were the Nationalist Party (Voldemarists), the Christian Democrats, the Social Democratic Party, the Peasant Populist Union, the *Tautininkai* (Nationalist Union), the Union of Lithuanian Freedom Fighters, and the Lithuanian Front.

The *Lietuviu Frontas*, or Lithuanian Front, was a reconstituted branch of the LAF, made up mostly of young Catholics and intellectuals. Its leadership came from an old, outlawed Catholic Action group. The group was diversified, having a number of military and nonmilitary sections. The Lithuanian Front's military section stockpiled a cache of arms and trained for combat in the event of a German collapse on the Russian front; if this happened, the group would be armed and ready to defend against the advance of the Bolsheviks. The Lithuanian Front published a variety of influential newspapers and other publications for various purposes, including *I Laisve* (*Toward Freedom*), a newspaper begun in January 1943, and a weekly, mimeographed political bulletin called *Lietuviu Biuletenis* (*Lithuanian Bulletin*). Subunits of the Lithuanian Front published a listing of native Nazi collaborators, called *Lietuvos Judas* (*Judas of Lithuanian*), and the satirical *Pogrindzio Kuntaplis* (*The Underground Pantofle*), and another newspaper called *Vardan Tiesos* (*In the Name of Truth*).

The Lithuanian Unity Movement (*Vienybés Sajudis*) was composed of youth, mostly university students of Kaunas and Vilnius, and their instructors. Its underground newspaper was called *Atzalynas* (*The Sapling*). The group was founded in the fall of 1942 and remained youthfully heterogeneous until one of its leaders was apprehended by the Gestapo, after which it became part of the Christian Democrats.

The *Lietuvos Laisves Armija*, or Lithuanian Free Army, was founded in February 1942 by former army officers. It steered clear of political affiliations and existed only as a military instrument. It began small, but later had enough members for company-sized military units stationed throughout Lithuania.

LLKS (*Lietuvos Laisves Kovotoju Sajung* or Union of Lithuanian Freedom Fighters) began early, on December 26, 1940, in opposition to the Soviets. Youthful liberals started the group when it mimeographed pamphlets called *LLKS Instructions*. It later published a popular underground paper *Laisves Kovotojas* (*Freedom Fighter*). Beginning in early 1944, it even used the airwaves to carry its message, establishing a clandestine radio station called "Free Lithuania's Radio Vilnius." Before the end of the German occupation, LLKS became one of the largest and most influential of resistance groups. LLKS supported attempts to unite other patriotic resistance groups against the Nazis.

Since these organizations and other smaller ones all shared the ultimate objective of Lithuanian independence, two central leadership organizations emerged: VLK (*Vyriausias Lietuviu* or Supreme Lithuanian Committee) headed leftist resistance movements, and *Lietuvos Taryba* (Lithuanian Council) headed the Catholic resistance movements. By late 1943, the two merged to create VLIK (*Vyriausias Lietuvos Islaisvinimo Komitetas* or the Supreme Committee for Liberation of Lithuania). This committee united the Social Democrats, Christian Democrats, the Lithuanian Nationalist League, Labor Federation, Farmers Union, Populists, and others that were formed. VLIK would later have ties to Lithuania's Home Formation. The VLIK suffered a major setback on April 22, 1944, when a courier en route to Stockholm, Sweden, was captured in a Gestapo counterespionage operation against the Estonian resistance in Tallinn. He had been sent by VLIK to meet with Swedish weapon makers to negotiate a large purchase. Gestapo torture extracted the names of the VLIK leadership, which led to their arrest and confinement in Bayreuth prison in Bavaria. VLIK continued operations with replacements.

The Voldemarists or Nationalist Party did not have a clearly defined agenda. For a time, the Voldemarists, named after pro-German Lithuanian politician Augustinas Voldemaras, collaborated openly with the Nazis to fill the ranks of five Defense Battalions to fight against the Soviets. The group even patterned itself after the Nazi party, but when its members had the audacity to criticize the *Zivilverwaltung* in a memo, the Germans banned the party. The group went underground and began anti-Nazi activity.

There were even pro-Soviet resistance groups, coordinated by the Central Committee of the Communist Party of Lithuania. These groups were supplied with arms by the Russians and coordinated some of their actions with movement of Red Army units at the front.

In Estonia, the resistance groups congealed around people of the same occupations, pre-Soviet political parties, and specific regions. After fragmented resistance during the first years of occupation, resistance groups in Tallinn and Tartu formed the EVRK (*Eesti Vaba Riigi Rahvus Komitee* or National Committee of the Estonian Republic) in March 1944.

The EVRK invited representation from other Estonian resistance groups, in hopes of uniting all resistance leadership and reestablishing a provisional government as the Germans withdrew. The EVRK and other resistance groups were just beginning to come to terms, setting aside old political differences, when the Gestapo launched a reign of arrests. Increased resistance activity had provoked the arrest of some 200 in April and May 1944.

Most resistance leaders succeeded in evading the Gestapo net, but negotiations and other activities were suspended until mid-June. At that time, agreements between them were reached, and the committee became a functioning governing body for the resistance.

Estonia enjoyed an advantage of geography that actually made travel by boat possible to Finland and Sweden. Resistance groups in Tallinn and Tartu were thereby able to maintain intermittent contact with the outside world—namely, Stockholm and London—through an Estonian envoy in Finland.

EVRK granted the resistance of the other two Baltic States some privileges of this service. The sea journey was dangerous, as was crossing state borders and traveling to Tallinn to make the journey. Lithuanian resisters made regular use of the service, but faced double peril—crossing two borders overland to reach a seaport and *then* crossing the Gulf of Finland. Rita Cavalouski remembered the loss of a courier on that route and fearing for her family for its part in the Lithuanian resistance. She explained, "When my father communicated through Estonia with a resistance group in Finland [where the Finns too were becoming disillusioned with the Germans], one messenger was arrested on one of his trips north. But he did not talk, and our family is alive because he died so very silently."

By summer 1944, a regular shuttle using a swift boat made the trip twice monthly between Tallinn and Stockholm. In Stockholm, a prominent Social Democrat named Ausut Rei was the committee's main contact.

Through Rei, a communication released to the foreign press told of the committee's existence in Estonia and that it had the objective of establishing a provisional government in the event of German retreat. This raised the wrath of the Germans who soon heard about it, because it was publicized in the free world's newspapers. Relentless Gestapo searches for the committee members no doubt would have followed, along with severe reprisals, but by then the German hold on Estonia was collapsing.

In September 1944, the Red Army was battering the weakened German line in the east. Estonian resisters launched attacks on the rear areas of the German line, as the Wehrmacht began widespread retreat. While the Germans fell back, Estonian forces set up a short-lived perimeter east of Tallinn in anticipation of the Red Army advance. On September 22, Russian troops crushed the perimeter defenses and occupied Tallinn.

The Latvian resistance also created the *Latvija Centrala Komitee* (Latvian Central Committee) in 1943. Led by a liberal named Konstantins Cakste, the committee's primary objective was to coordinate the forest brothers and all other resistance activity on a national level. Its most notable acts were communication with the outside world through memoranda to the Western Allies. In some of these communications, the committee sought to overcome what they thought was a perception in the West that Latvia was a willing supporter of Germany. In a February 1944 communication, the committee openly proclaimed Latvia as an independent republic once again.

By fall 1944, the Gestapo hunted down members of the committee. Among them was Cakste, who was deported like all those found. He perished in the camps. Now lacking a central command for resistance, Latvia's forest brothers continued operating in a fragmented way.

Some efforts to coordinate resistance for all three Baltic States were attempted late in the German occupation. In January 1944, leaders of Lithuanian and Latvian resistance met in conference. In April, leaders from all three states met twice. All the conferences took place in Riga. Even with their combined forces, the resistance leaders knew that the Baltic States faced overwhelming powers in both Russia and Germany. Chances for victory were slim. Still, if they united, perhaps they could win time for the Allies to intervene on their behalf to fulfill promises of the Atlantic Charter . . .


As conditions of the occupation became harsher, the Nazis decided to institute their final solution for the Baltic Jewish population. Concentration camps were built in Latvia at Salaspils, in Estonia at Klooga, and in Lithuania at Dimitra. Jews from Germany, Austria, Holland, and Czechoslovakia were brought to the Baltics to perish.

There were practically no Jews in Estonia (fewer than 5,000 in 1939). Latvia and Lithuania had larger Jewish populations, with approximately 90,000 and 200,000 respectively. The grim story was much like that of Poland's, but on a smaller scale. After segregating many of the Jews into ghettoes, the Nazi extermination teams were sent to begin the final solution. During the first three months of occupation, more than 71,000 were executed in Lithuania and slightly more than 30,000 in Latvia. Rita Cavalouski wrote: "The mind refused to accept this as possible, until one day in Marijampole [Lithuania] all the Jews were herded together, stripped of all their valuable possessions including wedding rings, made to dig a mass grave, and then shot."

Out of an approximate total of 300,000 Baltic Jewish residents in 1939, some sources estimate that 170,000 were killed during the Nazi occupation. (Some of the original number had actually been evacuated by the Soviets or drafted into the Red Army before the German invasion.) Native anti-Semite thugs are known to have taken part in the killings, with the nodding approval of the Nazis, but such murderers were the exceptions and not the rule among the Baltic population. The vast majority of Jews met death in the horrific concentration camps.

The Nazis ruthlessly imposed conscription for both the military and labor service. When a call for free-will volunteers failed, a program of forced labor began in December 1941. It required all Baltic citizens aged 17 to 45 to register. Avoiding registration carried penalties of three months imprisonment and a 1,000-mark fine, followed by work in the labor service.

When the "Baltic *Untermenschen*" still didn't recognize their destiny of slavery to the Master Race, and people refused to come forward for the labor service, the Nazis resorted to dragnets targeting able-bodied workers. The Gestapo surrounded churches, theaters, and restaurants—anywhere that young people were likely to gather—and took them forcibly to depots for transport to German factories. In the fall of 1942, whole villages in Latgalia (eastern Latvia) were surrounded and adults marched to railway depots, leaving only children behind.

There was a great outcry of public protest against these tactics, and in one case the people were actually heard. Citing the unlawfulness of policy under the Hague Convention, a Latvian agency won release for 3,000 Estonian and 10,000 young Latvian women just before transport to Germany for compulsory labor in April 1943.

Still, 126,000 Baltic citizens were conscripted for work in Germany, according to a memo from Rosenberg to Himmler, dated July 20, 1944. Even among the masses sent to work in the slave-like conditions of German factories, resistance cells formed with a mixture of Balts, Slavs, and others from occupied countries. As the war went on and increasing Allied strategic bombing devastated German industry, many were able to escape to their homeland amidst the confusion and upheaval.

Compulsory military service met with greater resistance than the labor service. The Germans hoped that the Balt's well-known anti-Soviet attitude would draw in the large numbers they needed, but their actions had alienated too many people and caused an equally vehement anti-German attitude. At one time, the Germans had been supremely confident that they could defeat Hitler's "real enemy" before the winter of 1941–1942. Now, with reversals at Stalingrad and other places in the east, the Wehrmacht desperately needed cannon fodder for the Russian front. The Germans were forced to "relax their standards" to accept Baltic recruits for so-called defense battalions as the Russian campaign dragged on into the second half of 1942.

The few homegrown Nazis came forward at this point. Others who came forward were enraged survivors wanting revenge for deaths of loved ones killed by the Soviets. But the numbers were small, and far short of German demands. Total estimates of "volunteers" for the defense battalions from each of the states numbered approximately 20,000 from Lithuania, 15,000 for Latvia, and 10,000 for Estonia.

When even the former soldiers—the same soldiers who had deserted the Red Army and willingly came over to the side of the Wehrmacht in June 1941—did not "volunteer," the Germans became more forceful, dictating that the alternative to military service was confinement in a POW camp.

The Germans had given assurances that the "defense battalions" would be used as their name implied—in defense of the homeland. But all had been sent to the Russian front, at first as reserves for the German front-line units, and later shoved forward on the front lines. Eventually, some units were also sent to Poland and Yugoslavia for treacherous antiguerrilla operations.

In the fall of 1942, the Germans tried recruiting a second wave of soldiers. This time they abandoned the euphemistic façade of "defense battalions" and called them National Waffen SS Legions— or, for each of the respective countries, simply the Estonian SS Legion, Latvian SS Legion, and Lithuanian SS Legion.

"When the Nazis issued the first order for the formation of a 'Lithuanian SS Legion' the press countered with: 'No one in history has ever fought to become enslaved and deprived of his rights,'" commented Rita Cavalouski. "The registration centers remained empty."

It was left to Rosenberg to find a way to improve relations and get the military manpower needed. He issued a decree that overturned the fundamental Soviet tenet and restored right of private ownership. He also approved the formation of national assemblies to provide governmental representation in each of the states. Buried in the decree was the "privilege" or, actually obligation, to muster national legions in each of the states to help preserve Europe from the Bolsheviks.

Despite Rosenberg's attempt to moderate occupation policies in hopes of inducing recruitment, Baltic citizens saw German motives for what they were.

Next, the Germans authorities went to the other extreme, leveraging whatever they could. One standing threat was compulsory labor service, and this was used to induce "volunteering" for military service. It was common knowledge that conditions in the labor service had worsened as the war years went on. So the Baltic citizens were essentially offered the "choice"—military service or labor—as a way for the Germans to put pressure on for enlistment. This worked to some degree in Estonia and Latvia, but Lithuanians remained stubborn and evaded conscription in either service.

Many of the former Lithuanian soldiers were already active in the resistance or were in partisan bands, or they took to the forests now. The students, too, disappeared into the forests, leaving the Legions with empty ranks. The enraged Germans roared that Lithuanians weren't worthy of the German uniform and halted recruitment there. They blamed the failure of the military mobilization on those who they felt could influence the youth: priests, university faculty, lawyers, and other intelligentsia. Many were arrested and deported to concentration camps for this reason. Deportations were followed by the closing of all institutions for higher education.

Under the German edicts, manpower trickled into the ranks of the SS Legions. Of course, the only *real* motivation capable of mobilizing forces in the Baltic States was the collapse of German lines, allowing Russian penetration of Baltic borders. That was coming, and people sensed it.

By January 1944, the front was pushed back almost all the way to the Estonian border. Narva was evacuated. Jüri Uluots, the last legitimate prime minister of Estonia prior to its fall to the Soviet Union in 1940, delivered an impassioned radio address that implored all able-bodied men born from 1904 through 1923 to report for military service. (Before this, Uluots had adamantly opposed mobilization.)

The call drew support from all across the country: 38,000 volunteers jammed registration centers, astonishing the Germans and surpassing the expectations of Estonian leaders. Several thousand Estonians who had joined the Finnish army even came back across the Gulf of Finland to join the forces of their homeland.

In Latvia, administrators also decided to support the mobilization. As the Red Army approached, the Latvian SS Legion surged in strength to 40,000. Within the next four or five months, another 20,000 would join.[36] The great willingness to volunteer, of course, had nothing to do with supporting the Germans. The hope from the beginning was for Nazi Germany to surrender to the Allies, and keep the Russian invaders at bay, so that the countries could remain free and independent—as the Atlantic Charter guaranteed. In Latvia and Estonia, this was fairly clear-cut.

In Lithuania, it was not clear-cut, and mobilization took different twists. Two major recruiting pushes by the Germans had failed miserably, each attempt followed by vicious reprisals in which many citizens were deported or killed. The underground press had done a masterful job of convincing people to stay away from registration centers.

The precipitating factor that did draw volunteers to military service was a marked increase in Soviet partisan activity in northeastern Lithuania. These partisans terrorized the local people, plundering, raping, and killing at will. To combat them, Lithuanian General Povilas Plechavicius proposed the "Home Formation," which would remain within Lithuanian territory and have Lithuanian leadership. Plechavicius was a charismatic and influential leader who became popular during the insurgence against the Soviet occupation.

Although negotiations with the Germans nearly ended in failure, they finally agreed to establishment of the Home Formation to fight the Soviet partisans and any other Soviet threat to its borders.

Recruiting for the Home Formation brought more volunteers than seemed possible during 1942 and 1943: 20,000 volunteers responded—twice the number Plechavicius proposed for his 14 battalions. The Germans, however, refused to equip these battalions with proper uniforms, weapons, and ammunition, even though stocks were ample enough. The Germans disrupted operations of the Home Formation in any way they could, short of forcibly disbanding it. The Home Formation, for its part, was openly patriotic, playing the Lithuanian National Anthem, and even being contemptuous of the Germans. Finally in April 1944, the Gestapo secretly intercepted a dispatch from the Home Formation, intended for foreign countries, and uncovered ties to the VLIK.

The following month, General Plechavicius and some of his staff were tricked into meeting with the Germans. He and the rest of the Lithuanian leadership were arrested, sent to Riga, and then deported to Kirchholm. The Germans went to disarm the Home

Formation battalions, but found many had dispersed into the woods, taking their weapons and equipment. Out of the Home Formation's 10,000 soldiers, 3,400 were found and captured. Every tenth soldier was executed in reprisal for those who "deserted."

No aid from the Western Allies would come to combat the Soviet annexation. The Western Allies gave lip service in protest, not recognizing the incorporation of the Baltics into the Soviet Union and even demanding restoration of Baltic States' independence before 1940. But the major concern of the United States and Great Britain was to "maintain the Soviet-Western alliance in the fight against Nazi Germany."

The first Baltic area to witness the return of the Red Army was Narva, on the Estonian-Russian border in the far north. That was January 1944, but the Russian offensive paused there until summer. At that time, the Germans expected an attack south of the Pripet Marshes because of the massed troops already in Poland. Instead, the Red Army attacked north of there, in Belorussia, where Hitler ordered the German Army Group Center to stand fast. Group Center fell in June, which opened the door for the Red Army's advance. In late July, the Russians advanced all the way to Kaunas. By the fall of 1944, most of the Baltic region was in Russian hands again. All that remained of the German occupation forces was in a seaside pocket of Latvia called the Courland. This kept dim hopes alive for restoration of a free republic in Latvia, even after the Soviets crossed the Latvian border. With the Soviet invasion, the forest brothers reportedly began receiving small arms and some supplies from German forces in the Courland. Since the Courland was still occupied by the Wehrmacht in May 1945 when Germany surrendered, hopes remained alive to the very last that the Western Powers would intervene and seize the pocket. But hopes were dashed again, as the Soviets soon took control of Latvia completely.

The Baltic hope of biding time so that a German surrender might happen before the Russian return was lost. The Red Army presence was every bit as savage as before, with raping, pillaging, and executions as the front passed through on the way to Germany.

Baltic citizens thronged the roads trying to get out of the way of the advancing Russians as the German lines disintegrated. The Germans wanted nothing of value left for the enemy to use, so they adopted the same scorched earth policy as the Russians had in *their* 1941 retreat.

"The Germans were burning everything on their retreat with a special vindictiveness," Rita Cavalouski remembered. "The sky stayed red for the whole night as . . . we moved slowly westward. . . . Our road was clogged with dusty and terrified German soldiers. Could they be the same proud men of 1941?"

The Balts would not learn for some time the true extent of Nazi duplicity: That, even as the Wehrmacht was welcomed as the great liberator from the Red Terror in June 1941, they had agreed to the Russian occupation to begin with. The German-Soviet Nonaggression Pact, signed in August 1939, had already sealed the Baltics' fate. At the same time Poland was carved like two sides of beef, Germany agreed that Russia would take the three Baltic States as "protectorates." This would restore the buffer zone once enjoyed by old-time czarist Russia. (Initially, Germany was to take Lithuania and Russia the other two, but Germany had ceded on this point.)

The Balts did not know the postwar fate they were to face, had Germany been victorious. Reich Minister Rosenberg's well-laid plans for the postwar colonization were laid open in files found in Berlin after the war, and in the testimony of defendants interrogated at Nuremberg. The information was gathered by the U.S. State Department and published in a report titled *Nazi Conspiracy and Aggression.* The document cited a German memorandum of April 2, 1941:

> *The necessary removal of considerable sections of the intelligentsia—particularly in Latvia—to the Russian nucleus area would have to be organized. The settlement of a German rural population in considerable numbers would have to be started— possibly a large continent of German settlers suitable for this purpose could be taken from among the Volga Germans, after the undesirable elements have been eliminated. Settlements there of Danes, Norwegians, Dutch and—after the war has been brought to a victorious end—of Englishmen too, might be considered so that, in the course of one or two generations, this area can be joined up with the German nucleus area as a new germanized country. In this case we must not neglect the deportation of considerable groups of racially inferior sections of the population from Lithuania.*

This policy would have sent two-thirds of the Baltic population into veritable slavery to the Aryan master. Those allowed to remain would have needed to be judged of racially pure enough Nordic blood to be worthy of germanization. These were the long-range goals; deportations were not to commence until after complete German victory. All plans were kept secret to prevent citizen unrest before the appointed time.

The Allies' policies of unconditional surrender and no "separate peace" ensured that the Baltic States would not share in liberty after the victory over the Axis. And there would be no independence and freedom, regardless of the Atlantic Charter's promises. Hanging on to meager hopes for a repeat of what happened in 1918, provisional governments were once again set up, but they lasted only a few days before the Russians stomped them out.

With the demise of the Third Reich, one cruel occupation gave way to another. Only the uniform of the occupier changed; the oppression stayed the same. And the Baltic resistance continued without interruption.

Remembering her family's exodus from the Baltics, Rita Cavalouski observed, "We did not know it then, but we were moving over ground that would soon be red with the blood of our Freedom Fighters . . . who would continue to fight from the forests for many years."

# Epilogue

As Europe threw off the yoke of Nazi tyranny, an army of statisticians was already at work tallying World War II's cost in terms
of bombs, bullets, money, and human lives, as well as what was
achieved for that cost. For the Allied military, it was a straightfor-
ward process, because most of the information was well documented through existing quartermaster records, combat reports, and unit
histories. The Statistical and Accounting Branch, Office of the
Adjutant General, neatly quantified and packaged the war's carnage
into rows of numbers, aligned and impressive like soldiers at attention in platoon formation.

No such official documents encapsulate the resistance in World
War II.

There's good reason for that, of course. By nature, acts of resistance
were mostly clandestine and small, often carried out individually, not
measurable and, for the resisters' well-being, not documented. This
leaves us with little in the way of a concrete record to show the resistance's costs and accomplishments.

In the years since World War II, there's been a lot of discussion—
in fact, heated debates—about just what the resistance *did* accomplish.
Fueled by legitimately heroic biographies and autobiographies, and
exaggerated novels based on fact, some of the more revolutionary chron-
iclers portray the resistance as the determining factor that won the war,
or could have if left on its own. Others go to the opposite extreme, saying the resistance achieved very little and dismiss it as inconsequential
in the bigger picture of the war when compared to the battles fought by
conventional military. The truth, according to the sketchy facts that do
exist, points somewhere in between. Neither an inconsequential factor
nor the determining factor, the resistance did take a toll on the Nazi
occupiers both materially and psychologically. It did reduce casualties for
Allied soldiers and took some obstacles out of their way. Its collective
work probably shortened the war, and certainly contributed to victory
over Nazi Germany. "A people who want to live free do not wait for
someone to bring their freedom. They take it. In so doing, they help
themselves as well as those who would come to their aid," wrote Albert
Camus in the resistance newspaper *Combat*.

A few accomplishments of the resistance can be put into numerical form—some quite impressive. For instance, it is known that more
than 33,000 Allied servicemen, mostly British and American airmen
and escaped POWs, were shuttled on escape lines to safety in neutral
or Allied countries. More than 7,000 Jews, 90 percent, were saved in
Denmark's famous and remarkable story, and more than 15,000 Dutch

Jews survived the Holocaust, hidden by sympathetic citizens in the Netherlands. Some sources credit the resistance for killing as many as 22,000 enemy troops in Greece, another 22,000 in Poland, and 25,000 in Czechoslovakia.

Still, it's very difficult to cast the resistance in terms of numbers with any precision. Even if there were a precise total of enemy soldiers killed, communications lines cut, bridges blown, trains derailed, and intelligence messages delivered, it would not give an accurate picture, simply because black-and-white numbers do not measure the *importance* of the acts. For instance, a delaying action that kept *Das Reich* away from the D-Day beaches for even one extra day might have been far more valuable than wiping out the Gestapo in a major city, or assassinating a leader like Heydrich. And contrary to the historians who begrudge value to the resistance except in cases in which guerrillas kept enemy divisions away from the fighting front, quiet sabotage of the war industry might have had far-reaching effects that sustained guerrilla action could not.

There simply is no adequate way to total the value of weakening the occupier's discipline and resolve through continuous opposition both large and small. The inverse is true, too. As the occupiers' spirit sank, the resisters' spirit inversely buoyed up, giving hope that saw them through the harshest of Nazi rule. And no statisticians' columns can add up the value of patriotism and the insatiable will to win back freedom.

The price for freedom was high, by any account. Attaching figures to show just how high is difficult—as difficult as pinpointing what the resistance accomplished. But it's possible to show representative figures from the smaller countries in the west where records survived the war. Government sources in the Low Countries, for example, state that fully 6,000 Luxembourgers lost their lives in the service of the resistance, either killed in action or after capture by summary execution or maltreatment in concentration camps; this is out of a total estimate of 8,000 Luxembourgers killed in the war. Approximately 16,000 Belgian resisters paid the ultimate price; this is out of a total estimate of 40,000 Belgians killed (not including 26,800 Belgian Jews who were deported and died in the Holocaust). More than 10,000 Dutch citizens died in resistance activities; another 2,000 Dutch men and women were executed in reprisals and terror actions.

The larger countries naturally had larger figures. In France, approximately 24,000 maquisards were killed in action. Another 75,000 French men and women "connected with the resistance" died in concentration camps.

Soon after the war, communist sources tried to put figures around their underground forces in the east and west, and along with it they estimated the number of noncommunist resisters. In round and reckless numbers, they assert that 4.5 million men and women participated in organized, anti-Nazi resistance, and that fully 1 million were killed.

For all its dangers and high cost, why did Europeans choose to resist the Nazi occupiers? Some would explain it in very direct terms. Without a millisecond's hesitation, French resister Elizabeth Sevier responded: "Because they killed my father. I wanted revenge."

For others, the brutality of treatment left no other recourse. As Rita Cavalouski stated, "Death did not seem much worse than life, and so everyone was very brave."

Most would tell you in essence that it simply *had* to be done, and not something they had to think about, not something they searched their minds to find a reason for. "I could not see myself doing anything else," said Belgian Gaston Vandermeerssche.

"My motivations were patriotism and self-respect," said Dutch resister Epko Weert. "Not waiting with your arms crossed as the Allies suffered all the losses to beat Hitler. We internally had to do something. If it would help, you could not know. In the meantime, you did whatever you could."

Mary Sigillo Barraco explained, "We were determined to stop the Nazi oppressors. We didn't think about how long we had to fight or what we had to sacrifice. We just knew we had to do it. And what kept me going on, even in my darkest hours—like in solitary confinement and interrogation rooms at Brussels' Gestapo headquarters at 347 Avenue Louise—was the thought that we *would* prevail. While in my cell, I heard American bombers flying overhead in July 1943. Another prisoner heard them, too, and immediately tapped on the pipe in code that the Americans had just landed in Sicily. It gave me the courage to endure, to accept anything that was happening, because I knew one day the Nazis would fall, and freedom would be ours again. It was in those moments that I learned freedom is beyond price."

When the Allies crossed the borders and liberation finally came, those in the resistance could hold their heads high and look the liberators in the eye, knowing they had earned their freedom.

# Resistance Organizations

Note: This list is by no means all-inclusive, but is representative of organizations noted in the text.

| Name | Translation | Leadership |
| --- | --- | --- |
| **Czech** | | |
| *Obrana Naroda* (ON) | Defense of the Nation | Military officers |
| *Politicke Ústredi* (PÚ) | Political Center | Politicians and intellectuals |
| *Sokol* (OSVO) | Falcon | Young athletes |
| *Peticni vybor Verni zustaneme* (PVVZ) | "We Will Stay True" Committee | Social democrats and leftist intellectuals |
| *Ústredni vybor odboje domaciho* (ÚVOD) | Central Leadership of the Home Resistance | Coalition |
| KSC | Communist Party of Czechoslovakia | Communist |
| R 3 | Council of the Three | Former PVVZ |
| **Slovakia** | | |
| Slovak Revolutionary Youth | | Youth |
| Association of Lutheran Youth | | Lutheran clergy |
| *Slovenska narodna rada* (SNR) | Slovak National Council | Democratic and communist |
| **Poland** | | |
| *Zwiazek Walki Zbrojnej* (ZWZ) | Association for Armed Struggle | Military officers |
| *Armia Krajowa* (AK) | Home Army | Former ZWZ |
| *Narodowe Sily Zbrojne* (NSZ) | National Armed Forces | Fascist |
| *Armia Ludowa* (AL) | People's Army | Communist/People's Guards |

| Name | Translation | Leadership |
|---|---|---|
| **Denmark** | | |
| *Prinser* | The Princes | Military intelligence officers |
| *Dansk Samling* | Danish Coalition | Right-wing activists |
| *Frit Danmark* | Free Denmark | |
| *Ringen* | The Circle | |
| *Friheds Raadet* | Freedom Council | Coalition of previous three |
| **Norway** | | |
| *Militaer Organisation* (Milorg) | Military Organization | Military officers |
| *Civil Organisation* (Civorg) | Civilian Organization | Political leaders |
| X-U | | Military intelligence officers |
| *Norge Fritt* | Free Norway | Communist |
| Home Front | | Milorg spinoff |
| **The Netherlands** | | |
| *Orde Dienst* (OD) | Law and Order Service | Military officers |
| *Trotskist* | Revolutionary Socialist Party | Socialist |
| *Raad van Verzet* | Resistance Council | Left-wing politicians |
| *Knokploegen* | | Calvinist and Catholic (specializing in sabotage) |
| *Landelijke Organisatie* | National Organization | Calvinist and Catholic (specializing in the care of *onderduikers*) |
| Communist party | | Communist |
| *Nederlandse Binnenlandse Strijdkrachten* | Dutch Home Forces | Coalition under Prince Bernhard |

| Name | Translation | Leadership |
|------|-------------|------------|
| **Belgium** | | |
| *Mouvement National Belge* | Belgian National Movement | |
| *Group G* | Group G | Engineers |
| *Lègion Belge* | Belgian Legion | Military officers |
| *Armèe Belge des Partisans du Front de l'Independence et de la Liberation* | Belgian Partisan Army of the Independence and Liberation Front | Communist |
| *l'Armée Secrete* | Secret Army | Military officers |
| *les Milices Patriotiques* | Patriotic Militia | |
| *le Mouvement National Royaliste* | Royal Nationalist Movement | Supporters of the king |
| *les Partisans l'Armées* | Partisan Army | Military officers |
| | | |
| **Luxembourg** | | |
| *Roude Léif* (LRL) | Red Lion | |
| *Letzeburger Partiote Liga* (LPL) | Luxembourg Patriotic League | |
| *Letzeburger Volleks Legioun* (LVL) | Luxembourg Peoples Legion | |
| *Letzeburger Freihétskämpfer* (LFB) | Luxembourg Freedom Fighters | |
| *Unioun vun de Resistenzmouvementer* | Union of Resistance Movements | Coalition |
| *Letzeburger Legioun* (LL) (Raths) | Luxembourg Legion | Catholic Boy Scouts |

| Name | Translation | Leadership |
|------|-------------|------------|
| **France** | | |
| *Libération Sud* | Liberation South | Trade union (de la Vigerie) |
| *Libération Nord* | Liberation North | Trade union |
| *France au Combat* | France at Combat | Professional class (Frenay) |
| *Organisation de Resistance de l'Armée* | Organization of the Army's Resistance | Military officers |
| *Front National* | Front National | Communist |
| *Bureau Central de Renseignements et d'Action* (BCRA) | Central Information and Action Bureau | Military intelligence officers (de Gaulle) |
| *Confrérie Notre-Dame* | Brotherhood of Our Lady | BCRA (Rémy) |
| *Mouvements Unis de la Résistance* | United Resistance Movements | Coalition created by Jean Moulin in old southern zone |
| *l'Armée Secrète* | Secret Army | Military (Delestraint) |
| *Conseil National de la Résistance* | National Resistance Council | Coalition (Delestraint, ultimately de Gaulle) |
| *Franc-Tireur* | | Catholic |
| *Franc-Tireurs et Partisans* | Snipers and Partisans | Communist (Duclos) |
| *Forces Françaises de l'Interieur* (FFI) | French Forces of the Interior | Coalition (de Gaulle) |
| **Greece** | | |
| *Ethniko Apeleftherotiko Metopo* (EAM) | National Liberation Front | Communist |
| *Ethniko Laikos Apeleftherotiko Stratos* (ELAS) | National Popular Liberation Army | EAM (Klaras) |
| *Ethnikos Dimokratikos Ellinikos Syndesmos* (EDES) | National Democratic Greek League | (Zervas) |
| *Ethniki ke Kinoniki Apeleftherosis* (EKKA) | National and Social Liberation Army | (Saraphis) |

| Name | Translation | Leadership |
|---|---|---|
| **Yugoslavia** | | |
| Chetniks | Chetniks | Monarchist (Mihailovic) |
| Partisans | Partisans | Communist (Tito) |
| | | |
| **The Baltic States** | | |
| Lithuania: | | |
| LAF | Lithuanian Activist Front | Nationalist (Skirpa) |
| *Vienybés Sajudis* | Lithuanian Unity Movement | University faculty |
| *Lietuvos Laisves Armija* | Lithuanian Free Army | Military officers |
| *Lietuviu Frontas* | Lithuanian Front | Catholic |
| *Lietuvos Laisves Kovotoju Sajung* (LLKS) | Union of Lithuanian Freedom Fighters | Nationalist |
| *Vyrianusias Lietuviu Lictuvos Taryba* (VLK) | Supreme Lithuanian Committee Lithuanian Council | Coalition Catholic |
| *Vyrianusias Lietuvos Islaisvinimo Komitetas* (VLIK) | Supreme Committee for Liberation of Lithuania | Coalition |
| | | |
| Estonia: | | |
| *Metsavennad* | Forest Brothers | Military officers |
| *Eesti Vaba Riigi Rahvus Komitee* (EVRK) | National Committee of the Estonian Republic | Coalition |
| | | |
| Latvia: | | |
| *Metsavennad* | Forest Brothers | Military officers |
| *Latvija Centrala Komitee* | Latvian Central Committee | Coalition (Cakste) |

# Notes

1.  Campert's original phrasing in Dutch: "Jezelf een vraag stellen, daarmee begint verzet. En dan die vraag aan een ander stellen."
2.  French historian Henri Michel outlined forms of resistance this way: Passive and administrative; secret tracts and newspapers; escape lines; information; sabotage (including strikes); maquis and guerrillas; and ultimately, a liberation movement. British historian M.R.D. Foot more compactly summarized the resistance's four main types as military intelligence, escape lines, guerrilla or other semiclandestine combat, and political activity.
3.  The German Army's security and intelligence organization, independent of the Gestapo and SS.
4.  He would later divulge the details for the invasion of Poland, Norway, the Netherlands, Belgium, and France. About a year in advance, he also communicated the invasion of the Soviet Union.
5.  Moravek, not to be confused with Frantisek *Moravec*, head of Czech intelligence, and certainly not Emanuel *Marvec*, a notorious Nazi collaborator. Vaclav Moravek was an army staff officer left behind by Moravec to organize resistance and set up communications with Czechoslovak intelligence in London.
6.  Many Czechs like Pavelka joined the Czech Legion in Poland soon after the German occupation and escaped Continental Europe during the evacuation of survivors of the British Expeditionary Forces from Dunkirk.
7.  During the six years of occupation, more than 350,000 Czechs were deported to concentration camps. Only 100,000 returned.
8.  Curda survived the war only to be hanged for treason.
9.  General Dwight Eisenhower had agreed to leave the region to Soviet control.
10. Many of these were rescued at Dunkirk.
11. When Hitler invaded Poland the previous year, Denmark's troops had numbered 36,000; within the next six months the number dropped to 14,000.
12. At the Nuremberg trials, an aide to Adolf Eichmann, testified: "I know that the [Danish] Foreign Ministry adopted the attitude that . . . deportation of the Jews was politically unacceptable."
13. Kaj Munk had been among the distinguished writers for Denmark's underground newspapers. While the Germans no doubt suspected this, he had not been tried and sentenced to death. His was a terror killing.

14. Kings Christian and Haakon (formerly Prince Carl) were both sons of King Frederick VIII of Denmark. When Norway separated from Sweden in 1905, Norway's parliament chose Prince Carl to be their monarch, Haakon VII. King Haakon reigned until his death in 1957.

15. British historian B.H. Liddell Hart has chastised Allied (mainly British and French) actions that provoked Hitler's invasion of Norway, writing vehemently in *The History of the Second World War* that when this charge of unprovoked war was leveled at Nazi leaders in the Nuremberg trials, it was "one of the most palpable cases of hypocrisy in history."

16. A lack of preparation was evident in smaller ways, too. Like when the Germans tacked up dozens of large posters with propaganda messages for "The Norwegian *Volk.*" Norwegians spell *folk* not with a "V" but with an "F," like in English. Subtle slips like this gave Norwegians a foretaste of how the Germans would impose themselves and their ideologies on the country in the days to come.

17. In 1943, Hitler issued an order that "Norwegians are to be treated with 'consideration.'" Hartung told Freyer about this order in July 1943 and said he disagreed with it. "But since it was *'Führer-befehl,'* it had to be obeyed," Freyer explained. "At the time this might have saved . . . us."

18. Exceptions were the Communist Party in Holland and the Revolutionary Socialist (*Trotskist*) Party that drew a minor following in Holland's western communities.

19. As many as 1,500 airmen would be spirited away, as well as another 3,000 escapees of all nationalities who became "passengers" aboard escape lines into Belgium.

20. Even when NSB membership swelled to 50,000 (Mussert claimed 80,000) as smaller fascist parties were absorbed into it, the Nazi regime still would not appoint him to the post.

21. The *Landstorm* also joined in the fighting against British airborne troops at Arnhem in October 1944.

22. Before Colonel Bastin could unify them, the Gestapo arrested him.

23. "WIM," named after Queen Wilhelmina.

24. Watt found out later that no one in the small Belgian villages of Hamme or Zele had been arrested on account of him. Most survived to meet with him on a peaceful return trip in 1984.

25. A temporary setback was yet to come with the Battle of the Bulge, the last German offensive, which came at year's end.

26. Translated by Britain's Ministry of Information.

27. Rewarded for his successes against the resistance, Darnand would later head all French police forces.

28. Out of the huge numbers of German soldiers stationed in France (60 divisions in 1944), virtually none had direct responsibility for internal security duties. This was left to the Gestapo and its collaborationist contingents. At most there were only 6,500 Germans nationwide in the policing role. The small numbers of German security forces can be viewed as signifying two things: It exemplified German efficiency and belied the extent of collaboration. Only later, when the maquis came above ground, was there open warfare that involved combat divisions.

29. *Boche* was a derogatory French word meaning "thick heads" or "cabbage heads."

30. Metaxas was the soldier-politician who executed a *coup d'etat* to become Greece's dictator in August 1936. He also carried the title of prime minister, but first and foremost he was a military general—commander-in-chief of Greece's armed forces.

31. Since the British could not hold Greece, they decided to hold at least Crete. If taken, the Germans thought, Crete-based Luftwaffe units could break the Royal Navy's hold on the eastern Mediterranean. So within a few weeks, elite German airborne troops began the offensive against Crete. The operation was disaster for Germany, as more than 12,000 parachutists were killed in this attack. The Germans eventually turned the tide and took Crete, but the severity of their losses was disproportionate to the gains in holding the island.

32. Often adopted by resistance leaders, an alias was used to protect one's self and family from reprisals.

33. In the early 1940s, the word *partisan* (like *Chetnik*) was used interchangeably with "guerrilla." Any resistance group waging guerrilla warfare might be called partisans, which led to great confusion for the British. They had indiscriminately ascribed all monarchist activities to "partisans."

34. Only Poland faced a similar dilemma, although the Poles had not known the complete Russian occupation like the Baltic States had and, in the desperation of the Warsaw Rising, the Poles were readily accepting of Soviet help.

35. Latvians reported it was possible to bribe some German officials, even in the Gestapo, whereas it had been impossible to bribe their Russian counterparts in the 1940–1941 occupation.

36. All told, as many as 150,000 Latvians served in the German army during the occupation. More than 50,000 were killed.

# Bibliography

Adamson, Hans Christian, and Per Klem. *Blood on the Midnight Sun.* New York: W.W. Norton & Company, Inc., 1964.

Ash, Bernard. *Norway: 1940.* London: Cassell Publishers, 1964.

Aubrac, Lucie. *Outwitting the Gestapo.* Lincoln: University of Nebraska Press, 1993.

Auty, Phyllis. *Tito.* New York: McGraw-Hill Book Company, 1970.

Auty, Phyllis. "The Rise of Tito." *History of the Second World War*, pp. 1,392–1,400.

Bird, Michael J. *The Secret Battalion.* New York: Holt, Rinehart and Winston, 1964.

Block, Gay, and Malka Drucker. *Rescuers: Portraits of Moral Courage in the Holocaust.* New York: Homes & Meier Publishers, Inc., 1992.

Blodnieks, Adolfs. *The Undefeated Nation.* New York: Robert Speller & Sons Publishers, Inc., 1960.

Cavalouski, Rita. "Liberation of the Baltic States." *History of the Second World War*, pp. 2,136–2,140.

Chambard, Claude. *The Maquis.* Indianapolis: The Bobbs-Merrill Company, Inc., 1976.

Cissold, Stephen. *A Short History of Yugoslavia.* Cambridge: Cambridge University Press, 1966.

Collier, Richard. *10,000 Eyes.* New York: Pyramid Books, 1958.

Cottam, Kazimiera J. *Women in War and Resistance.* Nepean, Canada: New Military Publishing, 1998.

de Gaulle, Charles. *The Complete War Memoirs of Charles de Gaulle.* New York: Simon and Schuster, 1964.

de Ridder Files, Yvonne. *The Quest for Freedom: Belgian Resistance in World War II.* Santa Barbara: Fithian Press, 1991.

Deighton, Len. *Blood, Tears and Folly.* New York: HarperCollinsPublishers, 1993.

Ehrlich, Blake. *Resistance: France.* New York: Little, Brown and Company, 1965.

Eisenhower, Dwight D. *Crusade in Europe.* Garden City, New York: Doubleday & Company, Inc., 1948.

Faitelson, Alex. *Heroism & Bravery in Lithuania 1941–1945.* New York: Gefen Books, 1996.

Flender, Harold. *Rescue in Denmark.* New York: Simon and Schuster, 1963.

Foot, M.R.D. *Resistance: European Resistance to Nazism 1940–45.* New York: McGraw-Hill Book Company, 1977.

Foot, M.R.D., and J.M. Langley. *MI9.* Boston: Little, Brown and Company, 1979.

Frenay, Henri. *The Night Will End: Memoirs of a Revolutionary.* New York: McGraw-Hill Companies, 1976.

Gallagher, Thomas. *Assault in Norway: Sabotaging the Nazi Nuclear Bomb.* New York: Harcourt Brace Jovanovich, 1975.

Garlinski, Józef. *Poland, SOE and the Allies.* London: Allen Unwin Publishers, 1969.

Garlinski, Józef. *Poland in the Second World War.* New York: Hippocrene Books Inc., 1985.

Gerolymatos, Andre. *British Intelligence and Guerrilla Warfare Operations in the Second World War: Greece, 1941–1944.* Ph.D. dissertation for McGill University, Montreal, 1991.

Giskes, Hermann. *London Calling Northpole.* London: Kimber, 1953.

Gjelsvik, Tore. *Norwegian Resistance 1940–1945.* Montreal: McGill-Queen's University Press, 1979.

Gordon, Gerd Strey. *The Norwegian Resistance During the German Occupation 1940–1945.* Ph.D. dissertation for the University of Pittsburgh, 1978.

Goris, Jan-Albert. *Belgium.* London: Cambridge University Press, 1945.

Goris, Jan-Albert. *Belgium in Bondage.* New York: L.B. Fischer, 1943.

Haestrup, Jorgen. *European Resistance Movements, 1939–1945: A Complete History.* Westport, CT: Meckler Publishing, 1981.

Hammond, H.G.L. *The Allied Military Mission and the Resistance in West Macedonia.* Thessaloniki: Institute for Balkan Studies, 1993.

Hawes, Stephen, and Ralph White. *Resistance in Europe, 1939–1945.* London: Penguin Books Ltd, 1975.

Hazelhoff, Erik. *Soldier of Orange.* New York: Holland Heritage Society, 1980.

Hondros, John Louis. *Occupation and Resistance: The Greek Agony 1941–1944.* New York: Pella Publishing Company, 1983.

Hong, Nathaniel. *The Illegal Press in German Occupied Denmark.* Ph.D. dissertation for the University of Washington, 1993.

Huggett, Frank E. *Modern Belgium.* New York: Frederick A. Praeger, Publishers, 1969.

Irving, David. *Hitler's War.* New York: The Viking Press, 1977.

Ivanov, Miroslav. *Target: Heydrich.* New York: Macmillan Publishing Co., Inc., 1973.

Ivinskis, Zenonas. "Lithuania During the War: Resistance Against the Soviet and Nazi Occupants," in V.S. Vardys (ed.), *Lithuania Under the Soviets, 1940–1965,* pp. 61–84. New York, 1965.

Jurado, Carlos Caballero. *Resistance Warfare, 1940–45.* London: Osprey, 1985.

Kapral, Zdena. *Tomorrow Will Be Better.* Tucson: Harbinger House, 1990.

Keegan, John. *The Second World War.* New York: Viking Penguin, 1989.

Klukowski, Zygmunt. *Diary from the Years of Occupation.* Urbana: University of Illinois Press, 1993.

Korbel, Josef. *The Communist Subversion of Czechoslovakia 1938–1948.* Princeton, New Jersey: Princeton University Press, 1959.

Korbonski, Stefan. *Fighting Warsaw.* New York: Funk and Wagnalls, 1968.

Kosinski, Jerzy. *The Painted Bird.* New York: Scientia-Factum, 1967.

Kraus, René. *Europe in Revolt.* New York: The Macmillan Company, 1942.

Kulski, Julian Eugeniusz. *Dying, We Live.* New York: Holt, Rinehart and Winston, 1979.

Laar, Mart. *War in the Woods: Estonia's Struggle for Survival 1944–1956.* Washington: The Compass Press, 1992.

Lacouture, Jean. *De Gaulle the Rebel 1890–1944.* New York: W.W. Norton & Company, Inc., 1990.

Leckie, Robert. *Delivered from Evil.* New York: HarperCollins Publishers, 1987.

Lees, Michael. *The Rape of Serbia.* New York: Harcourt Brace Jovanovich, Publishers, 1990.

Lehmkuhl, Herman K. *Journey to London: The Story of the Norwegian Government at War.* London: Hutchinson, not dated.

Lemkin, Raphael. *Axis Rule in Occupied Europe.* Washington: Carnegie Endowment for International Peace, 1944.

Lieven, Anatol. *The Baltic Revolution.* New Haven: Yale University Press, 1993.

Lindsay, Franklin. *Beacons in the Night.* Stanford, California: Stanford University Press, 1993.

Lukacs, John. *The Last European War.* New York: Doubleday, 1976.

Maass, Walter B. *The Netherlands at War: 1940–1945.* London: Abelard-Schuman, 1970.

Mamatey, Victor, and Radomir Luza. *A History of the Czechoslovak Republic 1918–1948.* Princeton: Princeton University Press, 1973.

Manchester, William. *The Arms of Krupp.* New York: Little, Brown and Company, 1964.

Manning, Olivia. "The Greeks at War." *History of the Second World War,* pp. 272–275.

Marres, Juliette. "Nazi Overlords." *History of the Second World War,* pp. 449–459.

Mastny, Vojtech. *The Czechs Under Nazi Rule.* New York: Columbia University Press, 1971.

Mayer, Allan. *Gaston's War.* Novato, California: Presidio Press, 1988.

Mazower, Mark. *Inside Hitler's Greece.* New Haven: Yale University Press, 1993.

Michael, Maurice. *Haakon, King of Norway*. New York: The Macmillan Company, 1958.

Michel, Henri. *The Second World War*. New York: Praeger Publishers, 1975.

Michel, Henri. *The Shadow War*. New York: Harper & Row, Publishers, 1972.

Milazzo, Matteo J. *The Chetnik Movement & the Yugoslav Resistance*. Baltimore: The Johns Hopkins University Press, 1975.

Miller, Francis Trevelyan. *The Complete History of World War II*. Chicago: Readers' Service Bureau, 1947.

Miller, Russell. *The Resistance*. Alexandria, Virginia: Time-Life Books, 1979.

Misiunas, Romuald J., and Rein Taagepera. *The Baltic States: Years of Dependence 1940–1980*. Berkeley: University of California Press, 1983.

Moravec, Frantisek. *Master of Spies: The Memoirs of General Frantisek Moravec*. Garden City, New York: Doubleday & Company, Inc., 1975.

Moulton, J.L. *Battle for Antwerp*. New York: Hippocrene Books, Inc., 1978.

Neave, Airey. *Escape Room*. Garden City, New York: Doubleday & Company, Inc., 1970.

Nissen, Henrik S. *Scandinavia During the Second World War*. Minneapolis: The University of Minnesota Press, 1983.

Orbaan, Albert. *Duel in the Shadows*. Garden City, New York: Doubleday & Company, Inc., 1965.

Pearson, Michael. *Tears of Glory: The Heroes of Vercors, 1944*. Garden City, New York: Doubleday & Company, Inc., 1978.

Piekalkiewicz, Janusz. *Secret Agents, Spies, and Saboteurs*. New York: William Morrow & Company Inc., 1969.

Rings, Werver. *Life with the Enemy*. Garden City, New York: Doubleday & Company, Inc., 1982.

Ripka, Hubert. *Czechoslovakia Enslaved*. London: Victor Gollancz Ltd., 1950.

Rougeyron, Andre. *Agents for Escape*. Baton Rouge: Lousiana State University Press, 1997.

Rowinski, Leokadia. *That the Nightingale Return: A Memoir of the Polish Resistance, the Warsaw Uprising and German P.O.W. Camps*. Jefferson, North Carolina: McFarland & Company, Inc., 1999.

Ryan, Cornelius. *A Bridge Too Far*. New York: Simon and Schuster, 1974.

Sarafis, Stefanos. *ELAS: Greek Resistance Army*. New Jersey: Humanities Press, 1980.

Schoenbrun, David. *Soldiers of the Night: The Story of the French Resistance*. New York: E.P. Dutton, 1980.

Shiber, Etta. *Paris—Underground*. New York: Charles Scribner's Sons, 1943.

Spekke, Arnolds. *History of Latvia*. Stockholm: M. Goppers, 1957.

Suhl, Yuri. *They Fought Back: The Story of the Jewish Resistance in Nazi Europe*. New York: Crown Publishers, Inc., 1967.

Sweets, John F. *The Politics of Resistance in France, 1940–1944*. DeKalb: Northern Illinois University Press, 1976.

Tec, Nechama. *Defiance: The Bielski Partisans*. Oxford: Oxford University Press, 1993.

Thomas, John Oram. *The Giant-Killers: The Danish Resistance Movement 1940/5*. New York: Taplinger Publishing Company, 1976.

Tsatsos, Ioanna (Jeanne). *The Sword's Fierce Edge*. Vanderbilt University Press, 1969.

Watt, George. *The Comet Connection*. Lexington: University of Kentucky Press, 1990.

Winterbotham, F.W. *The Ultra Secret*. New York: Harper & Row, Publishers, 1974.

Woodhouse, C.M. *Apple of Discord*. London: Hutchinson & Co. Ltd., 1948.

Woodhouse, C.M. *A Short History of Modern Greece*. New York: Frederick A. Praeger, 1968.

Woodhouse, C.M. *The Struggle for Greece, 1941–1949*. Brooklyn Heights, New York: Beekman/Esanu Publishers, Inc., 1976.

Zawodny, J.K. *Nothing but Honour*. Stanford, California: Hoover Institution Press, 1978.

# Index

Albania, 159, 161, 162, 167,
173–175, 178
Astrup, Poul, 63
Austria, 33, 96, 114, 142, 175, 197
Barraco, Mary Sigillo, 207
Belgian resistance groups:
Armée Belge des Partisans du
Front de l'Independence et
de la Liberation, 129
Armée de la Liberation, 129
Armée Secrète, 129
la Brigade Blanche Fidelio, 141
le Mouvement National
Royaliste, 141
Group G, 139
Légion Belge, 128, 129
les Insoumis, 129
les Milices Patriotiques, 141
les Partisans Armées, 14
Mouvement National Belge,
128
Witte Brigade, 129
Belgian underground newspapers:
La Libre Belgique, 127, 128
Belgium, 91, 93, 124–142, 151
Benes, Edvard, 16–21, 23, 25, 31,
32
Beran, Rudolf, 16, 19
Best, Karl Werner, 58, 61–63
Bily, Josef, 24
Blitzkrieg, 36, 40, 126, 151, 187
Bohemia, 18–20, 22, 23, 29–31
Bohr, Niels, 65, 66
Bor-Komorowski, Tadeusz, 47, 48
Bosnians, 174
Broz, Josip, 177–185
Buhl, Vilhelm, 58
Bulgaria, 158, 161, 162, 167, 170,
171, 173–175
Camus, Albert, 148, 205
Cavalouski, Rita, 207
Chamberlain, Neville, 17
Chetniks, 176–178, 180–184
Churchill, Winston, 41, 42, 47, 84,
124, 131, 160, 168, 172, 184,
185

Comet Line, 133, 134, 136, 137
Crete, 160, 162, 171
Croatia, 172–176, 178, 179
Czechoslovakia, 15–35, 42, 65, 73,
86, 155, 177, 189, 197, 206
Czechoslovakian resistance groups:
Obrana Naroda, (ON) 20, 21,
27, 28
Peticni vybor Verni zustaneme
(PVVZ), 21, 29
Politicke Ustredi (PÚ), 20, 21,
22, 28
SNR, 32, 33, 34
ÚVOD, 21, 23
Czechoslovakian underground
newspapers:
Czech Mail, 23
Into Battle, 23
Red Law, 23
V Boj, 23
Daladier, Edouard, 17
de Gaulle, Charles, 143–147, 150,
152–157
Danish resistance groups:
The Churchill Club, 57
Dansk Samling, 61
Frit Danmark, 61
Holger Danske, 61
Ringen, 61
Danish underground newspapers:
Boycott, 54
De Frie Danske, 53
Frit Danmark, 53
Denmark, 52–71, 73, 74, 85, 86,
93, 96, 114, 125, 137, 205
Dutch resistance groups:
Knokploegen, 92, 93, 119, 120
Landelijke Organisatie, 119,
120
Orde Dienst (OD,) 92, 93, 117,
118, 120, 122, 123
Raad van Verzet, 92, 93, 120,
121
Strijdkrachten, 120
Dutch underground newspapers:
De Waarheid, 96

Ege, Richard, 63, 64
Egypt, 162, 163, 168
Eichmann, Adolf, 65
Eliàs, Alois, 19, 24
England, 19, 29, 80, 87, 89, 93, 94,
  117, 118, 125, 131, 194
Estonia, 186–188, 192, 196–200
Estonian resistance groups:
  Forest brothers, 187, 188, 192
von Falkenhausen, Gen Alexander,
  127
Finland, 188, 196
France, 19, 39, 40, 72, 91, 93, 94,
  116, 126, 127, 130, 132, 134,
  138, 140, 142–157, 182, 206
Franco. Francisco, 136
Frenay, Henri, 146, 148, 151, 154
French resistance groups:
  Arc, 148
  Armée des Volontaires, 148
  Bataillons de la Mort, 148
  Ceux de la Libération, 148
  Ceux de la Résistance, 148
  Franc-Tireurs et Partisans, 154
  France au Combat, 148
  France d'Abord, 148
  Francs-Tireur et Partisans, 147
  l'Armée Secrète, 140, 141, 154
  l'Organisation Civile et
    Militaire, 148–157
  Le Coq Enchainé, 148
  Libération Nord, 148
  Libération Sud, 147
  Libérer et Fédérer, 148
  Maquis, 151, 153, 155, 156
  Mouvement Nationale
    Révolutionnaire, 148
  Organisation de Resistance de
    l'Armée, 148
  Pantagruel, 148
  Valmy, 148
French underground newspapers:
  Combat, 148
  Défense de la France, 148
  Résistance, 148
Gabcik, Josef, 25–27
Gestapo, 19, 20, 22–28, 40, 41, 45,
  57, 58, 62, 63, 65, 74, 76,
  82–84, 114, 120, 130–132, 135,
  146, 148, 149, 154, 176, 190,
  193, 195–198, 206, 207
Giskes, Hermann, 117, 118

Goebbels, Dr. Joseph, 28, 124
Göring, Hermann, 47
Grazzi, Emmanuel, 158
Great Britain, 19, 22, 55, 59, 78,
  81, 93, 145, 160, 169, 191, 202
Greece, 73, 146, 157–173, 181,
  182, 185, 206
Greek resistance groups:
  Ethniko Apeleftherotiko
    Metopo (EAM), 164, 167,
    169
  Ethniko Laikos Apeleftherotiko
    Stratos (ELAS), 164–171
  Ethnikos Draseos (EDES),
    164–170
Hàcha, Emil, 19
von Hanneken, Lt Gen. Hermann,
  58–61
Heydrich, Reinhard, 24–28, 45,
  206
Himmler, Heinrich, 25, 28, 47, 49,
  50, 63, 64, 198
Hitler, Adolf, 17–19, 24, 28, 31,
  34–37, 40, 41, 45, 46, 52, 53,
  57, 60, 63, 68, 72, 74, 75,
  84–86, 91, 93, 113, 136, 138,
  141, 144, 145, 157–163, 168,
  170, 172–175, 181, 186, 188,
  192, 199, 207
Hungary, 19, 34, 158, 163,
  173–175
Italy, 28, 48, 170, 172, 174, 175
Kaltenbrunner, Ernst, 28
Kapral, Zdena, 17, 26
King Christian, X 52, 53, 57, 61
King George II, 162
King Gustav, 65
King Haakon VII, 70–73, 79, 90
King Leopold III, 125, 137, 141,
  142
Klaras, Thanases, 164
Kosovo, 175
Kriegsmarine, 82
Kubis, Jan, 25–27
Latvia, 186–188, 192, 197–200,
  202, 203
Latvian underground newspapers:
  Neatkariga Latvija, 193
Laval, Pierre, 146, 149, 157
Lie, Jonas, 82, 89, 90
Linge, Martin, 77–80, 86, 87
Lithuania, 130, 186–189, 192, 194,

196–201, 203
Lithuanian resistance groups:
Lietuviu Frontas, 194
Lietuvos Laisves Armija, 195
Lietuvos Laisves Kovotoju
Sajung (LLKS), 195
Lithuanian Activist Front
(LAF), 192, 194
Lithuanian Freedom Fighters,
194
Nationalist Party
(Voldemarists), 194, 195
Peasant Populist Union, 194
Tautininkai, 194
Vyriausias Lietuvos Islaisvinimo
Komitetas (VLIK), 195, 201
Lithuanian underground
newspapers:
Atzalynas, 194
I Laisve, 194
Laisves Kovotojas, 195
Lietuviu Biuletenis, 194
Lietuvos Judas, 194
Lietuvos Laisves Kovotoju
Sajung (LKKS), 195
Nepriklausoma Lietuva, 193
Pogrindzio Kuntaplis, 194
Vardan Tiesos, 194
Luftwaffe, 37, 52, 72, 82, 84, 93,
131, 160–162, 169
Luxembourg, 42, 73, 91, 124–142
Luxembourgian resistance groups:
Letzeburger Freihétskämpfer,
129
Letzeburger Partiote Liga, 129
Letzeburger Volleks Legioun,
129
Patriotes Independants, 129
Unioun vun de
Resistenzmouvementer, 129
Luza, Radomir, 20, 22, 23, 27
Macedonia, 175, 179
Manhattan Project, the, 65
Marthinsen, Karl, 82
Metaxas, Ioannis, 158–161, 164
Meyer, Arnold, 116
Mihailovich, Col. Draza, 176–178,
180–185
Montenegro, 174, 175, 178, 179,
184
Moravec, Frantisek, 15–18, 22, 23,
25, 29, 32

Moravia, 18–20, 23, 28–31
Munich pact, 19, 20, 31
Mussert, Anton, 116
Mussolini, Benito, 17, 60, 136,
158–160, 162, 172, 175
Myers, Col. Edmund, 166–168,
170
The Netherlands, 16, 73, 91-123,
206
von Neurath, Freiherr, 19, 24
Norway, 52, 70-90, 93, 96, 116,
125, 128, 177
Norwegian resistance groups:
Civorg, 77
Milorg, 77–80, 83–86, 89
Norge Fritt, 77
X-U, 77
Onderduikers, 113, 114, 119–121,
149
Operation Animals, 168
Operation Barbarossa, 37, 77, 96,
150, 160, 162, 173, 175, 180,
186
Operation Doomsday, 89
Operation Gemsbock, 169
Operation Jupiter, 84
Operation Manna, 171
Operation Marita, 160
Operation Nordpol 118
Operation Overlord, 154
Operation Panther, 169
Operation Punishment, 173
Operation Sea Lion, 22
Operation Steinadler, 169
Operation Torch, 150, 151
Palestine, 163
Pancke, Gen. Günther, 62
Pavelic, Ante, 175, 182, 183
Pecanac, Kosta, 176
Pétain, Mar. Henri Phillipe,
144–147, 152, 154, 157
Poland, 19, 24, 33, 34, 36–51, 52,
73, 89, 114, 116, 137, 177, 189,
198, 199, 203, 206
Polish resistance groups:
Armia Krajowa (AK), 38, 45,
47–51
Armia Ludowa (AL), 48
Narodowe Sily Zbrojne (NSZ),
48
Zwiazek Walki Zbrojnej,
(ZWZ), 38

Polish underground newspapers:
  Biuletyn Informacyjny, 45
Queen Elizabeth, 137
Queen Wilhelmina, 91, 92, 94, 132
Quisling, Maj. Vidkun, 74, 75, 78, 81, 82, 85, 89, 90
Raczkiewicz, Wladyslaw, 39
Radio Berlin, 46
Radio Warsaw, 37
Raths, Aloyse, 125, 126, 130
von Renthe-Fink, Cecil, 57, 58
Reynaud, Paul ,144
Romania, 32, 37, 39, 158, 160, 163, 173, 174
Rommel, Gen. Erwin, 144, 162
Rosenberg, Alfred, 189, 198, 200, 203
Rowecki, Col. Stefan, 39, 46, 47
Royal Air Force, 42, 59, 60, 66, 87, 94, 118, 124, 161
Ruge, Otto, 70, 73, 76
Russia, 19, 21, 22, 29, 37, 46, 53, 56, 60, 130, 150, 151, 162, 186–188, 190, 193, 197, 203
Saraphis, Col. Stephanos, 167
Scavenius, Erik, 56, 58, 60, 61
Serbia, 172 175, 178, 182, 183
Seyss-Inquart, Arthur, 95, 116, 120, 123
Shetland Bus, the, 80–82, 93
Siberia, 187
Sicily, 60, 168, 169, 170, 207
Sikorski, Gen. Wladyslaw, 39, 46, 47
Simon, Gustav, 126, 131, 138
Skirpa, Col. Kazys, 192
Slovakia, 18, 19, 29, 31–35, 189
Slovenia, 172, 175, 178, 179
Sosnkowski, Gen. Kazimierz, 47, 48
Spain 93, 94, 114, 130, 132–134, 136, 151, 168

Spanish Civil War, 56, 130, 136
Special Operations Executive (SOE), 22, 25, 26, 29, 61, 68, 77–81, 83–85, 117, 128, 129, 131, 140, 141, 151, 152, 154, 165
Stalin, Joseph, 49, 50, 187
Stapo, 82, 84, 89
Stroop, Gen. Jürgen, 46
Sweden, 42, 55, 61, 62, 64, 65, 67, 71, 73, 75, 86, 88, 114, 195, 196
Switzerland, 93, 94, 118, 151
Terboven, Josef, 75
Thümmel, Paul, 15
Tiso, Jozef, 31–33
Tito, (See Broz, Josip)
Treaty of Versailles, 145
Tripartite pact, 172
Uluots, Jüri, 189
United States, 19, 56, 191, 202
USAAF, 94
Ustachi, 175, 176, 179
V-1 and V-2 flying bombs, 29, 42–44, 55, 131
Vandermeerssche, Gaston, 207
Weert, Epko, 93, 119, 120, 207
Wehrmacht, 18, 27, 30, 36, 37, 39, 42, 47, 54, 58, 61, 89, 91, 130, 138, 141, 146, 153, 156, 170, 173, 175, 188, 197, 199, 202, 203
Wilson, J.S., 80
Winkelman, Gen. H.G., 91
World War I, 36, 38, 50, 52, 56, 75, 92, 124, 127, 131, 133, 144, 173, 176
World War II 16, 35–37, 39, 46, 51, 56, 58, 65, 86, 129, 131, 141, 157, 172, 174, 176, 205
Yugoslavia, 73, 89, 95, 146, 157, 158, 160–163, 167–170, 172-185, 189, 192, 199
Yugoslavian resistance groups:
  Partisans, 177–179, 181–185
Zervas, Napoleon, 165–167, 169, 170